FASHION BY DESIGN

FASHION BY DESIGN

JANICE GREENBERG ELLINWOOD

MARYMOUNT UNIVERSITY

FAIRCHILD BOOKS
NEW YORK · LONDON · OXFORD · NEW DELHI · SYDNEY

FAIRCHILD BOOKS
Bloomsbury Publishing Inc
1385 Broadway, New York, NY 10018, USA
50 Bedford Square, London, WC1B 3DP, UK

BLOOMSBURY, FAIRCHILD BOOKS and the Fairchild Books logo are
trademarks of Bloomsbury Publishing Plc

First published in the United States of America 2011
Reprinted 2017, 2018, 2019

Cover design: Carolyn Eckert
Cover image © Photo byMino La Franca; Back Cover: Collection of the
Kyoto Costume Institute, photo by Richard Haughton

Library of Congress Cataloging-in-Publication Data
LC record available at http://lccn.loc.gov/2009934620

ISBN: PB: 978-1-5636-7848-6
ePDF: 978-1-6289-2192-2

Printed and bound in the United States of America

To find out more about our authors and books visit www.fairchildbooks.com
and sign up for our newsletter.

CONTENTS

EXTENDED CONTENTS

PREFACE

FASHION BY DESIGN provides the student of fashion design, or the interested layperson, with a foundation for artistic decision making. Its focus is the design theory that originated with the Bauhaus artists of the 1920s and 1930s and how it applies to fashion. The chapters examine the design process, along with each element of design—line, shape, form, space, texture, light, pattern, color, and value—as well as each principle of design—balance, emphasis, rhythm, proportion, and unity. The reader moves step-by-step through each topic, all supported by colorful illustrations from the worlds of art, architecture, and most importantly, fashion. The fashions in the book come from the world's most famous designers. In addition, profiles of selected designers provide insight into their artistic thinking and sources of inspiration, capitalizing on the most recent historical research and fashion reporting. Art projects at the end of each chapter invite the reader to experiment with each element or principle, with the intent of developing discriminating decision-making skills and a sophisticated eye for fashion.

The introductory Chapter 1, "About Design," outlines the creative design process, the Bauhaus artists and their development of design theory, the elements and principles of design, as well as the structural design (e.g., draped, architectural, and deconstructional) and the functional design of a garment. It also identifies the terminology used in the communication of fashion. Designer profiles include Madeleine Vionnet, Charles James, and Claire McCardell.

Part I: "The Elements of Design" includes Chapters 2 through 7.

Chapter 2, "Line," focuses on types of line, the interpretation of line in fashion, and line direction and quality. Designers profiled are Coco Chanel, Karl Lagerfeld, and Rudi Gernreich.

Chapter 3 covers "Form, Shape, and Space." In this chapter, we explore the feeling designers have for the human form as well as the importance of form in the structure of clothing parts. We equate shape to silhouette and examine an overview of historic silhouettes. We also see how designers interpret shape within the garment design and the flat pattern. Space is defined from the Japanese perspective, by its importance in Western fashion history, and in terms of theater and dance costume. There is also discourse on the relationship between positive and negative space. Profiles spotlight Christian Dior, Rei Kawakubo, and Issey Miyake.

Chapter 4, "Texture and Light," is divided between these two subjects. The topic of texture encompasses the kinds of texture, fabric structure, fabric terminology, aesthetic properties of texture, and texture caused both by construction techniques and by nontraditional materials. We look at types of light as well as the ways that designers use light in their designs and its purpose in fashion. Designer profiles include Yves Saint Laurent and Mariano Fortuny.

Chapter 5 covers "Pattern." Topics include the sources and interpretations of motifs, common patterns used in fashion, patterns that result from fabric structure, application to the fabric surface, and pattern that emerges from threads and yarns applied through the fabric surface. This chapter also includes an explanation of how to make a pattern, the types of layouts, and how to prepare the pattern design. We also look at the relationship between pattern, designing apparel, and industry trends. Gianni Versace is the designer profiled.

Chapter 6 examines "Color and Value." Beginning with color as light, the chapter includes the evolution of the Standard Color Wheel, color relationships, color temperature, and visual color interactions. The section on value comprises value scale, contrast, and influences on perception. The designer profile features Roberto Capucci.

Chapter 7 focuses on "Color and Industry." It covers color and dyes, color forecasting, the consideration of color in designing mass fashion, consumer concerns, color psychology, symbolism, and cultural meaning. This chapter includes an overview of how designers choose colors for their collections. Valentino and Vivienne Westwood are profiled.

Part II, "The Principles of Design," includes Chapters 8 through 12.

Chapter 8, "Balance," explores kinds of balance, such as horizontal and vertical balance, radial balance, balance of all-over pattern, and balance of three-dimensional form. This chapter also covers symmetry, asymmetry, and approximate symmetry. Hubert de Givenchy is the designer profiled.

Chapter 9 is about "Emphasis." This chapter summarizes James Laver's theories regarding the purpose of clothing, with special emphasis on the shifting of erogenous zones, supported by historic examples. The methods to implement emphasis are listed, such as isolation, contrast, placement, repetition, radiation, and construction techniques. The designer profiled is Elsa Schiaparelli. The focus on one designer is purposeful, in order to demonstrate how a talented eye can change at will the location of emphasis on a range of designs.

Chapter 10 introduces "Rhythm." The relationship between eacł ment and rhythm is discussed, as well as how rhythm is implemen. through structural expression. The kinds of rhythm are enumerated. Thı chapter includes a profile on Madame Grès.

Chapter 11 centers on "Proportion." Topics include the relationship of proportion to the human figure, to science, and to mathematics, including the golden mean and the Fibonacci series. This chapter also covers how designers determine proportion, the comparative proportionate relationships for fashion, and proportion's relationship to the design elements. The highlighted designer is Yohji Yamamoto.

Chapter 12 is on "Unity." Here we define variety, harmony, and the Gestalt Principles. Unity is discussed in relation to the garment, as well as to mass fashion. Designer influences include ideals of beauty and sources of inspiration. This chapter culminates with guidelines for maintaining unity across a group of fashions. Jeanne Lanvin is the final designer profiled.

Fashion by Design is written and presented with admiration for the great fashion designers who brought artistic inspiration to industry. They added beauty to our world, stimulated our intellect, and tantalized our creativity. We are forever in their debt!

ACKNOWLEDGMENTS

Writing *Fashion by Design* has been a wonderful opportunity to integrate my knowledge, teaching, and enthusiasm for fashion. However, I could only complete the task with the support and ideas of my colleagues at Marymount University: Dr. Pamela Stoessell, professor of fine and applied arts; Annette Ames, associate professor of fine and applied arts; the design expert and painter Judy Bass, professor of fine and applied arts; and Dr. Bridget May, furniture and interiors historian and professor of interior design. I also thank Dr. Hyun Jung for sharing her doctoral research at Hong-Ik University on fashion design and light. Dr. Jung has since taught at Texas Tech University. In addition, I want to thank my acquisitions reviewers Doris Treptow, Savannah College of Art and Design; Sass Brown, Fashion Institute of Technology; Lorynn Divita, Baylor University; Hyunjoo Im, Cal Poly, Pamona; Lombuso S. Khoza, University of Maryland, Eastern Shore; as well as my development reviewers, Su-Jeong Hwang Shin, PhD, Texas Tech University; Julia F. Cooper, Ohio State University; and Theresa M. Winge, PhD, Indiana University, for their contemplative feedback.

The team at Fairchild Books truly brought *Fashion by Design* to fruition. My gratitude goes to Robert Phelps, development editor, my mentor and a gifted writer; Elizabeth Greenberg, photo editor (and fashion historian); Carolyn Eckert, creative director; Jennifer Crane, editorial development director; Ginger Hillman, production director; Jessica Rozler, production editor; Joanne Slike, copyeditor, Noah Schwartzberg, ancillaries editor; and the incomparable executive editor Olga Kontzias, who embodies the vision of Fairchild Books.

Finally, I thank my family for their investment of a laptop in my efforts and their wonderful support: my sister, Dr. Donna Greenberg of Harvard Medical School and Massachusetts General Hospital, and my daughters Amy Rosenthal, Lindsey Rosenthal, and Samantha Rosenthal, who also generously lent both writing advice and technological expertise on command. Special love and appreciation go to my husband, Jamie Ellinwood, for all of his patience and advocacy along this journey.

ABOUT DESIGN

Fashion critics and buyers flock the runways each season in search of the most notable designs (FIGURE 1.1). They highlight them in the media and take notes back to the stores. How do critics and buyers know which designs are the best after seeing them only once on a runway, and after the blur of seeing so many collections in a single day? For that matter, how do designers know which of their ideas will impact the audience, the critics, their clients, and the stores?

Fashion is, especially at first impression, a visual product, and those who work in the fashion industry are visually oriented. They experience a sensual feeling of excitement whenever a winning design is spotted. Indeed, the first reaction is an emotional one. It may even take an old pro a few minutes to identify and describe why the fashion causes such reaction. Designers have the answer because they have developed an "eye" for good design, and with it, a language to articulate the attributes of design.

This chapter defines **design**, explains and lists the stages of the **design process**, and describes the three criteria by which a designer judges the success of a garment—**aesthetic design, structural design,** and **functional design.** It amplifies the designers' "language" in terms of the **elements** and **principles of design**, recounting where that language originated. Finally, it considers the terms that are most commonly used by the fashion industry to describe fashion: **silhouette, fabric, color, looks,** and **details**.

The term design refers to both product and process. As product, design is a tangible visual solution, an organism of an idea of a visual nature that also integrates materials and function. "Form follows function" is a maxim related to architecture of the twentieth century, credited to American architect Louis Sullivan (1856–1924), a champion of the Modernist movement. This movement preached a practical simplicity in the execution of a design, one based on the function of the product. Fashion is more often the application of creative thought to clothing where aesthetic execution is valued over function. In either case, design is the result of the organization and arrangement of parts into a final form. Even though spontaneity may have a role in its creation, it is really the result of many stages of thought, including research and analysis. That is what makes the process of designing so intriguing.

THE DESIGN PROCESS

In the fashion industry, an individual or a team may participate in the design process, depending on the size and structure of a company. Today's process defies the romantic image of the artist who, by a stroke of genius, spontaneously creates magnificence. It is actually a generation of several ideas that are edited and refined, whether by one designer or as a result of collaboration.

When a design problem presents itself, thinking through a series of steps will culminate in a sound solution:

1. PROBLEM IDENTIFICATION

Define and clarify the problem. What is it asking? How might it be interpreted? For the fashion designer this may involve the identification of the category of apparel (such as evening wear, or swimwear), a profile of the customer for whom the fashion is designed (by age range, income level, or lifestyle), and the **season**. In the classroom, the student must clarify the design project assignment, so that it is completely understood.

2. RESEARCH

Examine potential influences on the design problem, such as those from industry, culture, economy, history, or inspiration. The fashion designer may survey **fabric and color trends** anticipated for the coming season or search for a source of inspiration. In order to respond to a project assignment, students may investigate whether other artists or designers have solved similar problems, learn from their experiences, and then go beyond their solutions. They too may benefit from a new source of inspiration, depending on the design problem.

3. IDEATION

Determine alternative solutions. Of all the steps in the design process, this is probably the most important and the most enjoyable for the designer. That is because the task of designing is conducted again and again. The first solution may or may not be optimal. An individual will know for certain by comparing it with alternatives. When a large company determines the fashions for the season, different designers submit ideas, and the final choices are made by consensus. The student who creates several solutions is developing an eye for design in the process.

This stage is also an opportunity to think of ways to "push the boundaries" or to find options that are truly innovative. Pushing the boundaries means giving up preconceived notions that may limit creativity. Often these notions are self-imposed. Such reasoning is also called "thinking outside the box."

4. CONSTRAINT IDENTIFICATION

Consider limitations built into the problem. For the fashion designer, examples of limitations are time, the availability of fabric and materials, and cost. The student may experience the same limitations as the professional designer. The amount of time required to complete the project, the availability of materials and supplies, and the expense of purchasing them are real considerations.

5. SELECTION

Choose the best option. Make the decision based on research, the strengths of the alternative solutions, and a regard for the constraints. In the classroom, a professor may want to see the versions that have been eliminated as well as the chosen solution. Be prepared to give a related explanation, so that the reasons for the selection are readily understood. This may also occur in a work setting.

6. IMPLEMENTATION

Solve the problem. Execute, fabricate, or give form to the solution. For the fashion designer, this means making a sample of the design. For the student, it means constructing the solution for the assignment in the course.

7. EVALUATION

Examine the solution. Once the design is executed, the work is not finished. Consider how successful it is. A garment, for instance, is evaluated for **fit**, **workmanship**, aesthetic appearance, and cost. It is prudent for the design student to evaluate the solution to a design problem before the professor sees it, so factor into the implementation period the time to do that. Consider how original or innovative the solution is. How is the workmanship? How about the method of presentation?

8. REFINEMENT

React to the evaluation. It may indicate that more changes to the design are necessary. However, the amount of change is not likely to equal a new alternative solution, just a refinement of the final product. Refinements are a natural part of the design process and another enjoyable step for the designer.

9. PRESENTATION

Sell the solution. A manufacturer must promote a new fashion to store buyers in order to induce them to purchase it. The best method is to present an exemplary version of the design, but it is also necessary to verbally communicate its strengths. The student must do this as well. An oral presentation often accompanies a design solution in the classroom, or the student must make compelling comments during a group critique.

The final stage underscores the importance of communicating the design and the evaluation process. Designers from all fields, such as interior design, architecture, graphic design, textile design, and product design have the same need. Painters, sculptors, and everyone else who participates in the creation of a visual product also share this need. As a result, there is a shared language for that purpose. The application of this language to fashion design is the focus of this book.

AESTHETIC DESIGN

The concepts and terminology used for the evaluation of aesthetic de[...] are called "the elements and principles of design." How did designers fr[...] different fields become attuned to the same language? The answer date[...] back to an innovative school for German art education established in 1919 by architect Walter Gropius (1883–1969) called the Bauhaus.

THE BAUHAUS

The Bauhaus was a reaction both to the authoritative nature of the European art academies of the previous century and to the new wave of industrialization. One of its goals was to bring artistic integrity to machine-made products by marrying the forces of craftsmanship and art—one being precise and functional, and the other creative and imaginative. This philosophy was also a reaction against the historicism and romanticism of art in the nineteenth century. The hope was to furnish fresh inspiration for architecture and all areas of art and design, including painting, sculpture, home furnishings, textiles, graphic design, and theater. In an effort to reject the ornamentation and pretentiousness of the former century, the Bauhaus expressed its designs specifically through geometric form and the primary colors of red, blue, and yellow, as in the cradle by Peter Keler, table lamp by Wilhelm Wagenfeld, and the armchair by Gerrit Reitvald (FIGURES 1.2A–C).

1.2A Peter Keler's cradle (1922) is based on the Bauhaus commitment to primary colors and geometric forms.
KLASSIK STIFTUNG WEIMAR

1.2B The shapes used in this table lamp (1923–1924), designed by Wilhelm Wagenfeld in the Bauhaus metal workshop, adhere to the Bauhaus emphasis on geometric forms.
DIGITAL IMAGE © THE MUSEUM OF MODERN ART/LICENSED BY SCALA/ ART RESOURCE, NY

The school was organized in an unusual fashion. Instead of studios, there were workshops for every material used in applied art, including clay, glass, wood, stone, metal, and cloth. Each had a workshop master who was expert in the craft. In addition, there was an artist designated as the "Master of Form," who would introduce the students to the mysteries of creativity. There was also a preliminary course, the idea of the painter Johannes Itten (1888–1967), which taught the most basic concepts of creativity. It enabled students to experiment with materials in order to investigate forms, colors, textures, and tones in two and three dimensions. Through this organization, the Bauhaus attempted to educate a new generation of designers in an era of mass production and mass consumption, by achieving, through research, the development of a coherent and universally applicable language of design that did not depend on history.

The school was dissolved in 1933, due to the rise in power of the Nazis, causing its teachers to disperse and migrate to other countries. Some, including Itten, traveled to the United States and continued teaching there, spreading the unique Bauhaus philosophy, which became the basis for change in Amer-

1.2C This armchair was designed by Gerrit Reitvald in 1918. The color was added according to the Bauhaus tradition in 1923.

ican art education. The subsequent reorganization in American schools and universities endorsed a preliminary course, often referred to as a "foundation," from which students learn the universal language of design.

THE ELEMENTS AND PRINCIPLES OF DESIGN

This language works like a recipe for whipping up a satisfying design. The elements of design are the ingredients, and the methods by which the elements combine are called the principles of design. As such, they are guidelines. A student can try a wholly untested method to design a product, but it is helpful to know what has worked successfully in the past. Each chapter in this book discusses the different elements or principles in great detail.

The elements of design include the following:

1. **LINE**—a moving point or dot; a connection between two points.

2. **SHAPE**—a two-dimensional area enclosed by a line.

3. **FORM**—a three-dimensional area enclosed by a surface.

4. **SPACE**—empty area or extent; a two-dimensional emptiness or three-dimensional void.

5. **TEXTURE**—the visible and tangible structure of a surface.

6. **LIGHT**—the electromagnetic energy making things visible or radiant energy resulting from the vibration of electrons.

7. **PATTERN**—the result that occurs when any visual element is repeated over an extended area.

8. **COLOR**—a specific hue that is determined by its wavelength.

The principles of design are as follows:

1. **BALANCE**—The distribution of weight or force within a composition

2. **EMPHASIS**—Particular prominence in a part of the design

3. **RHYTHM**—The feeling of organized movement

4. **PROPORTION**—The comparative relationship of distances, sizes, amounts, degrees, or parts

5. **UNITY**—The sense of completed wholeness or cohesion

STRUCTURAL DESIGN   Structural design is that which determines form but not surface ornamentation. Regarding fashion, this involves the **cut of the fabric**, its texture, the **elements of construction**, how they relate to one another, and how they all relate to the figure. Not only does structural design contribute to the aesthetic attractiveness of the garment; it allows the garment to function. When creating the structure, the designer is always mindful of the human figure, which has its own form. The challenge is to make a flat piece of fabric that is two-dimensional conform in some way to body contours, which are three-dimensional. The fashion must envelop the body like a vessel, and the designer deliberates if it will fit closely and how much to allow for body movement, comfort, and ease. Such decisions are reliant to some extent on fashion trends and what is acceptable to the target customer (the particular customer envisioned by the designer's company and categorized by gender, age range, geographic location, and lifestyle), as well as on the designer's sensitivity to the elements and principles of design and the degree of innovation that is desired.

In order to obtain a shape that will adjust to the body or fit it clos[e,] is often necessary to cut sections of fabric and put them together using c[on]struction techniques. A **seam**, or line of stitching that attaches two pieces [of] fabric, is the most common method. Besides serving a function, a seam cre-ates a visual line in a garment. There are many kinds of seams, including one where the stitches are larger and looser so the fabric gathers into puffs of fabric. That type is called **gathering**. Another construction technique is called a **dart**. A dart is a method of stitching out a fold of fabric to remove excess in length or width, which enables the fabric to fit a body curve. It also appears as a line on the exterior of the garment, but shorter in length than a seam. These techniques are shown in FIGURE 1.3.

(a)

(b)

WORKMANSHIP

Excellence in arts and crafts is often determined by the level of craftsman-ship. Craftsmanship refers to mastery of the craft—for example, in the ceramist's ability to throw a pot or the jeweler's skill at hammering silver or gold. In relation to fashion, the comparable term is **workmanship**. Work-manship means excellence in the construction techniques used, such as the regularity of the stitching. Fine workmanship is a value belonging to all fashion designers. The structure of the suit in FIGURE 1.4, designed by French couturière Jeanne Lanvin (1867–1946) and dated 1940–1944, surely defines its beauty. The seams in the jacket subtly draw in the waist for a well-shaped, comfortable fit. They are repeated again in the matching skirt.

1.4 The quilted pockets, button tabs, and seams in this 1940s suit all demonstrate the excellent workmanship of French couturière Jeanne Lanvin.
COLLECTION OF THE KYOTO COSTUME INSTITUTE, PHOTO BY TAKASHI HATAKEYAMA

The repetitive stitching on the button tabs and pockets demonstrate excellence in workmanship, characteristic of the **haute couture** level of the fashion industry. Literally translated, haute couture means "high sewing," but refers to the level of the industry in which clothing is made of the best quality and sold at the highest prices on a custom-order basis. Lanvin was known for her use of stitching, and her design house still exists in Paris today.

FABRIC AND DESIGN

Fashion designers enjoy a personal relationship with fabric. They recogn[ize] fabric attributes by sight and touch and by experience. They understan[d] which are sturdy and stiff or drape in folds or stretch around the figure. They know which have a surface that reflects the light, feel woolly and warm, or appear light, translucent, and airy. From this sensitivity, designers decide how the fabric adorns the body. Is it cut and sewn? Knitted? Wrapped? Bunched? Folded? This is the opportunity for the designer to consider the cut of the fabric. Is the fabric used with its yarns **on-grain** in order to hang in a way that supports a traditional style, like a skirt that is gathered at the waist? On-grain means that the warp yarns (which run lengthwise in a woven fabric) and the weft yarns (which run crosswise) are at right angles. Or is it off-grain, or **bias cut**, enabling it to drape over the contours of the body as does a circle skirt? Off-grain means that the fabric is turned on its edge, with both the warp and weft yarns running on the diagonal. When that is the manner in which the fabric is used, the structure of the garment is referred to as **draped design**. Several designers have used this method, which is particularly characteristic of evening wear today, but surely the best known of them is the French couture designer, Madeleine Vionnet (BOX 1.1), whose contribution to the industry had such impact that we refer to her work several times in subsequent chapters.

ARCHITECTURE AND FASHION

Much has been written about architecture and fashion and the influence of one on the other. It has already been established that the aesthetic design of both is evaluated by the elements and principles of design. Architecture refers to a built environment, the structure of which is entirely self-supporting. Some fashions are designed in a similar manner but conceived as an environment for the body, rather than one for human beings to live and work within. These garments are executed with an actual or a visual rigidity of form that exists separately from the human body. When this approach is used, the structure of the garment is identified as **architectural design**. Rigidity is created with the use of a particular material that provides the garment's support through its understructure or foundation. Even garments required to convey an appearance of shape for aesthetic and performance value, as in Lanvin's suit in FIGURE 1.4, have something under the garment's surface, such as an **interlining** that enhances the jacket's shape, in addition to padding, which subtly raises and molds the jacket's shoulder. An interlining has a structure like a fabric and provides support without rigidity. Architectural garments that yield form independent of

BOX 1.1

MADELEINE
VIONNET

MADELEINE VIONNET ORIGINATED the bias cut in fashion, an innovation that continues to impact the fashion industry today. As a result, her designs were sleek and fluid, body clinging and elegant, all qualities associated with the fashions of the 1930s. Along with the bias cut, she developed two design details that capitalize on the cut of fabric: the cowl neck and the halter neckline. What were the influences that enabled her stroke of genius?

Vionnet was born outside Paris in 1876 to a modest family, but her mother left the family when she was three years old, and her father raised her. Although she was an avid student, her father chose to apprentice her to a seamstress when she turned 11, a decision that she always resented. Thus began her career as a "dress-maker," which is what she called herself. After a brief marriage, she moved to London, where she worked first for the English branch of Paquin's design house and then for the English dressmaker Kate Reilly. When she returned to Paris to be near her father, she sought a job with the Callot sisters, an opportunity that ultimately had great influence on her design work and which she described as the culmination of her days as an apprentice. This was because of her alliance with the oldest sister, Madame Marie Gerber, for whom she worked as a first assistant. In this role, she was responsible for executing the structure for Gerber's designs and witnessed her creative process. Gerber draped fabric on a live mannequin in order to experiment with ideas. She used muslin since the dress fabrics were so delicate and expensive, probably a first for the execution of haute couture. Vionnet's job was to interpret the design into a pattern, and later she fit the dress on the client. This provided her experience working with the body. She credited Gerber with the highest standard in workmanship and an exemplary taste in the best fabrics (Kirke, 1998, p. 32).

Vionnet opened her own design house in 1912 but had to close it because of the outbreak of war in 1914. She reopened in 1919. Because it was her own business, she could determine the designs. The opportunity piqued her creativity. She said that she was looking for a method to utilize a fabric's maximum suppleness, when she discovered that if she turned it on an angle, it gained more elasticity. This was due to her unique creative process. Vionnet did not know how to draw, so she created her designs on a 2-foot-high jointed wooden mannequin (FIGURE BOX 1.1A). She draped and pinned the fabric, turning the mannequin as she worked. This kept her aware of both the front and the back of the figure,

LEFT
FIGURE BOX 1.1A Madeleine Vionnet drapes on the figure in the round, circa 1935.
© APIC/GETTY IMAGES

RIGHT
FIGURE BOX 1.1B Madeleine Vionnet's 1933 bias cut evening dress drapes against the model's body.
GEORGE HOYNINGEN-HUENÉ © 1933 CONDÉ NAST PUBLICATIONS

OPPOSITE
FIGURE BOX 1.1C Vionnet's lovely bias-silk crepe evening pajamas in pink crepe romaine (1931).
GEORGE HOYNINGEN-HUENÉ © 1931 CONDÉ NAST PUBLICATIONS

as well as the structure of the garment she was building, similar to the thought process of an architect. In addition to her technique, she had a great visual sensitivity. She described how she regularly observed clothing on passersby, determining in her mind how she might change the design, thinking through her scissors, needle, and thread.

Vionnet's designs were characterized by delicacy and femininity, the result of the bias cut. However, she also applied lingerie techniques she had learned through her years of apprenticeship—pin-tucking, fagoting, and rolled hems—and she eliminated interfacing in order to enhance the fabric's drape against the body. The combination yielded designs that sensuously followed the lines of the body (FIGURE BOX 1.1B AND C).

Prior to Vionnet, the bias cut had only been used in sections of garments. Since her innovation, many subsequent designers have worked with the bias cut, including the French designer Alix Grès (1903–1993); the French-born, American designer Pauline Trigère (1908–2008); and American designer Mary McFadden (1938–). Madeleine Vionnet died in 1975.

body shape often use a more rigid material, like the metal hoops used in a bustle or the boning in a corset (FIGURES 1.5A AND B). Contemporary fashions utilize nonrigid materials to produce independent form, for instance, goose down or even air inflation for a style in the nature of a ski parka. Despite the unusual structure of the architectural design, a need remains for the garment to fit the figure in some fashion, for instance, at the shoulder, waist, bust, or hip. Fit is defined as the relationship between the cloth and the body, which is a static concept regardless of body movement. Designers sometimes engineer several layers beneath a fashion to create its structure. American designer Charles James (1906–1978) was especially adept at that process (BOX 1.2).

1.5A This British bustle (1871) is a cotton undergarment with metal threaded through each tier.
THE METROPOLITAN MUSEUM OF ART/ART RESOURCE, NY

1.5B This corset, made from red sateen and yellow leather in Great Britain in 1883, uses whalebone to provide its shape.
© V&A IMAGES, VICTORIA AND ALBERT MUSEUM

DECONSTRUCTION AND FASHION

In the 1980s and 1990s there was a trend that changed fashion structure. It was called **deconstruction**, and it originated with the writings of the French philosopher Jacques Derrida. Derrida's writings expressed a new approach to literary criticism—that literature could be analyzed not only by what was present in the text but also by what was absent from it. So deconstruction in literature means the search for hidden or alternative meanings. This trend affected modern art and architecture as well as fashion. The implication for architecture was no longer "form follows function," but that new and diverse forms express new functions. Architects strived to make contradictory or alternative statements to what was previously accepted. Instead of the traditional grid-shaped building, they created forms that unfolded, curved, undulated, and interpenetrated, like the building designed by architect Frank Gehry (1929–) in FIGURE 1.6. In fashion design, deconstruction meant a change to the traditional structures, challenging the traditional meaning of fashion, so that clothing appeared inside out, unfinished, or deteriorated. Construction techniques that were always hidden became visible and added a new visual dynamic to the

BOX 1.2

CHARLES JAMES

CHARLES JAMES IS considered an American designer, although he was born in England in 1906 and he lived and designed in both London and Paris during the 1930s. He began his career in fashion as a milliner in Chicago. Some credit his method for adorning the female figure to this beginning, because he approached his designs as if they were built on molded forms like a hat on a block. Some considered him an artistic genius, or at least, a wizard of dressmaking, including the most prominent designers of the twentieth century—Paul Poiret, Coco Chanel, Elsa Schiaparelli, Christian Dior, and Cristóbal Balenciaga. They understood that his purpose was to endow a woman with a shape that was perfection, unrelated to her own, and that he achieved this by building shapes and layers, shifting darts and seams, and forcing the fabric grain to fit his intention, rather than working with its natural flow, as in the manner of Madeleine Vionnet. He spent his career on his obsession with architectural design, and as a result, his designs did not follow fashion trends, and he never attained financial success in his endeavors.

James' brilliance with his craft is most profound in the 1948 photograph by the renowned Cecil Beaton, which featured eight of his most provocative ball gowns (FIGURE BOX 1.2A). They reflect a variation in design details, from asymmetrical and strapless necklines to deep décolletages and hip panels. Each gown, in its pastel hue, appears to float along with the body that wears it, recalling the splendor of a bygone era. In reality, this was hardly the case, as each was built on a hard shell that molded the figure to its ideal form. James then applied as many layers of pliant materials to the foundation as was required to convey the needed density and shape. Some of the garments weighed as much as 50 pounds, but the wearer managed because the designer's astute engineering distributed the weight.

When James assessed the contributions of his career, the design he rated the very highest was made for Mrs. William Randolph Hearst, Jr., to wear to the inaugural ball of President Dwight D. Eisenhower in 1953. She also wore it to the Coronation Ball of Queen Elizabeth II in London and to a subsequent affair at the Palace of Versailles (FIGURE BOX 1.2B AND C). He called it the "Abstract" or the "Cloverleaf" ball gown, as many of his designs were abstract interpretations of nature. Names of other dresses were "Swan,"

"Tulip," "Butterfly," and "Tree." The gown, of cream satin, flat black silk velvet and off-white faille, has a hemline formation that replicates a cloverleaf, thought to be the outline of his 1948 beret (Coleman, 1982, p. 65). The foundation was structured from several layers that float from the hips (FIGURE BOX 1.2C), creating the illusion, nevertheless, that the skirt floats as the wearer glides across a room. The entire design weighed 15 pounds. Despite the chore of carrying it, Mrs. Hearst was known to say that wearing a Charles James gown transformed her like Cinderella into a princess (Martin, 2006, p. 11).

James thought like an architect or engineer for his entire career. He was known to work over wired, structured forms that he built himself, after planning them out with precise dimensions. He was thoughtful about the positioning of seams, seeking to use them to emphasize a feature of the body. His goal was to compensate for deficiencies in the human figure. He raised or lowered the waist, sometimes positioning it differently in the front than in the back. He molded the bust using methods other than darts, but his varying pattern pieces regularly converged at the bust. Whatever the method, it was always hidden inside the dress' outer fabric. Other clients reported the difficulties in responding to his designs. It was not clear how to put on the clothes or to identify front from back. In some cases it was hard to walk or to sit down. However, because they marveled at his genius and felt beautiful in his designs, they were glad to sacrifice.

Later in his career, James developed a reputation for coats and jackets, in which the architectural approach varied from the ball gowns. The most famous was designed in 1937 (FIGURE BOX 1.2D), in which he used padding made of eiderdown for a silk evening jacket. Its quilted appearance was reminiscent of Chinese styling, and it maintained a structure separate from the human figure. Its innovation caused the artist Salvador Dali to call it the first example of soft sculpture, whereas James thought its function inspired the Air Force jackets used in World War II. It was later thought to be an influence for the American designer Halston (1932–1990), as a forerunner of the anorak.

Several of James' designs were donated to museums during his lifetime. Despite his financial failures, Charles James had opportunities to receive artistic recognition. He died alone in New York in 1978.

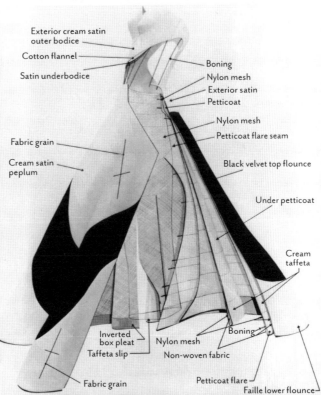

Exterior cream satin outer bodice
Cotton flannel
Satin underbodice
Boning
Nylon mesh
Exterior satin
Petticoat
Nylon mesh
Petticoat flare seam
Fabric grain
Cream satin peplum
Black velvet top flounce
Under petticoat
Cream taffeta
Inverted box pleat
Taffeta slip
Nylon mesh
Non-woven fabric
Boning
Fabric grain
Petticoat flare
Faille lower flounce

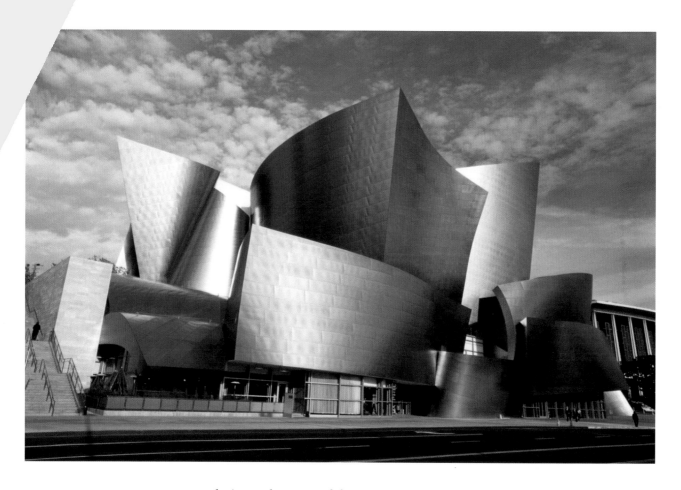

1.6 Frank Gehry's Walt Disney Concert Hall in Los Angeles is an example of deconstruction in architecture.
KURT KRIEGER/CORBIS

designs. Elements of deconstruction were detected as far back as the 1960s in the fashions of French designer Sonia Rykiel (1930–), where visible seams were sewn on the garment surface. Later examples of deconstruction appeared globally in the collections of British designer Vivienne Westwood (1941–), Japanese designer Yohji Yamamoto (1943–), and Belgian designer Martin Margiela (1959–). Yamamoto and Margiela utilized reversed seams, hanging threads, holes, and exposed zippers (FIGURES 1.7A AND B).

FUNCTIONAL DESIGN

Functional design refers to the way in which a fashion works or performs physically. The mechanics of the garment are the concern—how to put it on, how it opens and closes, how the body moves wearing it. Even a pocket demands mechanical considerations. What will it contain? What size is needed? Will it require a closure? The relationship of the garment to its purpose is also implied by the term. For instance, will a swimsuit function well in water? Will a coat provide sufficient warmth? Will a wedding gown allow a bride to dance? The consideration of the purpose often necessitates added research and experimentation. Functional design commands an even greater focus as the purpose becomes more specialized. Fashion

designers are not called upon to produce an astronaut's space suit or a suit for deep-sea diving. However, they may design airline uniforms or activewear for a specific sport. The discerning ones are able to identify new consumer needs as a result of changes in the lifestyles of the target market. For instance, increased use of technology, such as cell phones, personal data assistants, and MP3 players require the addition of an appropriately sized pocket to jackets and handbags. American designer Claire McCardell (1905–1958) was so clever at recognizing the lifestyle needs of her customers that her sensitivity for functional design foreshadowed the popularity of American sportswear (BOX 1.3).

THE COMPONENTS OF FASHION

Fashion designers are constantly in search of pleasing solutions in aesthetic design, structural design, and functional design. In that pursuit, they also are mindful of their clients' needs or their target market, and they utilize the elements and principles of design. This is certainly enough to preoccupy their attention during the design process. However, they are also aware of the manner in which those who interpret, critique, and order fashions perceive their designs. All of those individuals see their collections

BOX 1.3

CLAIRE
McCARDELL

CLAIRE MCCARDELL WAS famous for the focus on function in her timeless designs. Her contribution to the fashion industry was prolific, especially considering that her life was unusually shortened by illness. Born in Frederick, Maryland, in 1905, Claire was surrounded even in childhood by influences that would later affect her designs. From her three brothers, she gained an appreciation for the comfort and ease of menswear. Like them, she participated regularly in sports, so she came naturally to the idea of designing apparel with a specific purpose in mind. She left her study at Hood College in Maryland for the School of Fine and Applied Arts (later, Parsons School of Design) in New York City. During her education there, McCardell took a foundation course similar to the one taught in the Bauhaus system, and she had the opportunity to study in Paris. The sketchbook drawings made there underscored her knowledge and understanding of Madeleine Vionnet's bias cut. Along with her disposition for function, McCardell regularly integrated the bias cut into her designs. During her stay in Paris, McCardell also shopped flea markets and sample sales held by the couture houses, not intending to wear the clothes, but to take them apart in order to deduce the

methods of construction used by the most knowledgeable designers of the day. Hence, she used deconstruction to learn the way clothes worked, how they fastened, and how they felt.

McCardell's sensibilities were similar to the "form follows function" philosophy of the architects of her time. She thought of clothing as objects that must function instead of simply conveying decoration. She measured her own success by the performance of her clothes when worn by women, rather than by the comments of the press. She also thought of designing as a process of solving problems.

By 1930, Claire was employed by Townley Frocks in New York. There she came into her own as a designer, bringing forth the details for which she became known. Chief among these were pockets, which she constructed into every garment, even evening gowns, over the protests of her boss because of the added expense. She knew that pockets provided the ability to carry one's belongings, but also that women felt more at ease with a place to put their hands. She used the buckles from ski uniforms on her designs along with other hardware closings such as rivets, grommets, snaps, and hooks. She lifted the double stitching on blue jeans for reinforcement and style on elegant fabrics such as silk twill and organza (FIGURE BOX 1.3A). Her dresses were comfortable and easy to fit, because of her uncut and adjustable waistlines—often the result of spaghetti or shoestring ties—as well as sleeves cut in one with the bodice, dropped shoulders and deep armholes. These earmarks were nicknamed "McCardellisms."

Her popularity readily grew in the 1940s during the period of fabric restrictions because of U.S. participation in World War II and also because of the lack of communication with Paris couture houses during the Nazi occupation. McCardell worked around the regulations ingeniously, creating low-cost dresses and consistently identifying the needs of her customer due to their changes in lifestyle. One good example was the easy-to-pack wedding dress, made in soft wool for wartime brides to marry in unheated churches (FIGURE BOX 1.3B). Another was a dress designed for busy housewives and mothers who took over household duties from their staff during the period of war. It was called the "Popover," and its simple, wrap-front construction came complete with self-apron and attached oven mitt (FIGURE BOX 1.3C). The first version came in denim and cost $6.95, but it was remade in several other fabrics, including gingham, as its popularity increased. McCardell also designed the "Kitchen Dinner" dress, a cotton shirtwaist style, with dirndl skirt and matching apron, for the entertaining woman who liked to cook but did not want to appear that way.

McCardell's fame grew, thanks in part to the promotion of the store Lord & Taylor, a *Time* magazine cover, and even an award given by President Harry S. Truman. In addition to dresses, she went on to design travel separates, evening wear, swimwear, golf skirts, ski parkas, tennis clothes, ballet shoes, leotards, sweaters, and coats. She died of cancer in 1958 at the age of 52.

or lines concurrently with others during Fashion Week. Somehow they must make sense of the designs in the context of all that are offered for the season.

How is that accomplished?

This fashion-educated audience breaks down the fashions into their most basic components in order to make comparisons or identify similarities or trends. Some of these components overlap with the terminology for the elements of design, but their orientation and meanings are slightly different.

SILHOUETTE

First, they examine the fashions for their **silhouette**. The silhouette refers to the outer contour or shape of the fashions. The term is further discussed in Chapter 3, "Form, Shape, and Space." This is tremendously important, because similarities in silhouette are likely to appear across the collections. These similarities are retrospectively definitive of the period, and they facilitate the ability to describe the fashions for the season. Silhouettes continue for a longer time period than other garment components.

FABRIC

Fabric is second in importance. It is the medium in which the designer works. Traditionally, fabrics may vary from heavy wools or supple leathers for the fall season and comfortable cotton or translucent organza for the spring. However, a designer may choose an alternative material for the fabrication, such as vinyl or metal. These too are examined for trends or innovation, which are discussed further in Chapter 4, "Texture and Light."

COLOR

Then the fashions are examined for **color**. Color makes tremendous visual impact on the runway. Most colors are the result of forecasting for the season, because designers choose fabrics that are already manufactured and dyed. Typically, a particular spectrum of colors is highlighted. All the dynamics of color are described in Chapters 6 and 7, "Color and Value" and "Color and Industry." Sometimes, however, the choice of color is a personal one for the designer or is inspired by fabrics from a particular country or region. Comparisons are made across collections for similarities, or color choice may signify the exclusivity of a designer's collection.

LOOKS

Eventually, the comparisons of collections will reveal similarities among **looks**. The elements of the design combine to define a particular style or

look. Perhaps there is evidence of the style in a number of collect[...]
Sometimes the style has a traditional name, like a double-breasted suit [...]
blazer. Alternatively, the fashions resist traditional style names but suppo[...]
a common description, like the "space-age look." In that case, elements of [...]
the look filter through the collections but may not repeat in the exact same
form. However, the description identifies for the world what is new for the
season.

DETAILS

Finally, the focus shifts to garment **details**. Details are the changes in necklines, sleeves, waistlines, pockets, or any garment parts. They include trims
or surface embellishments, such as embroidery, fringes, buttons, appliqués,
bows, or even accessories like belts, handbags, or hats. Cumulative changes
in details drive new looks and ultimately modify silhouettes. An understanding of these terms prepares fashion designers for the public's reaction
to their ideas.

KEY TERMS

aesthetic design	elements of design	on-grain
architectural design	elements of construction	pattern
balance	emphasis	principles of design
bias cut	fabric	proportion
color	fabric trends	rhythm
color trends	fit	seam
cut of the fabric	form	season
dart	functional design	shape
deconstruction	haute couture	silhouette
design	interlining	space
design process	light	structural design
details	line	texture
draped design	looks	workmanship

PROJECTS

Follow the design process for each of these projects:

1. In your sketchbook, create six or more designs using the Bauhaus elements
   of geometric shapes and primary colors. In two-inch squares, combine the
   colors red, blue, and yellow with a triangle, circle, rectangle, or square in

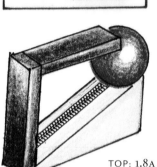

different arrangements. Use a straight edge or ruler, templates for the other shapes, and colored markers. Compare the alternatives. Which two are the strongest? Why? Transpose them into finished products, expanding the scale to four-inch squares on Bristol board and using colored paper in place of markers, if that enhances the impact of the design. Mount the squares on black mat board (FIGURE 1.8A).

2. Adapt the strongest of the preceding exercises into an accessory design, either a handbag, shoe, or umbrella. Practice in your sketchbook using colored markers. Transpose the final solution onto Bristol at a scale comparable to the four-inch squares, replacing the markers with colored paper, if that creates greater impact. Mount on black mat board (FIGURE 1.8B).

3. Turn the accessory design into a three-dimensional model at a similar scale. Use foam core, Styrofoam, dowels, colored papers or fabrics, and other craft materials. Tips: Use only fabric glue as an adhesive for fabric. An electric carving knife is especially effective in cutting foam core and Styrofoam. Nonelectric knives, X-ACTO knives, and mat knives also cut those materials. (Refer to FIGURE 1.9.)

TOP: 1.8A Project 1 example. ILLUSTRATION BY JANICE GREENBERG ELLINWOOD
MIDDLE: 1.8B Project 2 example. ILLUSTRATION BY JANICE GREENBERG ELLINWOOD
BOTTOM: 1.9 Project 3 example. ILLUSTRATION BY JANICE GREENBERG ELLINWOOD

REFERENCES

Bell-Price, S. (2004, October). Vivienne Westwood (born 1941) and the postmodern legacy of punk style. *Heilbrunn Timeline of Art History.* New York: The Metropolitan Museum of Art, 2000. Retrieved September 10, 2008, from http://www.metmuseum.org/toah/hd/vivw/hd_vivw.htm.

Coleman, E. A. (1982). *The genius of Charles James.* New York: The Brooklyn Museum.

Davis, M. L. (1996). *Visual design in dress* (3rd ed.). Upper Saddle River, NJ: Prentice Hall.

Frankel, Susannah. (2001). *Visionaries: Interviews with fashion designers.* London: V&A Publications.

Griffin, J., & Collins, P. (2007). *Wear your chair: When fashion meets interior design.* New York: Fairchild Books.

Harwood, B., May, B., & Sherman, C. (2009). *Architecture and interior design from the 19th century: An integrated history* (Vol. 2) Upper Saddle River, NJ: Pearson/Prentice Hall.

Kirke, B. (1993). *Madeleine Vionnet.* San Francisco: Chronicle Books.

Lambert, S. (n.d.). *Form follows function? Design in the 20th century.* London: Victoria & Albert Museum.

Lauer, D. A., & Pentak, S. (2005). *Design basics* (6th ed.). Belmont, California: Wadsworth.

Lee, S. T. (Ed.). (1975). *American fashion: The life and lines of Adrian, Mainbocher, McCardell, Norell, Trigere.* New York: The Fashion Institute of Technology.

Quinn, B. (2003). *The Fashion of architecture.* Oxford: Berg.

Roters, E. (1969). *Painters of the Bauhaus.* New York: Frederick A. Praeger.

Rowland, A. (1990). *Bauhaus source book.* New York: Van Nostrand Reinhold.

Shaeffer, C. (2001). *Sewing for the apparel industry.* New York: Prentice Hall.

Steele, V. (1991). *Women of fashion: Twentieth-century designers.* New York: Rizzoli.

Stewart, M. (2008). *Launching the imagination: A comprehensive guide to basic design* (3rd ed.). New York: McGraw-Hill.

Whitford, F. (1988). *Bauhaus.* London: Thames & Hudson.

Yohannan, K., & Nolf, N. (1998). *Claire McCardell: Redefining modernism.* New York: Harry N. Abrams.

Young, Frank M. (1985). *Visual studies: A foundation for artists and designers.* New Jersey: Prentice Hall.

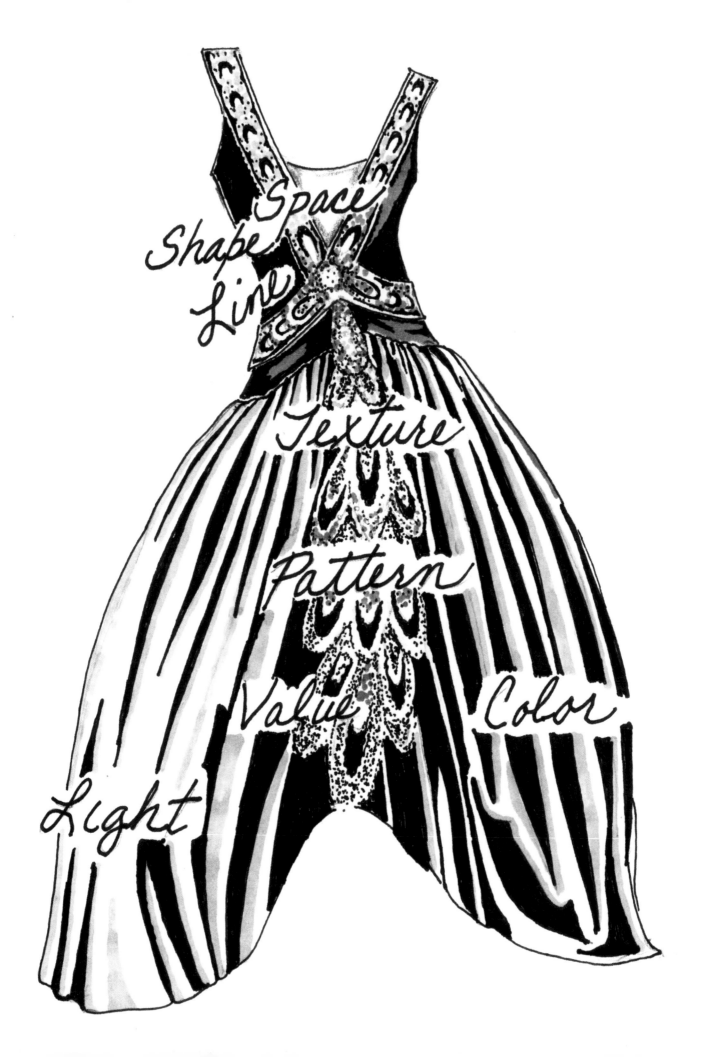

PART I | # THE ELEMENTS OF DESIGN

OPPOSITE
ILLUSTRATION BY
JANICE GREENBERG ELLINWOOD

| # LINE

OBJECTIVES

To enumerate the kinds of line a designer may use in a garment

To describe the ways in which a designer implements line in a garment

To explain how designers employ line direction and line quality in their designs

Line is the most familiar of all the design elements. Young children create lines and scribbles from the first time they are able to grasp a crayon or pencil and mark with it. So it is quite possibly the simplest design element and the easiest to understand. At the same time, it is the most versatile, because there are so many kinds that a designer may utilize. Ironically, the term has several definitions. Line has been called a **dot** or a point in motion. The dot is an even simpler element from the perspective of artists. Geometry defines a line as an infinite number of points. It is also considered the connection between two points or the implied connection between two points. The effect of a line is created by the edge of an object or shape, especially when there is no other **actual line** on the object's surface to distract the eye. Line provides a great benefit to the designer. It leads the eye in the direction the line travels. It activates a space. It divides the area through which it passes, acting as a compositional bridge. It even communicates a feeling or mood.

This chapter enumerates the various types of line, discusses the ways in which a fashion designer creates line in a garment, and describes the attributes of **line direction** and quality in relation to the design and to the human figure. It features supporting examples from the work of prominent fashion designers and artists.

TYPES OF LINE

Theorists agree that there are an infinite variety of kinds of line. However, they all divide them into two main categories: **straight** and **curved**. Beyond that, line varies in its path, thickness, evenness, continuity, sharpness of edge, consistency, length, and direction. It is through these variations that a mood or feeling is conveyed. Line quality is discussed later in this chapter.

As a line varies in its weight, direction, character, arrangement, or in the **contour** of a shape, it also carries a sense of **symbolism**. It reminds the viewer of a familiar object in the environment or in the natural world. That additionally colors the visual impact of the design. For instance, a spiral line might remind the viewer of a snail shell. Two diagonals in opposite directions may suggest a tent or the letter A.

Actual lines are those whose evidence and placement are by intended design. They are easily perceived. In other cases, the impression of a line is created as a result of arrangement. Whenever there is a series of shapes or dots placed in a linear arrangement, the result is an **implied line**. A designer manipulates both actual lines and implied lines.

LINE IN FASHION

A fashion designer incorporates line into a garment using both structural and decorative methods. Where structural methods are employed, designers often eliminate patterned fabrics so that the lines are not obscured. Lines are created by construction techniques, such as seams, darts, **tucks**, or **shirring**. Note the seams in the dress by Gabrielle "Coco" Chanel (1883–1971) in FIGURE BOX 2.1B (page 44). Designers also create line in the real or perceived edges of garment parts, such as the silhouette, edges of **collars**, **sleeves**, **hems**, **pockets**, or openings. (The term silhouette is examined more fully in Chapter 3, "Form, Shape, and Space.") The suit designed by John Galliano (1960–), designer for the House of Dior, pictured in FIGURE 2.1 is a good example, with its diagonally shaped silhouette and other garment parts. In yet another structural approach, designers utilize the creases

2.1 Diagonal line is perceived in the silhouette and garment parts of this suit designed by John Galliano for Christian Dior from the autumn-winter 1997 collection.
COLLECTION OF THE KYOTO COSTUME INSTITUTE, PHOTO BY TAKASHI HATAKEYAMA

2.2 Line is expressed in the draped folds of this silk jersey evening gown designed by Madame Grès. The date is thought to be between 1967 and 1985.
THE METROPOLITAN MUSEUM OF ART/ART RESOURCE, NY

or folds made by **pleats**, gathers, tucks, or draping for visual lines. The draped folds in FIGURE 2.2, a design by French couturière Alix Grès (1903–1993), illustrate this concept. In contrast, the decorative approach is where designers present lines on the surface of the garment, as in the case of fabric patterns such as **stripes**, **plaids**, **checks**, or **herringbones**. Other decorative approaches are those applied to the surface, such as **trims**, **braids**, **embroidery**, **ribbons**, **piping**, or rows of buttons. Chanel's trimmed suit in FIGURE BOX 2.1F (page 47) is a good example. **Topstitching**, **fagoting**, and **ruffles** are also used.

LINE DIRECTION AND QUALITY

Line direction is the key to the mood conveyed by a design. So it is important for a designer to understand its implications in order to make decisions that enhance both the visual design and the figure that wears it.

THE VERTICAL LINE

Vertical lines communicate a feeling of firmness, rigidity, strength, dignity, and tradition, much like the columns of a building, tin soldiers, or trees. They add height to the space in which they are placed. Therefore, designers use them to add the illusion of height to the human figure. By increasing height in proportion to width, vertical lines may also allow the human figure to appear slimmer. A fashion designer achieves this illusion with the use of seams, pleats, draped folds, rows of buttons, the elongated shape of a contrasting color, stripes, or trims, just to name a few options. Vertical lines may appear in repetition, or depending on the placement, one or more may divide the human figure symmetrically or asymmetrically. Choosing the placement affects the visual impact of the design.

THE HORIZONTAL LINE

Horizontal lines generate a very different feeling—one of rest, repose, and relaxation, like a sofa or chaise lounge or the distant horizon line on a lazy seashore. They add width to the space that they occupy. So, although they may appear in repetition, a designer is often careful about placement. Horizontal lines appear more readily in some kinds of apparel, such as sportswear and athletic attire, but the astute designer will have a reason behind the decision to add width to a particular body part. For instance, horizontal lines at the shoulders reinforce the message when fashions have emphasized the shoulder, as was the case with the military influence of the 1940s, or with the power attributed to career women in the 1980s. To create the illusion, designers utilize seams, stripes, **epaulettes**, pleating, or draping that results from **ruching**, among other alternatives.

THE LINE NETWORK

Rather than using one line or the other to excess, designers sometimes use the two kinds of line direction in combination, in an effort to achieve balance. (This concept is discussed at length in Chapter 8, "Balance.") When executed with repetition, the combination of vertical and horizontal lines create what artists call a **line network**.

MONDRIAN AND SAINT LAURENT

Piet Mondrian (1875–1944) was a famous painter whose best-known work combined vertical lines and horizontal lines with primary colors in various combinations. FIGURE 2.3 features one of these paintings. Mondrian was born in Holland and first studied painting there under the auspices of the leaders of the Barbizon School. His original work featured Dutch landscapes, and later, still taken with natural forms, he created a series of paintings that examined the structure of a flower. His work changed as a result of two influences. He had joined the religion of Theosophy, a late nineteenth-century form of Buddhism, and that encouraged in him a quest for spirituality. He also became aware of the art form called Cubism, a style perpetuated by the painters Georges Braque (1882–1963) and Pablo Picasso (1881–1973). From Cubism, he learned about and began to value **abstraction**, and he let the recognizable forms in his work disappear. That determined his direction on the journey to find his own distinctive art form.

Mondrian wrote about his ideas in the journal *De Stijl*, a term that also referred to a movement of artists and designers whose ideas were similar to Mondrian's. In his quest for a spiritual Utopia, Mondrian believed that art could express a true or pure reality, a metaphor for the harmony of universal relations, which could permeate all other aspects of life. For this he developed a nonrepresentational language that included both vertical and horizontal lines, which he thought was the essence of all that stands on the

2.3 Piet Mondrian painted "Composition with Red, Blue, and Yellow" in 1930. It is one in a series of paintings to combine horizontal and vertical line with the primary colors.
ERICH LESSING/ART RESOURCE, NY

earth or is spread over it. In addition, he chose to use red, blue, and yellow, the three primary colors that form the foundation of all other colors. With those, he used white, black, and gray, which were, in his mind, non-colors that could nevertheless define space and place. He spent the rest of his life combining these elements in different ways, attempting to attain a sense of unity every time. (This concept is further discussed in Chapter 12, "Unity.")

The French couture designer Yves Saint Laurent (1936–2008) had a prolific career. First representing the House of Dior and then operating under his own name, he brought forth memorable collections season after season. Inspired as he often was by artists, Saint Laurent's Fall 1965 collection featured a series of designs based on Piet Mondrian's paintings. One of them is shown in FIGURE 2.4. Each dress utilized the elements Mondrian identified as the most important—vertical line, horizontal line, red, blue, and yellow. Each combined these elements in a different manner, and each varied in its effect on the figure. The viewer might have the impression that these elements just ride the surface of each garment. However, each line and compartment is separated structurally by seams and made from a different fabric. The media of the day hailed the dresses and even compared

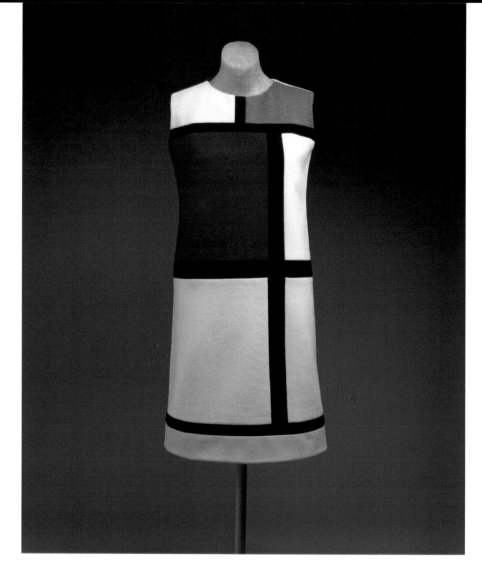

2.4 One of a series of dresses Yves Saint Laurent designed for his autumn 1965 collection based on the paintings of Piet Mondrian.
THE METROPOLITAN MUSEUM OF ART/ART RESOURCE, NY

the designs to a semaphore flag, a good example of the way in which the element of line communicates symbolism.

THE MODULAR GRID

Saint Laurent's collection occurred after Mondrian's death, and the artists of the 1960s had already moved on to a different formation of vertical and horizontal line. Their paintings and sculpture took the line network one more step, into the formation of a modular **grid**, like a checkerboard or graph. Artists of the 1960s called this formation a "nonrelational arrangement," as opposed to Mondrian's approach, which was a "relational structure." The difference is profound. A grid delineates a surface in a predictable fashion and is not **organic**. It runs the risk of boredom, has no potential for growth and development, but is a prime vehicle for repetition. In contrast, a T-formation in one of Mondrian's paintings might represent a figure with its arms spread, another example of symbolism. He also retained the option for a different outcome with each arrangement, the result of a trial-and-error process, a sound avenue to a gratifying design. (The grid is discussed in more detail in Chapter 5, "Pattern.")

Vertical and horizontal lines also characterize the **classic** fas
known as the Chanel suit, a design originated by French coutur
Gabrielle "Coco" Chanel. Its continual acceptance is a testimony to th
positive impact of that combination (BOX 2.1, pages 44 through 47;
FIGURE BOX 2.1A, page 44; AND FIGURE BOX 2.1F, page 47).

THE DIAGONAL LINE

Diagonal lines are quite different. Diagonal lines are dynamic; they suggest movement. They appear active and dramatic. The designer knows
that dividing the space diagonally is certain to attract the eye and that a
diagonal line commands the viewer's eye to travel along with it, as in the
case of FIGURE 2.5, a dress from American designer Zac Posen's (1980–)
2010 spring collection. Posen capitalizes on the diagonal lines to produce
pattern parts that are cut on the bias. Because of its association with
activity, diagonal lines are often considered most appropriate for sportswear. Some may caution against the use of too many diagonal lines and
suggest the balance of another directional line. Although that prescription may lead to a pleasing design, there is a unique synergy between
diagonal lines and the body. On a garment that has a close-fitting silhouette, diagonals swim around the body like spirals, placing a special accent
on the natural female anatomical curves. As a result, they flatter the
appearance. In addition to lines of other directions, prolific American
designer Rudi Gernreich (1922–1985) used diagonal lines often in his work
(BOX 2.2).

THE CURVILINEAR, OR ORGANIC, LINE

A **curvilinear** or organic line offers a different quality. This type is full of
curves, reminiscent of life forms—hence, the term organic. Such a line
may reference the contours of the human figure, flora, and fauna or even
the movement of water. As a result, a garment that features an organic line
in its structure or on its surface appears unified with the figure that wears
it. Note the example of the suit by designer Thierry Mugler (1946–) from
spring-summer 1990 in FIGURE 2.6. The horizontal, curved structural
lines in the jacket suggest the feeling of a landscape. Repeated organic lines
may also reinforce the anatomical curves of the female figure, as depicted
on the surface of the second suit by Mugler (autumn–winter 1990–1991) in
FIGURE 2.7. Such lines also reference computer technology, which was on
the rise at the time and has been since.

2.5 The diagonal lines in Zac Posen's dress (spring 2010) are seams that facilitate pattern parts of bias-cut fabric.
COURTESY OF WWD/JOHN AQUINO

RIGHT

The curved, structural seams Thierry Mugler's jacket from the spring/summer collection of 1990 accentuates the figure.

COLLECTION OF THE KYOTO COSTUME INSTITUTE, PHOTO BY TAKASHI HATAKEYAMA

BELOW

2.7 Thierry Mugler's jacket from his autumn/winter 1990–1991 collection is called "Anatomique Computer."

2009 MUSEUM ASSOCIATES/ LACMA/ART RESOURCE, NY

THE KINETIC LINE

Victor Vasarely (1906–1997) was a painter who used curvilinear or organic lines in his work. The painting in FIGURE 2.8 is a good example. The lines provide a sense of volume for the zebras that wear them. Vasarely, as well as the painter Bridget Riley (1931–), were both participants in the Op Art movement of the 1960s. Many of their paintings made use of **kinetic line**, line from which one perceives movement. In many, but not all, cases, their art takes organic or curvilinear line a step further, as in the example by Bridget Riley in FIGURE 2.9. The Op Art movement centered on images that create the illusion of perpetual motion. Its pinnacle was in 1965 when it was the subject of an exhibition called "The Responsive Eye" at the Museum of Modern Art in New York City. Simple elements, such as lines, dots, and stripes, were arranged in an organization that would distort the final image, creating afterimages, distortions of perspective, and other optical illusions. Artists appeared to consider the science of optical perception in their work, and the resulting art commanded the interaction of the observer. Op Art caught on in the fashion world immediately. Some art critics thought that was the reason for its demise, both because it degraded a concept thought to be "high art" and because it may have lead to its commercial saturation. A fashion editor for the New York *Herald Tribune* reported that an attendee to the exhibition was wearing a sheath and scarf made by

American designer Geoffrey Beene (1927–2004) of fabric designe
American artist Tzaims Luksus (1932–), which was described as optica
of black and gray circles scattered on white silk organdie.

A kinetic quality does not depend solely on organic lines. Designers can capture the quality by manipulating striped fabric. French couturier Christian Lacroix (1951–) has repeatedly used stripes in his designs, as in FIGURE 2.10. The sense of movement depends on the direction of the stripes that result from how the fabric for each pattern piece is cut and/or the effect created by tying or bunching it. Lacroix's interest in stripes originated from his love of historic costume as well as the wallpapers and draperies of historic interiors.

When the effects of line direction and quality are fully understood, the designer can choose the ones that most flatter the female figure and direct the viewer's eye throughout the design. For that reason, designers often choose to use different lines in combination. Gernreich's journal sketch in FIGURE 2.11 reveals the care with which he determined the best layout of lines for the figure. The design by Madame Grès in FIGURE 2.12 illustrates how that choice was made according to the placement and direction of the draped fabric against the figure. The example conveys that the cut of fabric was as important to Grès as it was to Madeleine Vionnet, who was profiled in the previous chapter. The difference, however, was that Vionnet focused on the body, while Grès' interest was in the movement of the fabric. She

BELOW LEFT
2.10 Christian Lacroix manipulates stripes in the evening jacket from his fall-winter 2004–2005 collection.
THE METROPOLITAN MUSEUM OF ART/ART RESOURCE, NY

BELOW RIGHT
2.11 Rudi Gernreich engineered the stripes in the design of the sketch from 1956.
2009 MUSEUM ASSOCIATES/ LACMA/ART RESOURCE, NY

used it in greater abundance and draped it carefully, pleat by pleat. Probably the most graphic example is the suit designed by American designer Adrian (1903–1959) in the 1940s (SEE FIGURE 2.13). Like Claire McCardell (1905–1958), Adrian was an American designer who was promoted by Lord & Taylor in New York during World War II, when the United States lacked communication with Paris. Adrian had worked as a costume designer during the Golden Era of Hollywood film in the 1930s. The pictured silhouette was obviously influenced by the military uniforms of the period. The suit is cut with great precision, which is evident from the variations in the direction of the striped fabric. He had to carefully appraise the female figure in order to make such decisions. It is a valuable lesson for any aspiring fashion designer.

abstraction	fagoting	pocket
actual line	grid	ribbon
braid	hem	ruching
checks	herringbone	ruffle
classic	horizontal line	shirring
collar	implied line	sleeve
contour	kinetic line	straight line
curved line	line direction	stripes
curvilinear line	line network	symbolism
diagonal line	organic line	top-stitching
dot	piping	trim
embroidery	plaid	tuck
epaulettes	pleats	vertical line

PROJECTS

1. In your sketchbook, create a series of Mondrian-like designs. Combine these elements—black vertical line, black horizontal line, white space, red, blue, yellow—into a different combination for each of six or more two-inch boxes. Sketch the boxes using a straight edge with pencil. Then use markers for color. Which two are the strongest designs? Why? Transfer the two best to four-inch squares of Bristol. Cut the squares from Bristol using a straight edge and X-ACTO knife. Use markers for color or choose black architectural tape for the lines and adhere construction paper for the colors. (SEE FIGURES 2.14A AND B.)

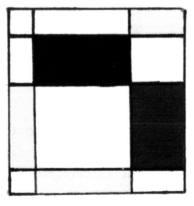

LEFT
2.14A Project 1 example.
ILLUSTRATION BY
JANICE GREENBERG ELLINWOOD

RIGHT
2.14B Project 1 example.
ILLUSTRATION BY
JANICE GREENBERG ELLINWOOD

2. Insert one of the two best designs from Project 1 into a compatible ment silhouette or shape. Use your sketchbook to experiment with differ-ent shapes. Cut the best one out of Bristol at a height of four inches, using the method described in Project 1. Hint: Choose a silhouette that is com-patible with the line direction for optimum unity. Use markers for color or choose black drafting tape and construction paper. Mount the two designs from Project 1, along with the garment silhouette, left to right, on a piece of black mat board, leaving adequate framing space around the products. (SEE FIGURE 2.15.)

2.15 Project 2 example.
ILLUSTRATION BY
JANICE GREENBERG ELLINWOOD

3. In your sketchbook, draw several garment silhouettes or shapes with pencil. Like Adrian did with his suit, divide each up using sections of stripes run-ning in vertical, horizontal, or diagonal directions. Use a 2B or softer pencil or a black marker for the stripes. Which of the designs is the most successful?

Which would flatter the wearer's figure better? Why? Choose the best of the series, and cut a larger silhouette out of Bristol. Use striped fabric or striped paper for the sections of stripes, cutting either medium into sections to fit the shape. Look for a maximum width of ¼-inch stripes. Craft stores carry many papers with stripe patterns in their scrap-booking supplies. Use white glue with a brush or glue stick to adhere the paper to the Bristol. Choose fabric glue to attach the sections of striped fabric to Bristol. Mount the garment design on black mat board, leaving adequate space around it.

2.16 Project 3 example.
ILLUSTRATION BY
JANICE GREENBERG ELLINWOOD

REFERENCES

Benaim, L. (2003). *Grès*. New York: Assouline Publishing.

Brainard, S. (1998). *A design manual* (2nd ed.). New York: Prentice Hall.

Britt, D. (Ed.). (2003). *Modern art: Impressionism to post-modernism*. London: Thames & Hudson.

Charles-Roux, E. (1981). *Chanel and her world*. London: Vendome Press.

Davis, M. L. (1996). *Visual design in dress* (3rd ed.). Upper Saddle River, NJ: Prentice Hall.

Koda, H., & Bolton, A. (2005). *Chanel.* New York: The Metropolitan Museum of Art.

Lee, S. T. (Ed.). (1975). *American fashion: The life and lines of Adrian, Mainbocher, McCardell, Norell, Trigere.* New York: The Fashion Institute of Technology.

Lacroix, C., Mauries, P., & Saillard, O. (2007) . *Christian Lacroix: Histoires de Mode.* Paris: Les Arts Décoratifs.

Locher, H. (1994). *Piet Mondrian: Colour, structure, and symbolism.* Bern: Verlag Gachnang & Springer.

Martinez, B., & Block, J. (1995). *Visual forces: An introduction to design* (2nd ed.). Upper Saddle River, NJ: Prentice Hall.

Moffitt, P., & Claxton, W. (1999). *The Rudi Gernreich book.* Köln: Benedikt Taschen Verlag.

Saint Laurent, Y., Vreeland, D., Huyghe, R., Berge, P., Picasso-Lopez, P., Agnelli, M., Deneuve, D., Michals, D., Boulat, P., Vreeland, N. (1983). *Yves Saint Laurent.* New York: The Metropolitan Museum of Art.

Sandler, I. (1998). *American Art of the 1960s.* New York: Harper & Row Publishers.

Steele, V. (2006). *Fifty years of fashion: New Look to now.* New Haven, CT: Yale University Press.

Steele, V. (1991). *Women of Fashion, Twentieth Century Designers.* New York: Rizzoli.

Stegemeyer, A. (2004). *Who's who in fashion* (4th ed.) New York: Fairchild Books.

Stewart, M. (2008). *Launching the imagination: A comprehensive guide to basic design* (3rd ed.). New York: McGraw-Hill.

BOX 2.1

CHANEL

CHANEL IS ONE of the most famous brands worldwide, due first to its namesake, the designer Gabrielle Chanel, and later, to the iconic designer who took over the design house some years after her death, Karl Lagerfeld. Gabrielle Chanel made great impact on the twentieth century for many reasons—the mystique of a hidden background, love affairs, and scandal, an opinionated and razor-sharp personality, and savvy fashion designs for women during two careers that were packed into one lifetime. The Chanel suit, the classic design that emphasized vertical and horizontal line, originated between 1955 and 1957, during the second of her two careers (FIGURE BOX 2.1A).

Gabrielle was born in 1883 to a French merchant and his "shop girl," whom he later married. When she died, however, he abandoned his children, and Gabrielle moved with a sister to a local orphanage. She was apprenticed to the needle trades, and then had a brief career as a café singer, where she adopted the nickname "Coco." In 1909, a lover named Etienne Balsan set her up in a millinery

business in Paris. By 1910, another lover, Arthur "Boy" Capel, enabled her to move her millinery shop to the most fashionable section of Paris and subsequently funded a shop in Deauville, to which she added casual outfits. He backed her first couture house in Biarritz in 1915. Her dresses sold at high prices, and she was finally able to become financially independent. She closed her business during World War I but reopened in 1919.

Chanel credited herself with appropriating men's clothing for women, including jackets, sweaters, sailor blouses, and dresses made of wool jersey, which she claimed liberated a woman's body. Jersey had previously been used only for men's underwear. The dress in FIGURE BOX 2.1B is a good example of her early design efforts, blurring the boundaries between *flou* (dressmaking) and *tailleur* (tailoring), with the goal of blending comfort, simplicity, and functionalism in her designs. She eliminated any elaborate decoration or stiff underpinnings. For her entire career, she neither made garments that clung to the body nor hung lose from it. Her silhouettes grazed the body at the bust, waist, and hip, pairing subtle shape with fluidity. Dresses made her success in the 1920s (FIGURE BOX 2.1C). She launched her signature fragrance Chanel No. 5 in 1921. Her "little black dresses" were famous by 1926. *Vogue* compared the style to a Ford, emphasizing that her brand name carried equal weight.

There are some who say that she was not an artistic designer, or an innovator of the craft like Madeleine Vionnet, but her genius was in knowing what women wanted to wear, sometimes before they did. That was probably because she designed for herself, and she was a well-known personality in Paris who was a recognized fashion leader, not unlike the public's infatuation for celebrities of present day. In the 1920s she set the trend for costume jewelry, believing it added elegance to any outfit. She wore it with evening clothes or over a

ABOVE
FIGURE BOX 2.1A This ensemble, designed by Karl Lagerfeld for his spring 2001 Chanel collection, adapts her trademark suit in an updated fashion.
COURTESY OF WWD/ GIOVANNI GIANNONI

OPPOSITE LEFT
FIGURE BOX 2.1B The wool jersey dress was designed by Coco Chanel in 1924. Note the lines in the torso expressed by seams, as well as the diagonal lines of trim and vertical button front.
THE METROPOLITAN MUSEUM OF ART/ART RESOURCE, NY

OPPOSITE RIGHT
FIGURE BOX 2.1C Coco Chanel's evening dress from 1926–1927 features a zigzag line pattern that vibrates its surface.
THE METROPOLITAN MUSEUM OF ART/ART RESOURCE, NY

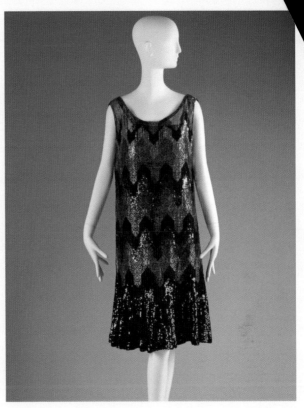

simple black sweater and baggy pants. When she cut her hair short, an international craze for bobbed hair followed. When she tanned in the sunshine, women followed suit. When she wore flat shoes or eyeglasses, women copied her. She even selected runway models that resembled her. She embodied the style that she created.

In the late 1920s and early 1930s, Chanel cultivated a relationship with the Duke of Westminster, reputed to be the richest man in England. It is said that he gave her a mill to design her own English tweeds, which she introduced into her collections along with cardigan sweaters at that time. Her suits included fitted jackets with long skirts. But the most famous designs of the 1930s were romantic evening dresses of white lace, tulle, or chiffon. That completed her "first" career, as World War II ensued in 1939, and she closed her design house to flee to the South of France. During the war years, her reputation suffered. She had an affair with a Nazi officer and was thought to have collaborated in Nazi intelligence. So the establishment of a new couture house in 1954 was truly a miracle.

At the age of 70, she opened her first collection, which was panned by the press. For a time, it appeared that Chanel had lost her touch. Staying true to her belief in physical ease, Chanel presented the iconic fashions still associated with her brand today: the beige and black, cap-toed, sling-back pump; the quilted shoulder bag; the slightly boxy suits framed with horizontal and vertical braid (FIGURE BOX 2.1F), jeweled costume necklaces, brooches, and chains. Her designs became a part of women's wardrobes everywhere during the 1960s. Coco Chanel died in 1971.

THE LAGERFELD ERA

The designs languished after her death, looking somewhat awkward against the continuing change of fashion. In 1983 Karl Lagerfeld was hired to design the collection. His reputation had already been established as the designer of both the Chloé and Fendi collections. His challenge in this new role was to design an existing product. In order to make it contemporary, he first had to assess the elements of design prevalent in Chanel's iconic fashions, such as the vertical and horizontal lines characteristic of the Chanel suit. He understood her use of geometry, which was even expressed in the packaging of her Chanel No. 5 perfume. One of Lagerfeld's updated versions of the suit from spring–summer 2009, with its closer fit and added touch of femininity, is pictured in FIGURE 2.1D. He sometimes expressed the same elements using implied line, as expressed by a row of buttons (FIGURE 2.1A). Lagerfeld adapted her fashions in many other ways. He brought new fabrics to the collections, such as leather, terrycloth, stretch fabrics, and denim. He altered the shape by widening the shoulders or tucking in the waist. He shortened the hemlines or lengthened them. He featured pants instead of skirts. He stayed true to the accessories but exaggerated their scale. In this way, he wooed a new customer. The customers who had worn Coco Chanel's designs were in their 50s, but Lagerfeld's designs attracted women who were in their 30s. He also brought her simple designs to a new level of luxury (FIGURE BOX 2.1E). Finally, Lagerfeld secured Chanel's place in the world as an international brand.

RIGHT
FIGURE BOX 2.1D Karl Lagerfeld interprets Coco Chanel's design elements in this suit from spring–summer 2009.
COURTESY OF WWD/
GIOVANNI GIANNONI

ABOVE
FIGURE BOX 2.1E Vertical
and horizontal lines are featured
in this gown designed by
Karl Lagerfeld in 2007.
DAVID SIMS © 2007 CONDÉ NAST
PUBLICATIONS

RIGHT
FIGURE BOX 2.1F The classic
Chanel suit, one of many designed
by Coco Chanel in the 1960s, uses
braid or trim to combine
vertical and horizontal line on
the garment's surface
COURTESY OF FAIRCHILD ARCHIVE

BOX 2.2
RUDI
ERNREICH

ABOVE LEFT
FIGURE BOX 2.2A The design
in this journal sketch by
Rudi Gernreich depends upon
his use of diagonal lines.
2009 MUSEUM ASSOCIATES/
LACMA/ART RESOURCE, NY

ABOVE RIGHT
FIGURE BOX 2.2B Clashing colors, geometric shape, and diagonal
stripes characterize this wool knit
minidress designed by
Rudi Gernreich in 1973.
2009 MUSEUM ASSOCIATES/
LACMA/ART RESOURCE, NY

OPPOSITE LEFT
FIGURE BOX 2.2C The diagonal
stripping in Gernreich's knitted
monokini from 1964
accentuates the body's curves.
COLLECTION OF THE KYOTO
COSTUME INSTITUTE, PHOTO BY
TAKASHI HATAKEYAMA

OPPOSITE RIGHT
FIGURE BOX 2.2D Rudi Gernre-
ich's knitted bathing suit from 1971
features diagonal lines that inter-
sect at critical points on the body.
COLLECTION OF THE KYOTO
COSTUME INSTITUTE, PHOTO BY
TAKASHI HATAKEYAMA

RUDI GERNREICH WAS the most avant-garde designer during the 1960s. Some think, in retrospect, that he was ahead of his time. Born in Austria in 1922, he migrated with his mother to the United States in 1938. He demonstrated his interest in fashion from boyhood but entered first into the field of dance. From that experience he learned to consider the way clothing looked and functioned in motion. In the 1940s he left dance to sell fabrics and tried earnestly to promote his own designs to fashion industry leaders. As early as 1951, they began to catch on.

His unorthodox view of clothing lead to concepts and changes that seemed shocking, and as a result, he was labeled a futurist. In a period when women were wearing fitted and feminine fashions, he took the inner construction out of bathing suits, showed cutouts in swimwear and dresses, used vinyl and plastic in his designs, introduced knitted tube dresses and the topless bathing suit. He engineered the no-bra look by creating a soft, transparent bra, designed the first see-through clothes, and originated the "total look," which interrelated dresses with tights, hats, gloves, and shoes. He developed the first designer jeans and the first thong. His fashions featured clashing colors, and he positioned checks with dots and stripes with diagonals. He thought in the geometric terms of barrels, triangles, fullness, slimness, and omitted waists. Rudi was defining a change in attitude more than a change in fashion. His greatest desire was to provide freedom for women.

Rudi's oeuvre provides several opportunities to examine how he used diagonal line to accentuate the figure and add visual movement. One example is the design in his journal sketch from 1958 (FIGURE BOX 2.2A). The repeated diagonal lines are dynamic in feeling, and they define the structure of the back. Another is Gernreich's striped minidress from 1973 (FIGURE BOX 2.2B). It featured the clashing colors, geometric shape, and diagonal lines characteristic of his work. Not only does the design facilitate visual and physical movement, Peggy Moffitt, Gernreich's favorite model, wore it as a maternity dress.

Of all his designs, the topless swimsuit or monokini caused the greatest public reaction. Originally, Gernreich designed it for a story about future trends in *Life* magazine. He thought that revealing the breasts was appropriate in an era focused on the emancipation of women, as was the case in 1964. *Newsweek* also ran a photograph of it. Store buyers placed orders for it. Over public objections, some 3,000 women bought the suit. FIGURE BOX 2.2C features the knitted design with diagonal striping, a pattern that underscored the body's curves. Another knitted swimsuit from 1971 experimented with diagonal lines that run in contrasting directions (FIGURE BOX 2.2D). Their intersections drew the eye to critical points on the body while encircling its anatomical curves.

After achieving the height of popularity and several fashion design awards, Gernreich took a leave of absence from the industry in 1968. He continued to work part-time with Harmon Knitwear, the company that produced his knitted swimwear. In 1971 he predicted that fashion trends would popularize androgyny. Before he died in 1985, he designed furniture as well as dance and exercise clothes. The colors, shapes, and patterns of his fashion designs were prevalent as late as 1991. They radiated on fashion runways from New York to Milan. Rudi Gernreich's modernity was indeed ahead of its time.

| # FORM, SHAPE, AND SPACE

OBJECTIVES

To illuminate the relationship between the human form and the creativity of the fashion designer

To enumerate the prominent silhouettes of the nineteenth and twentieth centuries

To explain how designers perceive silhouettes

To define space and describe how fashion designers and theater costumers utilize space in their creations

FORM, SHAPE, AND **space** are elements of design so intrinsically related that fashion designers seldom consider them separately when creating a new garment. But the manipulation of each is vitally important to the success of the final product, and the designer's interpretation of them contributes to the understanding and characterization of fashion for the period.

In its investigation of form, shape, and space, this chapter describes the value of the **human form** to the fashion designer as a vessel of and inspiration for his or her craft. In addition, it covers the primary **silhouettes** of the nineteenth and twentieth centuries and explains how a garment is subdivided into smaller shapes. Discussed here too are the ways in which designers utilize the space around the figure as part of a garment design and a comparison of the concept of space for the fashion designer and the theater costumer. Finally, the chapter examines the techniques designers have used to feature areas of space within the garment design.

FORM

Form is a three-dimensional area enclosed by a surface. So, in reference to fashion design, the term has two meanings. First, if the form is hollow, the interior is perceived as volume, and thus, form refers to structural clothing parts that relate to and complement the exterior contours of the body. Second, if the form is solid, its interior is described as mass, and so the term refers to the body itself, bounded by the contours, protrusions and concavities of the human anatomy, covered by skin. The human form is truly the designer's canvas, so the latter meaning is of primary importance.

THE BODY AS MUSE

Adoration of the human form is universal among designers. Its origin may vary according to personal experience, but every designer develops an appreciation of the human figure, its proportions and beauty. Anecdotes on this topic abound. Some tell of designers having a **muse**, an individual who especially inspires their designs. Today a muse is often a favorite model, client, or celebrity. But that may not be true in all cases.

Paul Poiret (1879–1944), the first prominent couturièr of the twentieth century, took credit for freeing women from the rigid shape of the **corset** by creating classically inspired garments that fell from two points at the shoulders, in the manner of the ancient Greek **chiton** (FIGURE 3.1). Originally, he executed the design in light fabrics, such as a supple gauze, chiffon, and crepe de Chine, and later, in heavier fabrics like lame, damask, and brocade. Along with the attire, he decreed the small head, with cropped hair, a confining bandeau, and lightweight rubber undergarments. The look was of one long line from head to toe (FIGURE 3.2).

When he was employed as a junior assistant to the famous couturièr Jacques Doucet (1853–1929), his mentor advised him to find a young woman to function as both his wife and model. That is exactly what Poiret did. About the time he originated his business in 1905 and his revolution in women's fashion, Poiret married the daughter of a family friend from the provinces, a woman who was thin and tall, considered by some as "gangly," despite carved classical facial features. He considered her to have the look of the future and used her to promote his designs. So his wife Denise personified Poiret's ideal of the female figure and the one he sought to convey to the women of his day.

3.1 An example of a Greek chiton, from which Paul Poiret derived his method of draping.
ILLUSTRATION BY
JANICE GREENBERG ELLINWOOD

3.2 Paul Poiret's ideal of the female figure wearing his design. 'AU CLAIR DE LA LUNE', DESIGN BY PAUL POIRET, 1913 BY GEORGES LEPAPE (1887–1971) PRIVATE COLLECTION/ THE BRIDGEMAN ART LIBRARY

Christian Dior (1905–1957), whose name is among the most recognized in the fashion world even today, was almost single-handedly responsible for bringing international attention back to Paris for fashion after World War II with his renowned **New Look of 1947** (FIGURE 3.3). Dior's New Look, also known as the *Corolle* line, was the opposite of what most women wore during the years of World War II, as a result of limits placed on fabric and the influence of the military uniform on fashion. In his first season, Dior designed skirts that used some 15—up to even 25—yards of material that reached almost to the ankles. Bodices were close fitting, with nipped-in waists, rounded breasts, and deemphasized shoulders. Although many thought the look was simply a reaction to the previous fashion, Dior actually was inspired by his mother's beauty in the form that Poiret ironically sought to free women from (Keenan, 1981, p. 12). Like the women of

3.3 The Bar Suit from the spring–summer 1947 collection was the epitome of Christian Dior's New Look.
AFP/GETTY IMAGES

her period, his mother wore a tiny, corseted, hand-span waist, tight-fitting bodice, and full rustling skirt. The impact of this collection was so profound and meaningful in fashion history that it is discussed again in this chapter and often in fashion literature. Here it is important to note that its origin was due to Dior's memory of his mother's figure.

Madeleine Vionnet's invention of the bias cut, as described in Chapter 1, could only have occurred through her devotion to the body. She thought that a dress must not hang on the body, but follow its lines. Her feminine ideal was the tall, slender woman with a long neck, which was in contrast to her own body. She thought of herself as short and dumpy, so she never designed for herself. Anatomy was so important to her that it dictated her approach for designing for each customer. Her goal was to dress the body, not simply to construct a dress.

Through these examples, you should understand the importance of the human form to the designer, both as inspiration and as part of the artistic product that he or she creates. That product is the summation of both the form that is composed of the structural clothing parts and the form that is the human body. It is through the clothing that the designer is able to manipulate the perception of the human figure. The body can be made taller, rounder, or more like an hourglass, all by how the clothing is organized around the figure. The volume created by the clothing's hollow forms appears to add mass to the human figure, or reduce it, as the case may be. Designers who work at the highest prices in the fashion industry can conceive of an idealized human form as they create, as in the cases of Poiret, Dior, and Vionnet. But the designer of a **mass-produced brand** or **moderate price point** must consider the real figure's attributes or flaws as characteristic of the **target market**. The challenge then is to implement the elements and principles of design to manipulate the perception of the clothing on the figure in order to make the result more idealized—taller, if the customer is short, for example, or slimmer, if the customer is heavier. The elements of form and shape are especially intriguing, because they have the capacity to express both psychological mood and visual illusion.

SHAPE

Shape is intimately related to form, because it is a subset of it. As opposed to the three-dimensional form, shape is defined as a flat, two-dimensional area, enclosed by a line. That line creates a silhouette or outline or edge of an interior area, and that appears flat. Shape is perceived in different ways in fashion.

Silhouette is the term used in fashion for the predominant shape of the garment that envelopes the figure. It is possibly the most defining element of design in fashion, because the outer shape is the first element to be seen from a distance. It can seem like women wear many different silhouettes simultaneously, but that is not the case. Research based on nineteenth-century fashions identified three dominant silhouettes, each lasting about 35 years, with an indication that they might rotate cyclically. These were the **tubular** (based on the **empire** style), **bell-shaped**, and **back-fullness** (based on the **bustle** style) silhouettes (FIGURES 3.4A AND B). The perception of this theory changed with the benefit of research on twentieth-century fashions, as noted in the paragraph that follows. However, it does appear that the outer shape of garments is generally consistent across a particular fashion period, for the duration of that period, indicating that the consumer identifies it as normal during the period and passé after it. Changes in

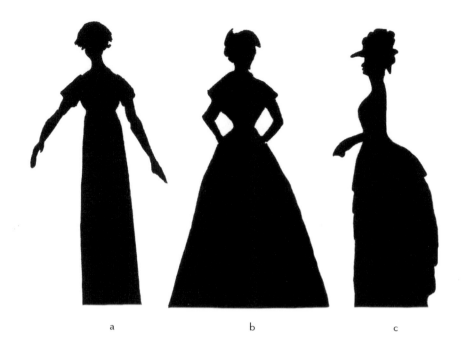

a   b   c

ABOVE
3.4A The (a) tubular, (b) bell-
shaped, and (c) back-
fullness silhouettes predominated
in the nineteenth century.
ILLUSTRATION BY
JANICE GREENBERG ELLINWOOD

RIGHT
3.4B This is an example of a
bustle-styled evening dress,
dated 1884–1886.
THE METROPOLITAN MUSEUM OF
ART/ART RESOURCE, NY

garment details may alter the silhouette in minor ways, until the cumulative effect is a complete change to the silhouette, and the subsequent dawn of a new fashion period.

Contemporary fashion researchers redefined the dominant silhouettes based on twentieth-century fashions, identifying them as **A-line**, bell-shaped, tubular, **wedge**, and **hourglass** (FIGURE 3.5A–E). Although the

a   b   c   d   e

shape based on the bustle style of the nineteenth century is omitted, several twentieth-century designers sought to rejuvenate it with a contemporary edge (FIGURE 3.6). In an era when many women are primarily concerned about comfort and functionality in their attire, it is unlikely that a bustle made of a rigid structure would have been widely accepted.

Theories regarding fashion silhouettes are traditionally based on what had been the mode in previous periods. Fashion designers face a range of possibilities as they design for the future. That is because potential silhouettes come in a full range of geometric and compound geometric shapes (FIGURE 3.7A AND B). The compound versions consist of two different geometric shapes in one silhouette. The range of possibilities challenge the designer to think through the construction methods necessary for fabric to support such shapes. For instance, in the 1940s Claire McCardell cultivated a singular geometric shape when she designed the bubble swimsuit and a compound one in her plaid silk playsuit (SEE FIGURE 3.8).

ABOVE LEFT
3.7A Here is a range of geometric shapes that may represent garment silhouettes.
ILLUSTRATION BY JANICE GREENBERG ELLINWOOD

ABOVE RIGHT
3.7B Compound geometric shapes may form silhouettes like the ones pictured here.
ILLUSTRATION BY JANICE GREENBERG ELLINWOOD

RIGHT
3.8 This bubble suit, designed by Claire McCardell in 1942, shows how a design results from a compound geometric shape.
UNTITLED, 1942, PHOTOGRAPH BY LOUISE DAHL-WOLFE, COLLECTION CENTER FOR CREATIVE PHOTOGRAPHY, UNIVERSITY OF ARIZONA © 1989 ARIZONA BOARD OF REGENTS

3.9 Christian Lacroix's 1987 eighteenth-century-inspired evening dress is the result of a compound geometrically shaped silhouette.
THE METROPOLITAN MUSEUM OF ART/ART RESOURCE, NY

Haute couture designer Christian Lacroix became legendary for his eighteenth-century **pouf** dress while he worked as a designer for the House of Patou. His evening dress, dated 1987, portrays the grandeur that results from a compound geometric silhouette, in which Lacroix placed the pouf shape below the hip (SEE FIGURE 3.9). Consider carefully how the fabric is constructed, manipulated, and fitted in order to support the shapes in these designs.

SHAPE AND MOOD

Shapes project the mood of the lines enclosing them and of the space within them, even though those executed in dress are rarely expressed in their simplest forms. Like lines, shapes can be classified as rectilinear or curvilinear. Rectangles and squares appear stable and confident, because of their horizontal and vertical sides and right angles. Those with diagonal sides, such as **triangles** and **inverted pyramids**, seem more dynamic. Curved edges provide an organic, natural feeling. Beginning with his New Look, Christian Dior knew well how to harness silhouette in his collections and often named them with a specific shape in mind (BOX 3.1).

BOX 3.1

CHRISTIAN DIOR

SHAPE, OR SILHOUETTE, was the definitive element of Christian Dior's designs.

Born in 1905 in Granville, France, Dior studied political science and ran an art gallery before he embarked on a career in fashion. Eventually he sold fashion sketches to Paris publications and found employment with Lucien Lelong (1889–1958), the designer who was responsible for preventing the Germans from moving French couture to Berlin or Vienna during World War II. From Lelong, he learned about the operations of a fashion house. So when the French textile magnate Marcel Boussac offered him financing, Dior knew he wanted to design according to the highest traditions of haute couture, with elaborate workmanship and aimed at a clientele of elegant women. Dior left Lelong to start his own fashion house in 1946.

His first collection, termed the New Look of 1947 or the *Corolle* line (FIGURE 3.3), was considered to be unprecedented, because of its contrast to the apparel worn during the war, with the squared shoulders of military uniforms and the limits on fabric demanded by the war effort. Dior's New Look featured skirts made from yards of material that draped to the ankles, tiny waists, and round shoulders. Hips were made fuller with pleats or pads, only to further enhance the smallness of the waists and underscore the curves of the female anatomy. *Corolle* referred to the flowerlike way the huge skirts blossomed from the slender waists.

This shape was further supported by skirts lined with tulle, which were then lined in fine silk to prevent the snagging of stockings. In addition to the hip pads and pleats, there were special boned corsets to cinch the waist and push up the breasts. The New Look was a revolution of international impact. At that point, it could not be anticipated that Christian Dior's career would last only ten more years. Each subsequent collection was also named, usually for the shape of Dior's designs.

In 1948 Dior created his collection *Envol*, meaning "flight" or "winged." Long skirts were caught up on one side or at the back like a bustle or with all the fullness pushed toward the derrière. Autumn 1948 brought the *Zig-Zag* collection, including one-shoulder dresses, one-sleeve dresses, or complicated draped and wrapped bodices. Skirts were sometimes uneven, reinforcing the Zig-Zag theme.

The *Trompe l'oeil* collection debuted in spring 1949. Dior utilized construction techniques to emphasize the width of the bust or provide movement for skirts without adding bulk. Giant collars overlapped shoulders, wings extended from the bodice or panels attached to the skirts (FIGURE BOX 3.1A).

He featured a straight, up-and-down look in spring 1950, which he called the Vertical line. Jackets were boxy, dresses made sleeveless, and coats omitted waists—all to emphasize a straight line between the shoulder and the hip. That collection was followed in autumn by the Oblique line. Dior slanted all construction to one side in that collection—tucks and seams spiraled around the body.

The year 1951 brought the Oval line, which meant that every edge was rounded. Raglan sleeves defined a smooth, curved shoulder, hips and breasts were rounded, and jackets hugged the figure (FIGURE BOX 3.1B). The *Sinuous* line of 1952 described clothes that were soft and fluid and that moved about the body. They were executed in soft fabrics of pastel colors.

The spring collection of 1953 was called the *Tulip*, because the silhouette was long and straight, but rounded at the bust in petal-like curves. It was followed in autumn with the *Cupola* collection, referring to the architectural term for a dome shape. Dior designed barrel-shaped coats and jackets with rounded shoulders. The skirt shapes of his evening dresses mirrored the same shape.

The autumn collection of 1954 was named the H line, which to Dior meant the tapered figure of a young girl. The distance between the bust and hips appeared elongated, by pushing the bust up and dropping the waist to the hips, where it represented the cross-bar of the H.

Dior created the *A* line for his spring 1955 collection. Dresses, coats, and suits favored narrow shoulders and flared out like triangles (FIGURE BOX 3.1C). The *A* line and the *H* line were revolutionary by comparison to previous fashions, because they directed attention away from the waist. Dior followed them with his Y line in the autumn collection. It was defined by a slender body with a top-heavy shape.

During these years, Dior was not always a healthy man, giving way to the moods that resulted from the pressures of his work. He was overweight. On a pre-collection trip in 1957, he died suddenly from a heart attack. His death was mourned by his fellow couturièrs, his staff, internationally known fashionable women, textile workers, friends from all art fields, and the press. However, his name, contribution to the fashion industry, and fashion house continue to present day.

SHAPE AND SYMBOLISM

Shapes also have symbolism. In other words, they can be associated with an object that is shaped in a similar manner. A circular shape may remind the viewer of a balloon, a sun, or an orange, and thereby provide a whimsical, happy feeling. A shape can also be distorted in a way that disregards its association with nature. On occasion a designer manipulates the outer shape of a garment to obscure the viewer's familiarity with the human form, testing, as a result, the viewer's concept of beauty. Rei Kawakubo (1942–) is a designer who delivered such a challenge to the fashion media and to her clientele (BOX 3.2).

SHAPES WITHIN SHAPES

Garment silhouettes are often subdivided into smaller shapes, as defined by construction details such as seams, pleats, pockets, collars, **yokes**, **waistbands**, ruffles, **patchwork**, top-stitching, and **quilting**, as well as surface embellishments such as **appliqué** and fabric pattern motifs. Even an added detail can express a shape that is an integral part of the overall design, such as a belt or a large button or broche. The designer must remain cognizant of the qualities inherent in the shape and what that brings to the overall organization of the form, meaning the garment and the perception of the figure it is on. For instance, shapes provide a sense of proportion when length is compared to width. So a short, wide midriff yoke shortens and widens the figure, while a long pant with a high waist lengthens it. Further, the designer must consider how the shapes relate to one another within the design.

TWO-DIMENSIONAL PATTERN INTO THREE-DIMENSIONAL FORM

Fashion designers must constantly negotiate between their understanding of the garment in its two-dimensional appearance and in its three-dimensional form. On the one hand, he or she envisions it as if in a runway photo or illustration, with the silhouette appearing as a flat shape and with the emphasis mainly on the front of the design. From that limited perspective, the designer is in danger of investing all of his or her creativity on the front of the design. On the other, the designer must see it in the round, as a three-dimensional form that is a counterpart of the three-dimensional human form, just as Vionnet did, using her small mannequin. This understanding is facilitated by the recognition of yet another kind of shape—that of the flat shape of the garment **pattern piece** as it is cut from fabric in order to enfold the figure or a particular portion of it (FIGURE 3.10). The designer becomes familiar with pattern shapes for a fitted bodice, slim skirt, or basic

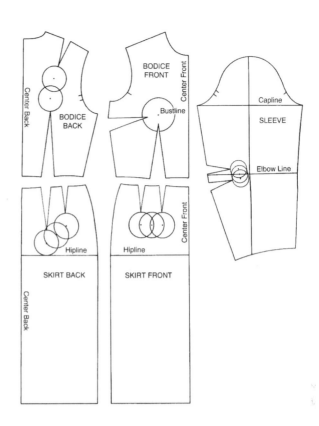

3.10 These are some of the flat shapes of garment pattern pieces.
ILLUSTRATION BY
NORA M. MACDONALD

sleeve and the process by which they can be adjusted to accommodate a new design idea. This can be accomplished by using the patternmaking processes of **flat pattern** (a system of adjusting the basic pattern shapes) or **pattern drafting** (where pattern shapes are developed from a combination of measurements). As the designer masters one or both of these methods, the designer can calculate how the shape must change in order to execute an original design concept. So design thinking occurs in two different "languages." When the garment is evaluated for its appeal, however, the assessment is based on how it appears on the figure, not on the pattern shapes that are cut from fabric. The structural design is the result of the transformation of the flat fabric into a three-dimensional garment, following the contours and movements of the human figure.

SPACE   Space is empty area or extent. Like shape, it relates to fashion design in two ways. First, it refers to the empty area or "air" surrounding the human form, which is infinitely intriguing to the fashion designer. It is a three-dimensional void that is hollow but has volume. The human form may be perceived as having space in several directions—forward, backward, side to side, and up/down. Alternatively, space may exist as a two-dimensional emptiness. As such, it has boundaries, but offers itself in contrast to shape and surface. It carries the potential to become something else. In this context, space serves as an integral part of the interior of the design.

BOX 3.2
REI
KAWAKUBO

KNOWN FOR DESIGNS that consistently challenge the fashion media and Western thinking, Rei Kawakubo graduated from Keio University in 1964. She introduced the Commes des Garçons label, which means "like some boys," in 1969. The business was formally established in Tokyo in 1971. International attention was directed her way with a collection that debuted in Paris in 1981, while Yohji Yamamoto was her partner.

The initial designs were black and oversized and hung loosely from the body (FIGURE BOX 3.2A). They were wrapped and draped, instead of cut and shaped like Western fashions. In addition, they were often ragged and distressed. This was an aesthetic that was not readily understood. The fashion media referred to it as the "Japanese bag lady look," along with other equally unflattering terms.

Under the Commes des Garçons label, Kawakubo presented several designs in 1997 that attempted to distort the shape of the human form. The collection began with a slender, ankle-length dress in pure-white stretch organza with fragile cape shoulders, from which two small kidney-shaped protuberances were positioned at the shoulder blades like angels' wings. Each of the subsequent designs, semi-sheer dresses in either red or blue gingham or prints, carried other apparent swellings, including lopsided bustles, padded hips, collar bones, humps, and fat snakes coiling around waists or rib cages (FIGURE BOX 3.2B). This was referred to as the *Bump* or *Lumps* collection. Unlike previous Western designers, who added padding to enhance the natural contours of the body, Kawakubo was extending the body in unlikely places, such as the torso, buttocks, or upper back and shoulders. Many found the collection to be disconcerting and unflattering. There was a range of reaction, joke telling, and discussion. *Vogue* and *Elle* chose to photograph the collection without its lumps, which was also the way many customers, but not all, chose to wear the designs.

Kawakubo explained that she was attempting to design from a different angle, changing the body itself, by means of stretch fabrics. She was already known for approaching the design process without preconception, while avoiding geometric shapes in preference for the organic. She expressed the ethos that "the body becomes dress becomes body," by which she described her attempt to erase the boundaries between fabric and skin. In so doing, Kawakubo also investigated the void, or space, around the human form, ultimately letting the garment dominate it.

Seeking a different aesthetic was more important to Kawakubo than financial success. Nevertheless, she operates a business in 33 countries, at more than $100 million wholesale per year, and mostly in Japan.

Attention to the space around the figure characterizes the Eastern approach to fashion design. That is because it derives from the **kimono**, the Japanese clothing that is part of the country's heritage and culture (FIGURE 3.11). The design of the kimono maximizes the use of space between the body and the cloth. It is actually a full-length garment that is assembled from rectangular pattern pieces, with a few tucks and easements, and the sleeves appear to hang about the space around the wearer. Its construction is the same regardless of gender, overlapping in front for both men and women. For this reason, kimonos are considered gender neutral. Any gender specificity is due to colors, fabrics, and prints and not silhouette or shape. Placed flat on a table, women's kimonos have a slit opening in the sleeve and men's do not. The ingenious advantage of the kimono design is that the garment adjusts its size to the wearer's needs; it is truly one-size-fits-all. Issey Miyake (1938–) was the first Japanese designer to show Eastern-inspired designs in Paris. The designs were in the spirit of the kimono, by bringing attention to the space between the body and the fabric (BOX 3.3).

3.11 The Japanese kimono pictured here, designed by Takuo Itoh in 1995, is typical of the cultural shape, decorated here with the *shibori* dying process.
THE METROPOLITAN MUSEUM OF ART/ART RESOURCE, NY

Rei Kawakubo, whose body-distorting garments were discuss relation to shape, showed several designs from the 1980s that demonstr an investigation of the space around the figure in the tradition of the kimono. Her expressions of shape and space also arise from the lack of gender definition characteristic of the kimono. Women's kimonos express a contourless body. Before a large-busted woman puts on a kimono, she first dons an undergarment to flatten the breasts. She might also add padding to her waist in order to create a cylindrical appearance that continues from the graceful slope of the shoulders. The kimono completely covers the body, leaving only the hands, neck, and face exposed. As a result, Kawakubo has never been comfortable expressing body definition or exposure in her designs, believing instead that fashion design should allow women to be what they are. It is her belief that the feeling of volume about the body is what provides variety and sensual pleasure for the wearer.

The exploration of space has been a characteristic of Western dress as well, sometimes to an exaggerated extent in fashion history. An example of such fashion excess existed as perceived extensions from the hip in eighteenth-century France (FIGURE 3.12). The garment parts that facilitated such extreme were termed **panniers**, which were worn in this manner by the royal court. Panniers originated from the French word *panier*, meaning

3.12 Panniers extend into the space from the hips in this British court dress (1750).
THE METROPOLITAN MUSEUM OF ART/ART RESOURCE, NY

BOX 3.3
Y MIYAKE

ABOVE
FIGURE BOX 3.3A The design of
Issey Miyake's ensemble illustrates
his interest in the space around
the figure which is
inherent in a kimono.
ISSEY MIYAKE, *TOP, DRESS COAT AND
TWO SASHES,* 1984. COTTON, WOOL,
NYLON, LINEN. NATIONAL GALLERY
OF AUSTRALIA, CANBERRA

OPPOSITE TOP
FIGURE BOX 3.3B Miyake's rattan
bodice from 1982 illustrates
his investigation of the space
beyond the shoulders.
ARTFORUM

OPPOSITE BOTTOM
FIGURE BOX 3.3C The Minaret
dress, designed by Issey Miyake,
is another example of his
investigation of the space
surrounding the body.
COLLECTION: POWERHOUSE
MUSEUM, SYDNEY.
PHOTO: SUE STAFFORD

WHEN ISSEY MIYAKE showed his Eastern-inspired designs in Paris, it was after years of study and apprenticeship in fashion. After education at Tama University, Bunka School of Fashion, and *l'Ecole de la Chambre Syndicale de la Couture,* Miyake apprenticed with French couturièr Guy Laroche (1923–1990). He served as assistant to another French couturièr, Hubert de Givenchy (1927–1995), and then worked for American designer Geoffrey Beene (1927–2004). Regardless of ample exposure to Western design, when he opened his own clothing business in the early 1970s, his designs consisted of irregularly shaped fabric, hung loosely about the body, utilizing the void referred heretofore as "space."

The designs were in the spirit of the kimono, bringing attention to where the body and fabric make only approximate contact (FIGURE BOX 3.3A). This was the result of research on Japanese folk culture, in which textiles and clothing used techniques such as wrapping and layering. He concentrated on the creation of garments from one piece of cloth with no visible seams or closures. The focus on space around the body also ensured that the wearer could move with complete ease, while garments were one-size-fits-all. Miyake offered this approach as an alternative to tailored Western fashion. In lacking structure, his designs appeared to lack perfection, but were democratic and comfortable.

In addition to designing, Miyake presented museum exhibitions that amplified his unorthodox approach to apparel. One that traveled from Tokyo to London, Los Angeles, and San Francisco between 1983 and 1985 called *Bodyworks* dramatized his exploration of the relationship between the body and the garment. In it he featured a red fiberglass bustier as well as a rattan cage bustier that fanned into the space above the shoulders and under the arms (FIGURE BOX 3.3B).

In 1988, after much experimentation with pleated fabric, Miyake opened a label called "Pleats Please." His design process was the reverse of the conventional one. Instead of cutting into already pleated fabric, he assembled a garment that was two-and-a-half to eight times its proper size in fabric. Afterward it was permanently pleated in a heated press. One of the best examples was the "Minaret" dress, where the pleated fabric expanded beyond the body in a shape like a Japanese lantern (FIGURE BOX 3.3C).

Miyake has continued a legacy of experimentation in the design of garments. A few characteristics have remained constant. One has been the exploration of materials, yielding a variety of textures. The second has been the variation in construction techniques. When the designs have been implemented in fabric, they included the use of layers, wrapping, draping, wrinkling, pleating, smocking, or the utilization of one piece of cloth. Finally, Miyake has continued to explore the space around the figure, often with the result that the clothing resembles sculpture.

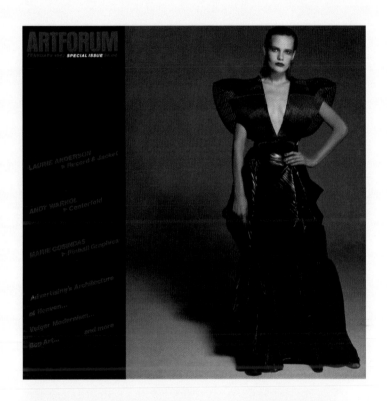

basket, which refers to the construction of the framework support. The framework was often covered with taffeta or brocade. In its most extreme form, panniers held out skirts like sandwich boards, and while worn with a bodice insert called a **stomacher**, covering the corset, underskirt, and petticoat, the result was a silhouette barely wider than the body in side view, but as expansive as nine feet wide from the front view. Women had to walk through a door sideways, and rails were installed along the edges of tables lest the panniers knock teacups off them as the wearer passed by.

SPACE AND THEATER COSTUME DESIGN

While this example of eighteenth-century formal attire and the garments executed by the Japanese designers provide sound examples of aesthetic attention paid to the space around the figure, it is worthwhile to examine briefly the meaning of space for theater costume designers. They too are preoccupied with the aesthetic impression of the garments, but often as seen from a distance, in terms of the mood expressed by the character wearing it and with the benefit of the special effects of artificially produced lighting. So the concept of space is considered in two separate ways: the immediate area around the figure, a concern similar to that of the fashion designer, and the total area of stage or screen space beyond the figure, which is not. The director and the costume designer manipulate the space by controlling areas of light and shadow, determining the colors of sets and costumes, and using the scenery in a variety of ways.

Oscar Schlemmer (1888–1943), an artist and costume designer who taught at the Bauhaus school in Germany in the 1920s, developed extensive theory about space in his work. He was a painter who served first as "Master of Form" in charge of the stone sculpture workshop. But he had already worked on sets and costume designs for ballet, and so it was an appropriate change when he took over the theater workshop in 1923. He was best known for his Triadic Ballet, which was first executed before he arrived at the Bauhaus. The costumes were based on his theory about space and the geometric forms that were valued by the Bauhaus. Each cut the space around the figure in a varying and interesting manner, employing shapes like discs and spheres that reach out from the figure (FIGURE 3.13). These appeared somewhat like Issey Miyake's Minaret dress, constructed of multi-pleated fabric stretched over circular frames that surround the body (FIGURE BOX 3.3C). Schlemmer's interest was focused on the movement of dance in relation to space, and he conducted an intensive investigation of it.

Schlemmer asserted that there were two measurable relations between the human form and space. The first he called a "planimetric relationship" to

3.13 Example of costume from Oscar Schlemmer's *Triadic Ballet*, 1926–1927.
APIC/GETTY IMAGES

cubic space, which he attributed to the innate consciousness of coordinates around each person. External space—apart from gravitation—is neutral, but everyone perceives its dimensions indirectly, and that is the reason our rooms are shaped as cubes. The person who stands up in front of others at first creates an invisible stage around himself, similar to the "stage box" of the theater. Today this concept is called **personal space**. This is space that can be tapped by the designer of our apparel. Schlemmer's conception of this space is a kind of architecture, pictured in cubic form, which has swollen into our surrounding space. The second relationship he called "stereometric" and refers more to the movements of dancers in space. It is the natural rotations of the dancer's organic movements that fill the space on a stage with vibrating radial motions.

SPACE WITHIN THE GARMENT

In addition to the void surrounding the human figure, the fashion designer is concerned with the manipulation of space within the garment design. For this purpose, space is a two-dimensional emptiness, which is actually defined by boundaries. It differs from shape, because shape is filled. Space is an area that is unfilled by the elements that make up the rest of the design. When that is the case, it often reveals the human form. Take, for example, the wool jersey halter bathing suit from 1945 by Claire McCardell (FIGURE 3.14). Because of the unique drape of the halter neckline, this artful designer was able to expose the midriff in a triangle, which flatters both the figure and the design to a greater extent than a rectangular space would have. The result is a successful design that is dependent both on the shapes of fabric and space presented.

Claire McCardell's wool ,ey halter bathing suit from 1945 cuts the figure in an unexpected way, exposing the midriff in a triangular space.
UNTITLED, 1945, PHOTOGRAPH BY LOUISE DAHL-WOLFE, COLLECTION CENTER FOR CREATIVE PHOTOGRAPHY, UNIVERSITY OF ARIZONA © 1989 ARIZONA BOARD OF REGENTS

POSITIVE AND NEGATIVE SPACES

Designers often use opposite terms to describe the relationship between shape and space. For instance, the term "filled" was juxtaposed with "unfilled" or "empty" to describe the two. Other common terms for shape include "figure" versus "ground" or "foreground" instead of "background." Even more common among artists are the terms "positive" for shape and "negative" for space.

Pierre Cardin (1922–), who designed in France from 1950 almost to the end of the century, was a genius at manipulating space in his designs. In the 1950s, 1960s, and 1970s, he sought to design for the "world of tomorrow" as it was conceived at that time. His influences were politics, economy, art, science, and technology, especially space travel. In order to express the future, he designed using a formal language derived from elementary geometric shapes, such as a circle, triangle, square, cylinder, sphere, and cone, and that became his signature. How ironic that he selected a similar language to the Bauhaus to express the future! Cardin was also a sculptor. He approached fashion design in a similar manner, draping his geometric language over body language.

Among his witty designs, Cardin cut shapes from the garment's interior, through which the viewer could nevertheless perceive space outside of

the figure, while guaranteeing the wearer a body-conscious fit. He made a practice of cutting out circular sections from his designs, thereby revealing parts of the figure—the midriff, chest, or legs. This approach exemplified the relationship of shape to space by showing filled parts of the designs (with shape, color, fabric) juxtaposed with empty ones. Sometimes his circular cutouts revealed fabric beneath them, either of the same type as the rest of the design or a contrasting one. Such examples illustrate the relationship of shape to space referred to as **figure and ground**. Something about the design provides the visual cue that a shape is advancing or closer to the viewer and the space is receding, which is often the result of overlapping fabrics. In other designs, Cardin conducted an investigation of the interplay between **positive space** and **negative space**. He juxtaposed a black shape against a colored one, almost like puzzle pieces, within the same dress silhouette. The natural response to this situation is for the eye to judge which of the two sections is more important, the black shape or the colored one. The one deemed less important becomes identified as space in relation to the other more prominent shape (FIGURES 3.15A AND B).

3.16 The Yang and Yin symbol denotes that opposites complement one another and do not conflict.
COURTESY OF ISTOCK PHOTO

NOTAN—YIN AND YANG

There is, however, a Japanese theory regarding positive and negative space, one that is most instructive for the designer. The theory is termed **notan**, which is a Japanese word meaning dark-light. The principle of *notan* is defined as the interaction between positive (light) and negative (dark) space. The idea behind the interaction is embodied by the ancient symbol of the Yang and the Yin, which consists of curved mirror shapes, one white and one black, revolving around a point of equilibrium (FIGURE 3.16). The two parts together make a whole created through opposites that have equal and inseparable value, and hence, contribute to a new unity. *Notan* teaches that opposites complement one another and do not conflict, as in the Yang and the Yin symbol. Nor does one part, either the dark or the light, dominate. It is the interaction of them that is important.

When considering the last of Cardin's previously discussed designs, the viewer may see the black shape as the dominant one for a moment or two. Another look lets the viewer define the colored shape, while the black one recedes. Then comes the realization that the two parts appear to be on the same plane. Alas! Both parts are needed to create an interesting and attractive dress design. Cardin was considered such an expert on "space" that ironically, he was the only other individual ever to wear the space suit of Neil Armstrong, the man who took a first step on the moon. In 1970, Cardin designed space suits for NASA.

THREE SEAMLESS ELEMENTS

The discussion in this chapter illustrates how fashion designers consider the elements of form, shape, and space in the design process. Of the three elements, designers vary according to which is the priority, depending on cultural orientation, purpose, and personal experience. But the designer may not consciously consider them separately as he or she works, because the three interrelate to such a great extent. Exploration of these elements, however, opens a true range of possibilities for the fashion designer.

KEY TERMS

A-line	chiton	form
appliqué	corset	hourglass
back-fullness	empire	inverted pyramid
bell-shaped	figure and ground	kimono
bustle	flat pattern	mass-produced brand

moderate price point	pattern piece	stomacher
muse	personal space	target market
negative space	positive space	triangle
New Look of 1947	pouf	tubular
notan	quilting	waistband
pannier	shape	wedge
patchwork	silhouette	yoke
pattern drafting	space	

PROJECTS

1. In a sketchbook, create five solid geometric shapes and five compound geometric shapes using a middle-value gray marker. Using either a white colored pencil or fine-tipped black marker, divide each with lines and shapes. Organize your marks symmetrically for some of them and asymmetrically for others. Which are more pleasing to the eye? Choose the most pleasing and adapt the designs into garments, picturing lines as seams, darts, pleats, and so on, and shapes as pockets, collars, yokes, and so on (FIGURE 3.17).

2. Build a garment around a half-scale form using colored tissue paper. Rely on paper folding and pins, making pencil marks to remind you later how to rebuild the design you ultimately obtain. Use scissors as necessary, in order to fashion parts of the design or to slice or curl the paper. Show the final design in two forms—flat on the table and dressed on the half-scale form.

3. Begin with a rectangular sheet of white drawing paper. Then select a piece of black construction paper that is the same height as the drawing paper but half the width of it. Create the shape of a motif at a scale that will dominate

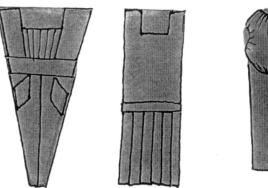

3.17 Project example 1.
ILLUSTRATION BY
JANICE GREENBERG ELLINWOOD

the black piece of paper. Using an X-ACTO knife, cut out the motif from the black piece of paper. Paste what is left of the black shape on the left side of the white sheet. Flip the black motif horizontally and place it in the center of the right half of the white sheet, so that the two shapes exist as mirror images on the same page. This is a process in which you develop positive and negative space. Share your solution with others in order to examine which solutions are the most successful and why. Now create a few simple garment silhouettes and place your mirror images within them. You might situate them on a dress bodice, a T-shirt, the hip yoke of the skirt, both top and bottom of a bikini, and so on. The choice is up to you. Render the garments and the motifs in black marker (FIGURE 3.18).

3.18 Project example 2.
ILLUSTRATION BY
JANICE GREENBERG ELLINWOOD

REFERENCES

Batterberry, M., & Ariane Batterberry, A. (1977). *Mirror mirror: A social history of fashion.* New York: Holt, Rinehart and Winston.

Davis, M. L. (1996). *Visual design in dress* (3rd ed.). Upper Saddle River, NJ: Prentice Hall.

Fiore, A. M., & Kimle, P. (1997). *Understanding aesthetics for the merchandising and design professional.* New York: Fairchild Books.

Frankel, S. (2001). *Visionaries: Interviews with fashion designers.* London: V&A Publications.

Issey Miyake making things. (1998). Paris: Fondation Cartier pour l'art contemporain.

Kawamura, Y. (2004). *The Japanese revolution in Paris fashion.* Oxford: Berg.

Keenan, B. (1981). *Dior in Vogue.* New York: Harmony Books.

Langle, E. (2005). *Pierre Cardin: Fifty years of fashion and design.* New York: Vendome Press.

Martin, R., & Koda, H. (1996). *Christian Dior.* New York: The Metropolitan Museum of Art.

Mitchell, L., (Ed.). (2005). *The cutting edge: Fashion from Japan.* Sydney: Powerhouse Museum.

Roters, E. (1969). *Painters of the Bauhaus.* New York: Frederick A. Praeger.

Rowland, A. (1990). *Bauhaus source book.* New York: Van Nostrand Reinhold.

Sparke, P. (1987). *Modern Japanese design.* New York: E. P. Dutton.

Steele, V. (1985). *Fashion and eroticism: Ideals of feminine beauty from the Victorian era to the Jazz Age.* New York: Oxford University Press.

Steele, V. (1991). *Women of fashion: Twentieth century designers.* New York: Rizzoli.

Tortora, P., & Eubank, K. (1989). *A survey of historic costume.* New York: Fairchild Books.

Whitford, F. (1984). *Bauhaus.* New York: Thames & Hudson.

Wilcox, R. T. (1958). *The mode in costume.* New York: Charles Scribner's Sons.

Yohannon, K., & Nolf, N. (1998). *Claire McCardell: Redefining modernism.* New York: Harry N. Abrams.

| # TEXTURE AND LIGHT

FASHION DESIGNERS INEVITABLY use texture to express their aesthetic perspective of apparel for a given season. It is also the element that effectively adds variety to their complete repertoire of designs. Texture refers to the surface of an object. Surface texture reveals itself by touch. The feel of apparel is critical, not only to the fingers but because it must feel good on the body. Like the other senses, touch becomes a part of experience, so sensations are stored in the brain and remembered. As a result, texture is also perceived visually. Seeing it reminds us of a previous experience or sensation.

The ability to see texture is also directly related to light and to what extent a material reflects or absorbs it. A surface with shine is often so smooth that it reflects a great deal of light. A matte surface, by contrast, is nonreflective.

This phenomenon is the reason that both texture and light are discussed in this chapter. First, we will look at texture in relation to all art forms and to the materials that an artist or designer uses. Because fashion designers choose to work with fabric most often, we will also consider its structure and terminology as well as its aesthetic properties and their importance to designers.

Light is defined and categorized by our perception of it, along with the way in which surfaces react to it. In this chapter we will also look at how fashion designers consider light in the creative process—the ways in which they use it and for what purpose.

TACTILE TEXTURE AND VISUAL TEXTURE

At the beginning of this chapter, we noted that there are two types of texture: tactile texture, or the result of touch, and visual texture, or our visual perception of the surface. These, and the following terms, apply to all art forms.

ACTUAL TEXTURE

Actual texture is used for the form the surface takes that causes the sensation when it is touched. Physical texture is another term for the same

4.1 The application of brush strokes in Vincent Van Gogh's *The Starry Night* (1889) is a texture that adds impact to the picture.

THE MUSEUM OF MODERN ART/LICENSED BY SCALA/ ART RESOURCE, NY

concept. The artist or designer creates the surface as part of the product. A good example is the oil painting *The Starry Night* by Post-Impressionist Vincent Van Gogh (1853–1890). (SEE FIGURE 4.1.) The texture caused by Van Gogh's brush strokes is an inimitable characteristic of his painting style, and in addition to the subject matter and colors, it has great impact on the viewer. It provides a sense of movement that suggests the wind. It makes the whirlpools of light twinkle. Its swirls direct the eye across the painting.

SIMULATED TEXTURE

Simulated texture is the faithful rendering of a real texture. In paintings, examples include wood grain, leather, and stone. Taken to an extreme, the approach can be so real that it causes a deception, where the viewer expects the authentic feel of the material on the painting's canvas. This effect is called trompe l'oeil, from a French term meaning "to fool the eye." The painting *Still Life—Violin and Music* by American painter William Michael Harnett (1848–1892) depicts the textures of wood and rusted metal (FIGURE 4.2). Harnett could not know that a subsequent school of twentieth-century painting, Magic Realism, would prescribe that artists combine their paints with substances that enable simulated textures, like brick, not only to look like the real thing but to feel like it. Trompe l'oeil is a technique that is also used in fashion. Franco Moschino (1950–1994) used it in his jacket from fall 2001 to express his humor about fashion (FIGURE 4.3). The jacket appears to have several closures and construction details—zippers, tab pocket, topstitching, belt and belt loops—but in reality, they are merely printed on the surface of the cloth.

RIGHT
4.2 The textures in Michael Harnett's *Still Life—Violin and Music* are so real that they could fool the eye.
THE METROPOLITAN MUSEUM OF ART/ART RESOURCE, NY

BELOW
4.3 This jacket by Franco Moschino (fall 2001) deceives the viewer into thinking there are zippers, topstitching, tab pocket, belt, and belt loops on it.
MOSCHINO (ITALIAN, FOUNDED 1983), JACKET, FALL 2001, PRINTED WOOL, PHOTO BY KEN HOWIE, COLLECTION OF PHOENIX ART MUSEUM, GIFT OF MRS. KELLY ELLMAN

ABSTRACT TEXTURE AND INVENTED TEXTURE

Artists employ two other types of texture. Abstract texture displays a simulated texture but then abstracts or simplifies it, like the use of the curving lines of wood grain, but without its color tones and literal surface quality. Invented texture is the pure invention by the artist or designer through the use of the media. This occurs most often in art that is nonobjective or abstract. The texture may result from the artist's brushwork, pen, wax crayon, collage, or other tools and media. A fashion designer may invent texture through a variety of means. One example is like collage, where a variety of fabrics or other materials are used together. The evening dress by American designer Geoffrey Beene juxtaposes three different fabrications, much like a two-dimensional artist chooses varying papers for a collage (FIGURE 4.4).

TEXTURE AND MATERIALS

The creation of texture is dependent on the materials chosen by the artist or designer, because each material has its own inherent quality and structure. Structural texture is the result of the elements of a substance or mate-

4.4 As an artist creates a collage, Geoffrey Beene combines three different textures in his short evening dress from 1991.
THE METROPOLITAN MUSEUM OF ART/ART RESOURCE, NY

4.5 Carolina Herrera chose raffia as the fiber for the jacket with braided collar from her spring 2010 collection.
COURTESY OF WWD/ THOMAS IANNACCONE

rial and the method of its construction. Fabric is the most common medium for the design of fashion, so an examination of its properties is sure to enhance its manipulation.

THE STRUCTURAL ELEMENTS OF FABRIC

The structural elements of fabric are fiber, yarn, construction, and finish.

FIBER

Fiber is the chemical substance from which fabrics are made. The fiber is a significant influence on a fabric's performance. There are two groups of fibers: natural and man-made. Natural fibers include those that come from animal or plant sources, such as cotton, **flax** (linen), **ramie**, **hemp**, **wool**, **mohair**, **angora**, **camel's hair**, **cashmere**, **alpaca**, **silk**, and other minor fibers. American designer Carolina Herrera (1939–) chose **raffia**, a fiber from a species of Madagascar palm, for a two-tone jacket with braided collar to go with an embroidered skirt in her spring 2010 collection (FIGURE 4.5). Man-made or synthetic fibers are **rayon**, **acetate**, **nylon**, **polyester**, **acrylic**, **modacrylic**, **spandex**, **Fiberglas**, **metallic fibers**, and others. Some of these are long fibers, as in the case of silk and synthetic fibers, called **filaments**. Filaments are shiny and smooth and have a cool touch. Short fibers, which are characteristic of cotton and wool, for instance, are called **staples**. They are dull, rough, and fuzzy, with a warm touch. Extremely fine polyester filaments are called **microfibers**. They are strong and take on bright colors extremely well.

YARN

Yarn is the result of fibers spun together in order to form its structure. Filament fiber yarns are generally smoother and more slippery. Yarns made from staple fibers are fuzzy, like those used for a cotton or wool flannel. Sometimes staple fibers are made parallel before being spun, so they have a smoother texture, which is appropriate for the worsted wool that is used in a suit. The extent of yarn twist, achieved while the yarn is being spun, is also an influence on the final product. Highly twisted yarns, like a crepe, create a pebbly surface, which is aesthetically valued and wrinkle resistant, but they do not result in fabric strength. Low yarn twist with lustrous filament fibers causes a shiny texture, and with fuzzy staple fibers, it results in a soft surface.

The number of strands that a yarn has twisted together contributes to its texture, thickness, and strength. Strands are referred to as **ply**. The higher the ply, the more desirable the fabric. The thickness of the yarn determines how many will fit into an inch, and that influences the fineness or coarseness of the texture.

Novelty yarns are created with interesting contours, bulges, and slubs, which are collections of tufts of fibers. Some have strands of different types spun together, and some vary in their direction or degree of twist, such as **bouclé**, which has a loopy texture. An elasticized yarn results in a fabric that has stretch. All of the novelties have an impact on fabric texture.

CONSTRUCTION

Fabric structure probably has the greatest impact on texture. It is the method used to interlock fibrous yarns together into a flat fabric. A weave is the formation of fabrics in which yarns are woven together. The yarns that run from front to back on a loom are called the **warp**. Those that run crosswise are called the **weft**. The simplest weave is when the warp and weft yarns interlock singly with one another. That construction is a **plain weave**.

A loom can manufacture more complex woven structures, as yarns are raised and lowered during the weaving process, causing them to float over and under one another in different numbers. Each complex woven structure has a different name and a different texture. **Twill** is the one used in denim jeans. A **satin** is recognized by its smooth, shiny appearance. Both a **dobby** and **jacquard** have a pattern woven into its structure, even though the full piece of fabric has one color. The pattern is perceived by the sheen of the motifs in comparison to their background. Some weaves have **pile**, which are cut yarns that cause a plush surface. Other woven structures are possible. Weaves are the strongest, most stable fabric structures, but they do not have much stretch. As a result, woven fabrics must be cut and sewn, using construction techniques like seams and darts, in order to enable flat fabric to fit a human figure.

Fashion designers form a preference for working with certain types of fabrics. The great couturièr Cristóbal Balenciaga (1895–1972) searched for a silk fabric with a new structure in order to execute the designs he sioned in the 1960s. He worked with the textile designer Gustav Zums and the Swiss textile manufacturer Abraham of Zurich in order to create ı The fabric was called silk **Gazar**, a heavily sized woven silk of even texture that is still in production today. Compared to previous decades, Balenciaga wanted to design simple, almost abstract, evening dresses, free of surface decoration. Although it was not the easiest fabric to work with, the heavy Gazar enabled him to drape designs with both crisp silhouette and the beautiful sheen characteristic of silk (FIGURE 4.6).

In Chapter 1, we noted the importance of grain in relation to garments that have draped structural design. It is worth repeating in relation to woven fabrics. The direction of the yarns, another term for grain, is pivotal in the determination of how a fabric will work. The lengthwise yarns, or warp, are the strongest, and therefore the part of the garment that receives the most stress in the wearing should reflect that direction: where knees or elbows bend or where a skirt is pulled when the body is seated. However, grain is an important consideration for aesthetic judgment as well. When

4.6 Balenciaga's use of silk Gazar enabled him to achieve a crisp silhouette as exemplified by this matching dress and cape from 1967.
© V&A IMAGES, VICTORIA AND ALBERT MUSEUM

the lengthwise and crosswise yarns are used on the diagonal, the fabric is said to be "on the bias." This enables the fabric to drape more flexibly, allowing soft and elegant shaping that reveals the body. The designer Madeleine Vionnet was the first to be credited for draping on the bias.

A **knit** is another type of fabric structure where needles are used to form a series of interconnecting loops from one or more yarns or a set of yarns. This process enables the fabric to be more flexible, wrinkle-resistant, and stretchy, and that allows the fabric to conform to the body without the need for seams and darts demanded by a woven fabric. A knit is less durable and stable than a weave, and the fabric may sag or stretch out of shape with extended use. There are several kinds of knits, including single, double, weft, warp, or pile. Knits are commonly used in the fashion industry for sweaters, T-shirts, underwear, and jogging suits, among other items. The benefit is that the elasticity helps apparel to adjust to variations in body size. As a result, fewer sizes in a range are necessary.

French designer Sonia Rykiel (1930–) is famous the world over for her knitwear. Through this medium she sought to express a lifestyle for modern women, a kind of sweaterlike head-to-toe dressing. She thought of it as a second skin that wraps the body with softness and comfort. Knits facilitate movement and, as a result, provide a sense of freedom. Together with these attributes, Rykiel is known to add color, fashion details, and other textures, such as **paillettes** and **lurex** yarns (FIGURE 4.7).

4.7 Sonia Rykiel is known for designing high fashion in knitwear.
COURTESY OF FAIRCHILD ARCHIVE/LARRY ROSSOW

American designer Norma Kamali (1945–), who is perhaps best known for her swimwear, commanded attention in the late 1970s and early 1980s for experimenting with another kind of knitted fabric—sweatshirt cloth. Her work coincided with the trend for physical exercise and highlighted the fitness of women. She creatively designed fashion with a fabric that was formerly considered appropriate only for athletic apparel (FIGURE 4.8).

There are other fabric structures that do not fall into either the category of weaves or knits. These include **felt**, where fibers adhere to each other without first being spun, **netting**, **lace**, **braid**, **crochet**, and **macramé** (knotting). The great couturièr Yves Saint Laurent capitalized on macramé for the design of his African dresses in the 1960s (FIGURE 4.9).

FINISH

Finishes used on the surface of textiles also create texture. Finishes are chemical or mechanical treatments that apply heat, pressure, and/or chemicals to affect the fabric surface and penetrate its fibers. Many of these have a functional purpose, often adding resistance to wrinkles, shrinking, water, moths, mildew, and flame. The focus of this chapter is on finishes that add texture for aesthetic purposes. A common example is the bleaching or use of other treatment on jean fabric to support a fashion trend and provide the jean consumer with added choice. For adding sheen to a fabric surface, the finishing options are **ciréing**, **glazing**, **schreinering**, and **calendering**. The finishing process used to create sheen in a water pattern is called **moiréing**. Napping causes fuzziness, while shearing gives pile an even surface.

There are many words used to describe fabric qualities, but it is critical to command the correct terminology to identify fabrics. For that purpose, the identifying terms include both the fiber content and the fabric structure, as in the case of Balenciaga's silk "Gazar." A wool **gabardine** may work best for a suit. For a summer skirt, an appropriate fabric is a cotton **seersucker** or **piqué**. Would an evening gown look better in polyester **jersey** or nylon **chiffon**?

EXPERIENCING FABRIC

What is the best way to learn about fabrics? The most valuable method is by experience. True familiarity does not come from a computer or classroom. Textiles must be seen and handled. Attend costume exhibits in museums to see how designers worked with fabrics in the past. Check out retail clothing stores and see how different fabrics are used today. Visit fabric stores regularly to examine the assortment and watch it change seasonally. Buy pieces of fabric that have special appeal and actually "play" with them. How do they hang, bunch, look under the light?

With this experience, designers discover methods to create their own texture. They know that texture can result from the use of construction techniques. For instance, Norma Kamali used drawstrings, gathers, and ruching to add texture to the flat surface of the silk and nylon in her evening ensemble from 1977 (FIGURE 4.10).

NON-TEXTILE CLOTHING

Not all clothing is made from textiles. Fashion designers also choose other materials. Nevertheless, the garment's texture depends on the structure of those materials, whether metals, plastics, furs, feathers, or paper, to name a few. Haute couture designer Paco Rabanne (1934–) began his career by creating garments from plastic discs and metal chains (FIGURE 4.11). He followed those by showing fur coats with leather patches. Later he used strips of

4.10 Norma Kamali added texture to her evening ensemble by utilizing construction techniques.
THE METROPOLITAN MUSEUM OF ART/ART RESOURCE, NY

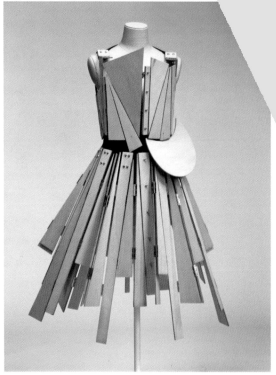

LEFT: 4.11 Paco Rabanne introduced designs in plastics and metals. COLLECTION OF THE KYOTO COSTUME INSTITUTE, PHOTO BY TAISHI HIROKAWA

RIGHT: 4.12 This garment made of wood and hinges over black wool was designed by Yohji Yamamoto in 1991. COLLECTION OF THE KYOTO COSTUME INSTITUTE, PHOTO BY TAKASHI HATAKEYAMA

aluminum laced with wire as well as ribbons and tassels. Yohji Yamamoto was introduced in Chapter 1 for his design statements related to deconstruction. He has also made a mark by using a diversity of textures in his work, as exemplified in his ensemble made of wood and hinges, with an understructure of black wool (FIGURE 4.12).

AESTHETIC PROPERTIES OF TEXTURE

Playing with fabrics reveals their aesthetic properties. There is a terminology for those too, and some of the terms have already been named, but not formally defined.

DRAPE

Drape is the way in which a fabric falls, which is a critical consideration when the purpose is to clothe the human figure. Fiber, yarn, and fabric structure all determine drape, but to differing degrees. Fine fibers produce softer drape, but fabric structure is the greatest determinant. Chiffon is free flowing, for instance, and a wonderful choice for a Grecian-style gown, where many folds are desirable. Satin is stiff and heavier, so it is the better choice for a bouffant ball gown.

HAND

Hand is the way fabric feels to the skin, also a critical concern of the designer's. Hand gives the wearer an intimate experience, leading to words of description, such as rough, coarse, fuzzy, nubby, crinkly, soft, slippery, smooth, stretchy, springy, stiff, and so forth.

Fabric is also handled as a three-dimensional substance. That means it is bent, crushed, stretched, twisted, folded, or squeezed in its manipulation. As this happens, qualities of hand become clear. For instance, **flexibility** expresses how supple or rigid a fabric is and whether it will drape softly or hold a crisp silhouette. **Compressibility** is how the fabric responds to squeezing. The ease of compressibility is extremely important where the body bends, such as the elbow, hip, or knee. **Extensibility** refers to the extent of stretch in the fabric. Stretch enables the fabric to conform to body contours and creates ease of fit. Designers desire more extensibility when the goal is a body-revealing silhouette. **Resilience** speaks to the ability of the fabric to spring back from squeezing or twisting. Consumers often prize a garment that will hold its original form after wearing.

DENSITY

Density is the weight per volume of a texture. The weight of a garment is important to the wearer for both comfort and ease of movement. Density is due to the fineness or coarseness of the yarn, how open or compact is the fabric structure, and how thin or thick it is. For example, a fine yarn can make a compact fabric, such as **percale**, or an open one, such as **tulle**. It can also be used in a thin one, such as **organdy**, or a thick one, such as **terry cloth**. Ironically, fabric is more air by volume and more fiber by weight—fabrics that seem bulky may have more air trapped between fibers and yarns and thereby weigh less than fabrics with a greater density of fiber.

LUSTER

Luster results from the way light is reflected by a surface. Fabrics with silk, a filament fiber, are usually lustrous, especially those with a smooth surface, like satin. Luster is a desirable quality for formal apparel. Short fibers, like wool or cotton, are low-luster and usually contribute to a fabric surface that is matte or dull.

SURFACE CONTOUR

Texture also results from the surface characteristics of fabrics. **Surface contour** means divergence from a flat plane in the fabric surface, indicating a range from smoothness to roughness. However, some structures with variation in the fabric surface are not considered rough, such as fleece or a ribbed knit. Surface friction indicates how fabric slides over itself or catches because of traction, with a range from slippery to harsh. A coat lining fabric should feel slippery, so that the wearer's arms can slide easily into the sleeves.

THERMAL CHARACTER

Thermal character is the apparent fabric temperature by comparison to skin temperature. A fabric that feels warm is uncomfortable in a warm season or climate. Comfort level may also have to do with the property of absorbency. Those that have greater absorbency, like wool, may feel warmer, while some less absorbent synthetics may feel cooler, like an athletic shirt made of nylon. While consumers may reject wool for warm weather, a bulky fabric that is airy may also receive a rejection, just because it looks like it feels warm.

TEXTURE AND THE DESIGNER

Fabric is a defining influence on a new design. In fact, many designers do not begin to design until they choose the fabric. It may actually inspire one or a group of garments. A fashion designer handles it to see how it drapes or if it is crisp or airy. Cuban-born designer Isabel Toledo's (1961–) creations are considered to be more works of art than clothing. She works directly with the fabric and does not sketch. If a sketch is necessary, she turns to her husband, illustrator Ruben Toledo. She reported to Harriet Mays Powell, the fashion director of *New York Magazine*: "The fabric gives me an emotion. I think about how I am going to wrap the fabric around the body—how I am going to anchor it" (Powell, 2009, p. 1). Toledo's design in FIGURE 4.13 demonstrates her concern for anchoring the fabric with each of its multiple sections of drapery, although the design probably evolved using the flat pattern method.

4.13 Isabel Toledo's multiple sections of drapery illustrate her concern for anchoring the fabric as it wraps around the body.
COURTESY OF THE MUSEUM AT FIT

Fabric also defines the garment's silhouette, as in the case of Balenciaga's development of Gazar, the heavy silk that gave his evening wear a definite form, separate from body shape.

FABRIC DICTATING DESIGN

Two subsequent designers idolized Balenciaga's work and also had a love for silk Gazar. They were Geoffrey Beene and the only American member of the French haute couture since the 1930s, Ralph Rucci (1957–).

Geoffrey Beene would say that fabric dictated his designs. At least, it spoke to him in a special way from the time he was a boy. At the age of eight years old, he persuaded his aunt to turn a favorite piece of fabric, a cotton print of orange flowers on a baby blue background, into a pair of beach pajamas. The process of seeing it transformed from a flat piece of fabric into three dimensions proved to be a lifelong inspiration. Later he reincarnated those pajamas into a jumpsuit, one of the fashions for which he became known. He used many fabrics, like wool jersey and gray flannel. Another story relates how he never cut into a piece of black and silver brocade, with a star motif, which he discovered near Cannes. He was so entranced by it that he felt no garment design could improve on it. Another tells of his search for a new fabrication, much like Balenciaga's. When he saw the thick wools loomed by the Lesotho tribe in Africa, he inquired whether one could be made in a lighter version. When they delivered to him the new product, a lightweight woolen weave, he adapted it into an evening coat edged in gold braid. He said that the greatest contribution to the fashion industry in the twentieth century was the capacity for stretch. Instead of fashion models, he featured his designs on dancers, who displayed the elasticity of his designs with their movements. He even made **challis** prints stretchable. He called wool jersey his dream fabric, because it behaved like a second skin. But Gazar was his greatest challenge; it was crisp silk that appeared to sail away. Yet he made a jacket that reversed men's shirting to it! He also used other combinations, being mindful of the textural beauty caused by light reflection, such as silk with metals or plastics (FIGURES 4.4, page 82, AND 4.14).

LISTENING TO FABRIC—LITERALLY

Ralph Rucci's philosophy has been to let the fabrics speak. Each fabric has a sensual quality that is revealed by its type, like the sound of **faille**, the whoosh of **taffeta**, the oomph of cashmere, or the ahh of chiffon. Rucci attributes his initial inspiration to the Spanish-born Balenciaga, whose work he observed in *Vogue* in the 1960s. There he found a bridal gown or dinner dress where the construction was dependent on the inherent qualities of Gazar. When cut on the bias, the fabric would achieve a conical form as the wearer moved and air caused the skirt to billow out. Rucci has created his own success with silk Gazar (FIGURE 4.15). But he also has been successful by adding original textures to a fabric's surface. He has used embroidery, hammered silk, leather-covered paillettes, Mongolian lamb, coq feathers, and hand-looped ribbon on his creations.

French couturièr Yves St. Laurent, introduced in Chapter 2 regarding his Mondrian-inspired dresses, was also a master of fabrics and all applied materials. Over his long career, his contribution was prolific. An examination of his work features many lessons on texture (BOX 4.1).

YVES SAINT LAURENT had an extensive career as an haute couture designer, so his contribution to the fashion industry was prolific. He was born in Oran, Algeria, and demonstrated an inclination for art during his boyhood. His interest in clothing began when he went to a theater production of *School for Wives* by Molière, a French playwright and actor, and saw the sets and costumes designed by Christian Bérard (1902–1949). After that, he occupied himself by making miniature costumes and sets. That was enough to prime his talent, because he won the first prize in the International Wool Secretariat contest at the age of 17. His design was an asymmetrically draped, one-sleeve cocktail dress. When he went to Paris in 1953, the editor of French *Vogue*, Michel de Brunhoff, was struck by the similarity between Yves' sketchbook designs and the forthcoming *A* line by Christian Dior, so he introduced them. Dior immediately hired him as his assistant.

When Dior died unexpectedly in 1957, Saint Laurent was named head designer for his House, an awesome responsibility at the age of 21. However, he began his work with gusto, featuring the "trapeze" look (lines extending outward from the shoulders) in the collection of 1958. Parisians shouted in the streets that Yves Saint Laurent had saved the economy.

His fate, however, was undetermined. In 1960, he was drafted into the French army and had a nervous collapse. He returned promptly to Paris, but the House of Dior had hired Marc Bohan in his place. Although this must have been disappointing for Saint Laurent, it created the opportunity for him to open his own couture house, in partnership with Pierre Bergé and a businessman from Atlanta, Georgia. The rest was history, as this began the myriad of couture and ready-to-wear collections he would create.

An examination of his collections reveals Saint Laurent's command of texture in all its varieties. The 1960s brought designs such as his Mondrian dresses from the autumn-winter 1965 collection described in Chapter 2 (FIGURE 2.4). At that time, he created a cocoonlike white wedding gown hand-knitted of Aran wool, which was so nontraditional that it has sometimes been described as "grotesque." He followed those in 1967 with "The

Smoking," a man's dinner suit for women, and dresses meant to commemorate the Pop Art movement. In the spring/summer 1967 collection, he designed a noted group of African-inspired dresses, using macramé along with wooden beads, shells, and raffia (FIGURE 4.9, page 87, AND FIGURE BOX 4.1A). By the end of the 1960s, he made evening and cocktail dresses completely of bird-of-paradise feathers (FIGURE BOX 4.1B). His Russian collection occurred in 1976–1977, featuring peasant blouses and gypsy skirts in fabrics such as mousseline de soie, moiré, taffeta, patterned lamé, and velvet, and trimmed with tassels, jet, glass, fur, and fringe (FIGURE BOX 4.1C). The fall–winter 1977–1978 collection featured Chinese-inspired ensembles, assembled with brocade, ciré, velvet, and chiffon, decorated with embroidery and sequins, and trimmed with tassels and passementerie. By the end of the decade, Saint Laurent's inspiration came from Picasso, and he applied Cubist shapes in reflective, colorful fabrics using appliqué on the surface of skirts and jackets. Known also for renown styles in cloth for women, such as the peacoat, trench coat, safari jacket, and tuxedo, his designs in the 1980s and 1990s continued with varying levels of opulence, in shantung and satin, suede, faille, sequins, beadwork, and touches of rhinestones.

His death in 2008 seemed inconceivable and signaled to many the end of great couture. The styles he originated, the interpretations of artistic inspiration, and the name, Yves Saint Laurent, remain memorable in the fashion world.

LIGHT

Light has long been a source of interest to artists and designers. Its qualities can lift emotions and provide aesthetic pleasure. Impressionist painters made it a focus as they painted outdoors or *en plein air*. Claude Monet (1840–1926), the father of Impressionism, painted the same subject at different times of the day and discovered, like the other artists of his movement, that color and atmospheric perception changes with the light. Two of his paintings of the Cathedral at Rouen demonstrate the difference (FIGURES 4.16A AND B).

Light is the portion of the electromagnetic or radiant spectrum that is visible to the human eye. Radiant energy includes X-ray, ultraviolet, infrared, and radio waves and results from the vibration of electrons. Light varies from the other forms of radiant energy in wavelength and frequency. **Wavelength** is the distance between the highest peak of one wave and the next. **Frequency** refers to the speed of the wave vibrations. Brightness or level of illumination is the result of the amount of energy radiating from its source.

BELOW LEFT
4.16A This view of the Cathedral de Rouen was painted by Claude Monet in 1894 in full sunlight.
SACLA/ART RESOURCE, NY

BELOW RIGHT
4.16B Compare the lighting of the Cathedral de Rouen at noontime, as perceived by the paint colors Monet chose in 1893–1894.
SCALA/ART RESOURCE, NY

LIGHT AND SURFACE

By observation, artists also know that light behaves differently depending the surface it strikes. For instance, light is refracted (or bent) when it hits a transparent surface like clear glass, creating a complex network of luminous shapes. By comparison, objects made from silver, steel, or mirrored glass are reflective, meaning they bounce light back into space. This dynamic also describes the interaction of light with satin, sequins, and gemstones. Surfaces that are dark or dull have more light absorption, which is characteristic of wool, velvet, and cotton. Translucent surfaces, like organza, which are not fully transparent or fully opaque, demonstrate light transmission.

The amount of light perception is also determined by the **angle of incidence**—the angle at which light hits an object. More light bounces off of a shiny surface if it strikes from a low, side angle, and that causes long shadows behind it. More is absorbed or reflected if it hits at a higher angle. Then short shadows fall behind the object.

LIGHT AND ENVIRONMENT

Perception is also due to light projection in the environment. Ambient light encompasses an entire space, like sunlight on a warm afternoon. Directed light is localized and focused like a spotlight. Light quality ranges from soft and diffused, or atmospheric, to sharp and bright. Diffused light reduces the contrast on surfaces and softens the contours on objects. Sharp light reinforces surface quality, accenting textures and depth. A spotlight, providing sharp focused light, creates strong highlights, dark shadows, and the feeling of drama—an effective way to feature draped folds and gathers.

Theater lighting designers and interior designers can determine the lighting of a space, but the fashion designer cannot. The intent is a design that is pleasing under a range of lighting and as the body moves. So the most effective method to obtaining the desired effects is by controlling the surfaces on which it will fall. However, with the increase of technology, there are new, innovative approaches that designers are using to link fashion with lighting, and they are enumerated in this chapter.

FASHION SHOW LIGHTING

One venue where the designer can control lighting is the fashion show. Lighting is one of the key elements of a fashion show, and a lighting plan is developed with consultation in advance. The fashion show is an important form of sales promotion at the introduction of a seasonal line or collection. Lighting must change to govern the viewer's eye as the garments travel down the runway. To that end, the constantly changing highlights and shadows are critical.

LIGHT AND TEMPERATURE

Light affects clothing in yet another way—the temperature of the surface it strikes. This is the result of an interaction between light and color. More light rays bounce off a pastel fabric, so the reverse side stays cooler. A dark color absorbs light rays and transforms it into heat. The implication, then, is that light, color, and fabric conspire to provide comfort for the wearer or a lack of it. Logic suggests that a navy or black wool coat is a good choice for winter wear, and the same is true for a white or pastel swimsuit in the summer.

FOUR CATEGORIES OF LIGHT

The research of Dr. Jung Hyun of Hong-lk University in Korea classifies contemporary fashion designers' use of light into four categories: reflected light, represented light, emitted light, and projected light. Designers are certain to further explore each of these avenues in order to visually impress their consumers and the public.

REFLECTED LIGHT

Reflected light is the term that describes the interaction between light and the fabric surface as presented in this chapter. The reflection is heightened by the use of metallic, crystalline, and holographic fabrications and materials, as in the nature of Paco Rabanne's design in FIGURE 4.11 (page 89).

REPRESENTED LIGHT

Represented light refers to a graphic interpretation that is symbolic of light, like the pattern on a garment from Emilio Pucci in the spring/summer 2008 collection (FIGURE 4.17).

EMITTED LIGHT

Emitted light is radiated from a source existing within the clothes. In the recent past, this phenomenon resulted from an electrical or battery source, but there is currently growth in non-electric luminous materials that are combined with textiles, such as phosphorescence, fluorescence, and chemical luminescence. Other interesting electrical sources include LED, laser, and optical fibers (FIGURE 4.18).

PROJECTED LIGHT

Projected light originates from a projector that propels a pattern on the clothing's surface. Alternatively, the image of light may come from a form of holography (FIGURE 4.19).

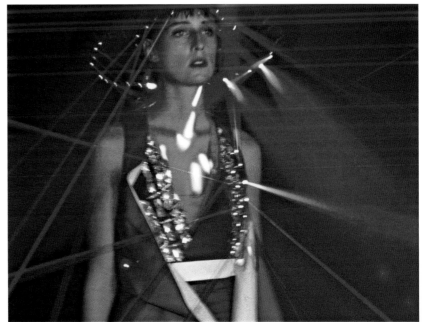

4.19 The light effect shown on this garment is the result of light projection.
COURTESY OF WWD/ GIOVANNI GIANNONI

LIGHT'S CAPTIVATING QUALITY

What other goals do we have for using light in our designs? Dr. Hyun's research concludes that light has many benefits, beginning with a sense of fantasy. Historically, light has implied mystical symbols related to religion or the cosmos. Fantasy assures the wearer psychologically of an opportunity for escape, a great selling point for the right consumer.

Designers may also stress sensuality and seduction, especially with the effects of glittering or flickering light that change the wearer into an object of fascination. The utilization of light alternatively presents an opportunity for play, especially when it is stimulated by touch or the visual product is kaleidoscopic.

There is also the opportunity for interactivity, when the moment, synchronism, and digital technologies involve the wearer in the clothes. Interactivity has high appeal for a generation used to video and computer games.

Finally, designers may choose the functional purpose of generating light for physical protection of the body or psychological stability.

Among the designers who have explored light in their creations is Mariano Fortuny (1871–1949), whose timeless designs had appeal over decades (BOX 4.2).

In addition to texture, experience with fabric and other materials reveals their interaction with light. The ones that have light reflection, absorption, and transmission become apparent. In addition, exploration of new fabrics and technologies present opportunities for innovative design. The effective utilization of texture and light in a fashion design is certain to enhance its aesthetic success.

KEY TERMS

absorption
abstract texture
acetate
acrylic
actual texture
alpaca
ambient light
angle of incidence
angora
bias
bleaching
bouclé
braid
brightness
brocade
calendaring
camel's hair
cashmere
challis
chiffon
ciréing
compressibility
cotton
crepe
crochet
density
diffused light
directed light
dobby
double knit
drape
embroidery
extensibility
faille
felt
fiber
Fiberglas
filament
finish
flannel
flax
fleece

flexibility
frequency
gabardine
Gazar
glazing
grain
hand
hemp
holographic materials
invented texture
jacquard
jersey
knit
lace
level of illumination
light
linen
lurex
luster
macramé
man-made fibers
men's shirting
metallic fibers
microfiber
modacrylic
mohair
moiréing
napping
natural fibers
netting
non-objective
nylon
organdy
paillettes
percale
physical texture
pile
pile knit
piqué
plain weave
ply
polyester

ramie
rayon
reflective
reflected light
resilience
ribbed knit
satin
schreinering
seersucker
sequins
shearing
silk
simulated texture
single knit
spandex
staples
structural texture
surface contour
surface friction
synthetic fiber
tactile texture
taffeta
terry cloth
texture
thermal character
translucent
transmission
transparent
tulle
twill
velvet
visual texture
warp
warp knit
wavelength
weave
weft
weft knit
wool
worsted wool
yarn

PROJECTS

1. Design a garment on a half-scale mannequin form using nontraditional materials, such as Q-tips, pipe cleaners, safety pins, paper clips, wrapping paper, tissue paper, mesh or netting, bubble wrap, feathers, thin wooden dowels, beads, buttons, twine, yarn, fake fur, cork, bark, and so on. Use them alone or in combination. Consider how to attach them to each other and how to "dress" the mannequin in a quick, functional fashion for the critique. What kinds of texture(s) are created? Hints: Browse stores for these or other materials before attempting to design. Use the sketchbook to think through different designs before purchasing the materials.

2. Draw the silhouette of the back and the front of a garment on a piece of Bristol. Apply the materials listed in Project 1 or others to the two-dimensional surface to simulate a garment design. What texture(s) are created? Then mount the silhouette on a neutral color board. Optional: Fill in the background with collaged materials or create a separate background using collage to set off the design. Hint: Use proper adhesives for the materials chosen—the appropriate glue, one- or two-sided tape, and so on.

3. Shop for swatches, pieces, or remnants of different fabrics of the same color and intensity. Assemble cut or torn shapes into a collage on thin cardboard or Bristol, (dimensions between 8 inches by 10 inches to 11 inches by 14 inches) using fabric glue. The success of the piece depends not only on the layout of shapes but also on the treatment of light on the fabric surfaces.

REFERENCES

Battista, A. (2009, August 5). Isabel Toledo: Fashion from the inside out. *Dazed Digital*. Retrieved August 7, 2009, from www.dazeddigital .com/Fashion/article/4272/1/Isabel_Toledo_F.

Cunningham, R. (1989). *The magic garment: Principles of costume design*. Long Grove, IL: Waveland Press.

Davis, M. L. (1996). *Visual design in dress* (3rd ed.). Upper Saddle River, NJ: Prentice Hall.

De Osma, G. (1994). *Fortuny: The life and work of Mariane Fortuny*. New York: Rizzoli.

Donofrio-Ferezza, L., & Hefferen, M. (2008). *Designing a knitwear collection from inspiration to finished garments*. New York: Fairchild Books.

Gordon, R., & Forge, A. (1989). *Monet*. New York: Harry N. Abrams.

Jung, H. (2008, June 30). The aesthetic characteristics of fashion design adopting light. [Doctoral dissertation]. Hong-Ik University.

Kadolph, S. J. (2007). *Textiles* (10th ed.). Upper Saddle River, NJ: Pearson Education.

Mauriès, P., & Rykiel, S. (1998). *Sonia Rykiel.* New York: Universe Publis ing and Vendome Press.

Milbank, C. R. (1985). *Couture: The great designers.* New York: Stewart, Tabori & Chang.

Miller, L. E. (2007). *Cristóbal Balenciaga (1895–1972): The couturiers' couturier.* London: V&A Publications.

Ocvirk, O. G., Stinson, R. E., Wigg, P. R., Bone, R. O. , & Cayton, D. L. (2002). *Art fundamentals: Theory and practice* (9th ed.). New York: McGraw-Hill.

Powell, H. M. (2009, June 16). Video: A tour of "Isabel Toledo: Fashion from the Inside Out." *New York* magazine. Retrieved October 12, 2009, from http://nymag.com/daily/fashion/2009/06/video_a_tour_ of_isabel_toledo.html.

Saint Laurent, Y., Vreeland D., Huyghe, R., Berge, P., Picasso-Lopez, P., Agnelli, M., Deneuve, D., Michals, D., Boulat, P., & Vreeland, N. (1983). *Yves Saint Laurent.* New York: The Metropolitan Museum of Art.

Steele, V. (1991). *Women of fashion: Twentieth-century designers.* New York: Rizzoli.

Steele, V. (1997). *Fifty years of fashion: New Look to now.* New Haven, CT: Yale University.

Steele, V., Patricia, M., and Sauro, C. (2007). *Ralph Rucci: The art of weightlessness.* New York: Fashion Institute of Technology.

Stegemeyer, A. (2004). *Who's who in fashion.* (4th ed.) New York: Fairchild Books.

Stewart, M. (2008). *Launching the imagination: A comprehensive guide to basic design* (3rd ed.). New York: McGraw-Hill.

Stoops, J., & Samuelson, J. (1983). *Design dialogue.* Worcester, MA: Davis Publications.

BOX 4.2

MARIANO FORTUNY

ACCORDING TO CAROLINE Reynolds Milbank in *Couture: The Great Designers,* the dresses designed by Mariano Fortuny are "paintings in light" (Milbank, 1985, p. 95). Fortuny was different from other fashion designers, because he had been both a painter and a lighting designer before he began a business in clothing and textiles.

He was born in Spain in 1871 to a family of painters. Although his father died when he was a boy, Fortuny grew up in an environment surrounded by collections of art and textiles. He was also educated in chemistry and physics. His family moved briefly to Paris and then to Venice, where he spent his time painting, drawing, and etching. Like Yves Saint Laurent, Fortuny's interests were transformed after seeing a theater production. Fortuny's transformative experience was caused by the opportunity see the work of composer Richard Wagner (1813–1883) in Bayreuth, Germany, where Wagner had built a theater especially designed for his operas. Fortuny had been enamored by Wagner's music, but perceiving it integrated with other art forms, such as poetry, painting, dance, and architecture, stimulated a passion for theater production. That pressed him to study electricity and its use in the creating of stage lighting and sets (De Osma, 1994, p. 23). Wagner had considered lighting to be one of the most important elements in theater production, and Fortuny knew a lot about light from his painting. He knew that it could be used to produce dramatic effects and that painting involved the relationship between color and light as much as it did producing a picture. Electricity was new at the end of the nineteenth century. Up until that time, lighting on the stage had been furnished by gas.

Ultimately, Fortuny made a great contribution to the craft of stage lighting, because of his perception of the stage as a three-dimensional picture and of the knowledge that colored lighting could be combined like paints on a palette. His conclusions were integrated into the Fortuny dome, a structure at the back of the stage that functioned both as a backdrop and screen. It operated a system of lighting by means of reflection that exploited all of the possibilities of indirect light and utilized projected light. By the early 1900s, Fortuny was ready for a new career and embarked on a clothing and textiles business, for which he became even more famous.

Because of his experience as a painter, he was more interested in clothing as an art form than as fashion and was influenced by the manner in which painters had pictured clothing on their canvases and by their adoration of the human form. In his mind, clothing was an art that was not subject to change, and in fact, his garments remained desirable for the rest of his life and beyond. Silk was the first fabric he chose, and his first garment was a large scarf, which he called the "Knossos." As a flat rectangle of cloth, the scarf could wrap the body in a number of ways, allowing freedom of expression for the wearer and ease of movement. The scarves were lightweight and could float about the body.

The first and best-known dress was called the "Delphos robe," made of pleated silk and hung loosely from the shoulders to the ground (FIGURE BOX 4.2A).

ABOVE
FIGURE BOX 4.2A These evening dresses (1910–1935) by Mariano Fortuny illustrate the designer's sense of light in his creations.
THE METROPOLITAN MUSEUM OF ART/ART RESOURCE, NY

OPPOSITE RIGHT
FIGURE BOX 4.2B The texture of this evening coat by Mariano Fortuny (circa 1930s) is an aesthetically rich companion to the one on the dress.
MARIANO FORTUNY (SPANISH WORKING IN VENICE, 1871–1949), DELPHOS DRESS AND JACKET, 1920S–1930S, SILK; SILK VELVET STENCILED WITH METALS, PHOTO BY KEN HOWIE, COLLECTION OF PHOENIX ART MUSEUM, GIFT OF MRS. BURTON TREMAINE (DRESS) AND GIFT OF MRS. JOSEPH MCMULLAN (JACKET)

The Delphos came at a time when most women were wearing corsets, so it provided the comfort of apparel in the nature of the Empire period but with the classicism characteristic of ancient Greek attire, although it was made of silk instead of wool or linen. A later version was based in its form on the Greek *chiton* (FIGURE 3.1). It was called the "Peplos." The fine pleating and soft colors of Fortuny's garments, such as white, soft yellow, pale pink, and aqua, also attracted women. In the coloring process, the silk was dipped many times into a transparent dye that made the fabric change according to light and movement. Although all of Fortuny's garments were made of flat shapes of fabric, there were other elements of construction that caused interest. The system of hand-pleating is today considered a mystery, although the process was patented in 1909. Pleats on the garments that remain today are still tight. Pleating also defined the best method of storage, which was to keep the garments rolled and twisted tightly from both ends like a skein of yarn. The hem of the dress, along with its companion over-blouse, sides, and the cuffs in later versions were finished with a series of small Venetian glass beads in different colors. The beads were ornamental but also weighted the garment to cause better contouring to the body.

Fortuny also created outer garments to be worn over these robes, along with pocket bags and simple beret hats. They were made of silk velvet, so they boasted a wonderful sheen, and were printed using woodblocks, Japanese *katagami* stencils, or silk screens in a photographically inspired printing process. Such garments offered a wonderful textural juxtaposition to the undulating silk dresses (FIGURE BOX 4.2B).

In addition to Europe, his garments were sold in New York, where they continued to be sold after his death in 1949. In subsequent years, the Fortuny products were condensed to fabrics alone. However, his dresses were worn extensively by celebrities and are featured in several museum collections today.

PATTERN

O N   A   G A R M E N T , **pattern** is the element most like the frosting on a cake because when it is employed, it attracts the eye so effectively. A pattern results when any visual element is repeated over an extended area. In fashion, a pattern occurs on a fabric's surface, in the fabric structure itself, or when it is attached to or applied through the fabric surface. Pattern is more complex than the other elements because it can be broken down into its own design components, such as line, shape, and space.

A term frequently associated with the word pattern is **motif**. This chapter explains the origin of a motif, how motifs are categorized into the most common textile designs, and how the **arrangement** of them indicates the most successful **layouts.** In addition, it examines the ways in which patterns are implemented on the garment's surface and which of them are most appropriate for different segments of the apparel industry.

The beauty of pattern is exemplified in the art of Gustav Klimt (1862–1918). The example in FIGURE 5.1 demonstrates the earmarks of the Austrian painter's work—the use of gold, jewel-like colors, and patterns in flat, forward-facing figures, almost like icons. Klimt was influenced by the German version of the international **Art Nouveau** movement, the goal of which was to free design from a reliance on historical forms and motifs. Designers emphasized nature instead, using sinuous, climbing vines, leaves, and lilies. Klimt was also inspired by Asian and Byzantine art, and later, by **Symbolism**, a late-nineteenth-century movement that espoused the evocation of feelings and ideas rather than representational nature and objects. An examination of pattern in Klimt's art reveals motifs that integrate all these influences in the nature of their shapes, lines, and colors.

MOTIF

Motifs are the building blocks of a pattern, making it recognizable by their repetition and arrangement. Each motif has its own shapes, lines, and spacing. The motif's design arises from a **source** that is classified in one of four categories. These categories are **natural objects**, **man-made objects**, **imagination**, and **symbolism**.

5.1 Pattern is a key element in *The Embrace* (1905–1909) by Gustav Klimt.
© AUSTRIAN ARCHIVE/SCALA, FLORENCE/ART RESOURCE, NY

NATURAL OBJECT AS SOURCE

Natural objects originate in nature, like flowers, leaves, waves, snowflakes, and seashells. Even an animal print, used so often in the fashion industry, comes from this category (FIGURE 5.2). Natural forms have an organic quality that lends itself easily to a pattern.

MAN-MADE OBJECT MOTIFS

Man-made objects represent those that are familiar as a result of experience. Examples are teapots, lipsticks, beach balls, golf clubs, or birdhouses. They carry special significance based on memory.

IMAGINATION-INSPIRED MOTIFS

Imagination-inspired motifs represent a cross-sensory interpretation; these often originate from geometric forms. One example is the graphic interpretation of light described in Chapter 4 (FIGURE 4.17).

SYMBOLISM AS SOURCE

Symbolism refers to motifs that represent a nonconcrete idea, like a political movement, religion, or organization. Examples include logos, flags, and religious or political symbols. Some symbols cause negative responses or superstitious beliefs. As a result, designers should avoid the ones that cause controversy—unless they intend their garments to provoke such reactions.

WORKING WITH MOTIFS

Each motif, regardless of category, receives an **interpretation** from the textile designer. For instance, flowers may feature a **realistic** presentation, where the motifs have their true colors, highlights, and shadows, and where the overlapping of them provides depth and perspective. This approach works with other natural and man-made objects as well. As an alternative, a textile designer may choose to **stylize** a motif. In that case the motif remains recognizable, but it is simplified, flattened, distorted, changed in color, or edged in line.

Some motifs are expressed in an **abstract** form. There is nothing representational or recognizable from the natural or man-made world. Rather, the motifs involve free-flowing forms, colors, values, lines, shapes, and spaces, the total of which suggests a feeling or mood. **Geometric** interpretations are a subset of the abstract ones. These motifs are characterized by geometric shapes but also include woven structures defined by lines, such as stripes, plaids, and checks. All of these interpretations are subject to fashion trends. Designers may introduce floral motifs after a period when geometrics have predominated. The consumer is ready to accept something new when one interpretation has saturated the market.

FLORAL PATTERNS

Motifs also determine the most common types of fabric designs. For instance, **floral** patterns have been a historical favorite. Flowers may vary in their scale or complexity, from mini-prints or lingerie prints to **chintz**. Chintz is polished or glazed cotton that may feature a floral with a realistic interpretation (FIGURE 5.3). The pattern may also include birds

and figures. In this form, chintz originated in the seventeenth century in India. A **botanical** is a pattern related to a floral, but the plants, flowers, and herbs are organized within blocks, reminiscent of the way they were pictured on pages of nineteenth-century books that enumerated plant species.

CONVERSATIONAL PATTERNS

By contrast, **conversational** patterns tell a story or communicate a message. The motifs are man-made objects or symbols, or they feature an element of the culture. As a result, conversational patterns are entertaining. One example from 1973 is a dress fabric that features the face of dancer/actor/entertainer Fred Astaire (FIGURE 5.4). (Astaire became popular in the Hollywood musical films of the 1930s and 1940s.) The repetition of his face shows the influence of the **Pop Art** movement, which was prevalent at that time. Its origin is discussed later in this chapter.

TRADITIONAL PATTERNS

Some patterns can be classified as **traditional** designs, because they have been treated the same way over many years. They are considered to be the

5.4 This conversational pattern from 1973 features the face of dancer-singer-entertainer Fred Astaire as its motif.
© V&A IMAGES, VICTORIA AND ALBERT MUSEUM

classics of the textile world. Among these are **foulards**, patterns with tiny geometric motifs t. repeat in a **set layout**, meaning in the format of grid. The grid is discussed at greater length later in this chapter. Foulards are often associated with men's neckties and convey a conservative effect, although they were seen in the fabrics of nineteenth-century dresses. **Paisley** is a design inherited from the cashmere shawls that were woven in Paisley, Scotland. The palm shape, originated in India, defines the design, which is repeated at either a very large or a small scale. Italian designer Gianni Versace (1946–1997) used it in his body-revealing design of 1992 (FIGURE 5.5). **Calico** prints have closely situated, tiny floral motifs in four-color combinations, usually with a dark or bright background. Some calicos have tiny geometric forms, stripes, or plaids. They have been associated historically with American country fabrics of the nineteenth century. They are chosen most commonly for dresses, aprons, children's apparel, and quilts. **Liberty** prints are named for the British department store called Liberty of London. Originally they sold fabrics with floral motifs at small or medium scale, although some featured fruits and birds. They favored soft colors and were easily recognized. Like the other traditional patterns, they convey a conservative feeling, and they are found in women's and children's apparel (FIGURE 5.6).

ABOVE
5.5 Designer Gianni Versace features a paisley pattern on his beachwear ensemble from spring–summer 1992.
THE METROPOLITAN MUSEUM OF ART/ART RESOURCE, NY

RIGHT
5.6 British designer Bill Gibb's long dress from 1972 displays printed fabrics from Liberty & Co. Ltd.
© V&A IMAGES, VICTORIA AND ALBERT MUSEUM

DOCUMENTARY DESIGNS

Documentary designs are the common term used for those that originate in historic periods, other countries and cultures, and international or ethnic styles.

BATIK

Batik is one example of a documentary design. Originating in China or India, the product comes from Indonesia most commonly today. The look of batik comes

from its dying method. Areas of the fabric are covered with liquid wax and then immersed in dye. The dye penetrates cracks in the wax, yielding the effect that gives batik its character. This is an example of the resist method of dying fabric. The process may occur more than once, using different colors of dye.

IKAT

Ikat is a pattern that results from a yarn-dying method. Yarns are individually tied and then dyed along different lengths. Then they are untied and woven. The characteristic pattern evolves when the weaver uses great skill and tension control for matching. The ikat process has been used in many regions of the world, including Central Asia, South America, Southeast Asia, and India. Noted international designer Oscar de la Renta (1932–) used ikat silks from Uzbekistan in his runway fashions of 2005 (FIGURE 5.7).

TOILE DE JOUY

Toile de Jouy means "cloth from Jouy," referring to a French town known for the print works that were founded in 1760. The pattern features romanticized landscapes and figures (FIGURE 5.8). Traditionally used for home fashions, fashion designers have made apparel with this pattern in recent years.

ABOVE
5.7 Oscar de la Renta's ready-to-wear design from spring 2005 features an ikat fabric from Uzbekistan.
COURTESY OF WWD/TALAYA CENTENO

RIGHT
5.8 Example from Waverly Fabrics of a contemporary toile fabric, featuring country scenes from France.
COURTESY OF WAVERLY FABRICS

FOLK PATTERNS

Folk patterns refer to those that originate in specific regions or countrie They picture figures, animals, plants, flowers, birds, scenes characteristic o the locale, and/or designs distinctive of the culture. The treatment of them varies; some are realistic, others are stylized or naïve. The United States, Afghanistan, China, Japan, Russia, Egypt, Indonesia, Mexico, Guatemala, Peru, and India are some of the countries with designs featured in the textile market.

A subset of regional folk patterns includes those that are **Country French**. They originated in the Provence region of France in the eighteenth century. Their designs were the result of the artisan's process of printing with woodblocks. Motifs from India and the Orient were featured using bright colors. A fashion designer may choose to feature the folk style from another favorite region. Christian Lacroix, for example, designed garments with the ornamentation distinctive of Arles in France (FIGURE 5.9).

ART NOUVEAU

Mentioned earlier in the chapter, Art Nouveau is the term for a pattern with the organic elaboration that descends specifically from that design period,

5.9 Christian Lacroix used the folk patterns of Arles in this dress and jacket from his spring/summer 1988 collection.

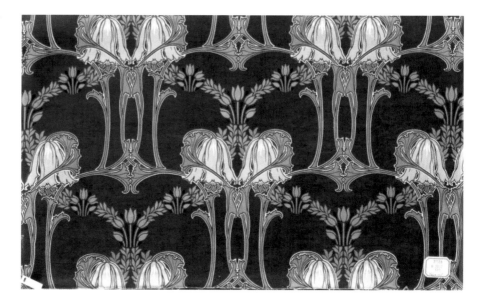

1890–1914, in Europe and North America. It was a response to the apparent clutter and eclecticism of the Victorian Age and advocated nature as the true source of all good design. The characteristics of the style were sinuous curved lines along with an asymmetrical arrangement of forms and patterns. They descended from natural forms such as grasses, lilies, vines, peacock feathers, butterflies, and insects (FIGURE 5.10).

ART DECO

Another pattern named for its period is called **Art Deco**. It is associated with the design influences during the 1920s and 1930s, the acceptance of industrialization, and the aesthetics of machines, which rejected the elaborate ornamentation of the preceding generations in favor of geometric shapes and simplicity of line (FIGURE 5.11).

CAMOUFLAGE

Camouflage is a pattern meant to present low visibility in the underbrush during a time of war (FIGURE 5.12). Made from spatters of different colors, such as red, green, yellow, blue, and brown, a different version of camouflage originated during World War I in the French, British, and American military services. Improvisations were introduced in subsequent wars in different countries worldwide, to culminate today in digital versions. Today the pattern is often chosen for men's, women's, and boys' casual apparel.

ABSTRACT AND GEOMETRIC PATTERNS

The category of abstract and geometric interpretations includes several familiar patterns. Geometric ones are designs composed of squares, trian-

5.12 This is an example of a camouflage pattern, meant to create low visibility of the wearer.
COURTESY OF ISTOCKPHOTO

gles, circles, cubes, cones, spheres, and lines (FIGURE 5.13). Of course, the most common repetition of the line is called the **stripe**. Stripes can range in their width, and sometimes another pattern is enclosed within a stripe, like the mitered rows of a **herringbone**. Lines intersected at a right angle by others form a **check**. Checks vary in their scale. The most familiar ones are the woven **gingham** and **houndstooth**, a pattern with motifs that appear to connect by tiny hooks.

5.13 Example from Waverly fabrics of a contemporary geometric pattern.
COURTESY OF WAVERLY FABRICS

Plaids are created when different width lines intersect one another. There are many types of plaids. Some of the most common are **tattersall**, **madras** (named for Madras, India), and **tartans** (FIGURES 5.14A AND B). Tartan plaids come from Scotland. Each is believed to represent a different family clan. The tartan pattern is distinctive because the bands of different colors and varying widths repeat in a sequence. The sequence, or **sett**, is exactly the same lengthwise and crosswise. Some of the names of familiar tartan plaids include Rob Roy, MacGregor, Wallace, Lennox, MacPherson, and Black Watch. Even the iconic plaid popularized by Burberry Ltd. is a tartan. Tartans are identified with the Scottish kilt, the garb of the family clans. However, Paul Poiret, Jacques Fath (1912–1954), Vivienne Westwood, John Galliano (1960–), Jean Paul Gaultier (1952–), and Marc Jacobs (1964–) are among the fashion designers who used tartans in their designs, as well as Commes des Garçons, whose garment is pictured in FIGURE 5.14B.

LEFT

5.14A Isaac Mizrahi designed this sundress in madras plaid for Target stores in the United States.

PHOTO BY AVITAL ARONOWITZ

RIGHT

5.14B Commes des Garcons featured tartan in their spring–summer 2006 collection.

COURTESY OF WWD/GIOVANNI GIANNONI

By comparison to most designers, however, Gianni Versace was kn[own] for harnessing bold prints in his luxurious designs (BOX 5.1).

PATTERNS IN FABRIC

When a pattern is the result of the weaving process, there is a presumption that it is on-grain. The pattern is created either from different-colored yarns or different weaves. Stripes, checks, and plaids all are created in the weaving process. Variations in the weaving process cause different numbers of weft and warp yarns to float over each other at differing distances. This is the method by which **damask**, a floral or scroll patterned fabric, is created when all of the yarns are the same color (FIGURE 5.15). Several colored yarns used in the same method produce a **jacquard** or **brocade**. The ikat pattern, previously discussed in this chapter, is produced when yarns are tied and then dyed at different lengths prior to the weaving process.

Many nonwoven fabric structures have pattern. It is possible to create a pattern in a knitted garment, for instance, based upon the numbers of ribs, cables, or other raised areas. Lace, crochet, and macramé all have patterns in their structures.

In addition, patterns are applied to the fabric surface using a variety of methods. **Direct printing** imparts motifs to the fabric via engraved rollers, wooden blocks, or a photo process. **Discharge printing** is when dark dyes are removed from dark backgrounds, causing light-colored motifs to occur. **Resist** methods indicate that a medium is applied to the fabric surface to prevent dye from reaching it. For instance, batik, also previously discussed in this chapter, uses wax to resist the dye, and the crackled effect of the minimal penetration characterizes

5.15 Example from Waverly fabrics of a contemporary damask fabric.
COURTESY OF WAVERLY FABRICS

GIANNI VERSACE

GIANNI VERSACE SECURED a significant place in fashion history despite his premature death, when he was assassinated in 1997. He presented looks and materials that had not previously been acceptable at the couture level of the industry. His feminine ideal was described as the "hooker" or prostitute, and that image lead to over-the-top design choices that bordered on vulgarity. The historical influences from which Versace created this image, however, are of critical relevance.

Born in Calabria, Italy, his comfort with fashion came from his mother, a dressmaker. After studying architecture, he designed knitwear in Florence and then moved to ready-to-wear firms in Milan. He first designed a collection of menswear under his own name in 1979.

For women his controversial materials included leather, denim, and metal mesh. He mixed them with a range of brash and opulent patterns. The looks hinted at sexuality, bondage, luxury, and extravagance. His bravado is typified by the animal print ensemble and paisley beachwear from his spring–summer 1992 collection (FIGURES 5.2 AND 5.5). Other fashions were decorated with gold Baroque motifs, Greek fret designs, stripes, *Vogue* magazine covers, Greek crosses, Byzantine ornamentation, floral prints, Art Deco patterning, quilting, lace, beading, Japanese characters, cutwork, and appliqué.

For several of these design decisions, the historical inspiration is obvious. Versace was greatly affected by both history and art. His choice of metals was attributed to the pageantry of the Renaissance. His gladiator boots came from Roman history and romance. He repeated Byzantine decoration, ancient Greek pattern, and Art Deco motifs.

Versace's favorite artists included Gustav Klimt, who was also inspired by Byzantine art, Sonia Delaunay (see Chapter 6, "Color and Value"), and Pop artist Andy Warhol. He designed garments in homage to Warhol and his icons of Marilyn Monroe and James Dean (FIGURE 5.21). He also saw fashion as an art of the media and drew inspiration from rock music, dance, performance, and street movements. The safety pin was a motif used regularly in his designs as a reference to Punk (FIGURE BOX 5.1).

In addition to his fascination with sexuality, history, and art, Versace demonstrated skill in draping that some thought equaled that of Madame Grès and Madeleine Vionnet. His focus was specifically on the organic curves of the female form.

With the opportunity to live a longer life, surely Gianni Versace would have continued to electrify his public and make an even grander contribution to the fashion industry. His sister Donatella took the reins of his fashion house after his death.

RIGHT

5.16 This grand eighteenth-century dress flaunts a warp printed floral pattern.
COLLECTION OF THE KYOTO COSTUME INSTITUTE, PHOTO BY TORU KOGURE

BOTTOM LEFT

5.17 Giorgio Armani's evening gown from spring 2009 is covered completely with embroidered flowers.
COURTESY OF FAIRCHILD BOOKS

BOTTOM RIGHT

5.18 Christian Lacroix's gown from his haute couture collection for spring–summer 2000 features patchwork and white boning.
AFP/GETTY IMAGES/PIERRE VERDY

its pattern. A **stencil** allows dye to pour through its holes but not through the plate itself. **Screen printing** works in a similar manner. Dye meets the fabric through a cutout adhered to a fine fabric screen. **Rotary screen printing** moves the dye through a finely perforated drum. When fabric is tied into gathers, pleats, tucks, or puckers and then is released after being submerged into dye, the process is called **tie-dyeing**. **Warp printing** has its own two-step operation. Warp yarns alone are first printed and then woven with a single-colored weft. The motifs have a shadowy effect, like the eighteenth-century French robe in FIGURE 5.16.

There are many decorative applications that generate pattern by threads or yarns running through the fabric surface. Among these is

embroidery, which is dramatically used in the stylized blossoms ado this 2009 runway design by Giorgio Armani (1934–) (FIGURE 5.17). Ferns also result from the thread-trimmed cutouts of eyelet, the running stitches of trapunto or quilting, and the juxtaposition of the fabric shapes and stitches of patchwork. Couture designer Christian Lacroix featured patchwork in a sheath dress from his spring–summer 2000 haute couture collection (FIGURE 5.18).

PATTERNING   One major design structure defines the organization of pattern, and that is the grid. The regular intersection of vertical and horizontal lines is also a defining force in architecture, graphic design, and art. Although that structure is characteristic of many historic buildings, it is also evident in modern architecture (FIGURE 5.19). For the graphic designer, the grid organizes the page, acting as a guide for the layout of copy and image.

POP ART AND THE GRID

Pop Art artist Andy Warhol (1928–1987) set up his images using the grid as a road map, as shown in his iconic work of actress Marilyn Monroe (FIGURE 5.20). The Pop Art movement began in the United Kingdom and in the United States in the 1950s. As one of the biggest art movements of the twentieth century, it drew its themes and techniques from popular mass culture such as television, movies, advertising, and comic books. Employing popular culture made art seem less elitist and enabled it to reach a large audience. Andy Warhol was the most famous artist of the movement. Beginning

5.19 The grid system is used for modern architecture.
ALAN SCHEIN/CORBIS

RIGHT
5.20 Andy Warhol presented icons like Marilyn Monroe in a grid format (1962).
THE ANDY WARHOL FOUNDATION, INC.

BELOW
5.21 Gianni Versace turned Andy Warhol's icons of Marilyn Monroe and James Dean into a print, used here on an evening dress (1991).
THE METROPOLITAN MUSEUM OF ART/ART RESOURCE, NY

as a commercial illustrator, Warhol executed the collective American state of mind in his art, in which the famous image of a person and the famous brand name replaced all other values. Other notable examples of his work pictured the faces of actress Elizabeth Taylor and former first lady Jacqueline Kennedy, as well as the packaged Campbell soup can. The grid format, utilized in his most famous pieces, is meant to mimic mass advertising and the condition of image overload in a media-saturated culture. It was a mechanism that triggered the use of repetition, a type of rhythm, the design principle discussed in Chapter 10, "Rhythm." Gianni Versace paid homage to Andy Warhol in his evening dress from the spring–summer collection of 1991 (FIGURE 5.21).

WILLIAM MORRIS PATTERNS AND THE GRID

William Morris (1834–1896) was famous for distinctive wallpaper and fabric patterns characteristic of the **Arts and Crafts** movement. This movement, lead in addition by other reform thinkers like John Ruskin (1819–1900), was a response to the tastes of the Victorian era and the growth of the Industrial Age, and it overlapped with and influenced the Art Nouveau period. Proponents believed that good design was linked to a good society. It was preferable for a worker to develop pride in craftsmanship and skill rather than suffer the brutality of working conditions found in factories. As a result, design could be a source of pleasure to both the maker and the user. Medieval guilds were a model for the ideal craft production system. So Arts and Crafts ornamentation was derived from Medi[...] European and Islamic sources, as well as some Japanese ideas.

Morris' interest in textiles grew from a journey that he made wit[...] artist Edward Burne-Jones to examine the Gothic cathedrals of Northern France. He was enamored with the carpets and tapestries. In the 1860s he decided to build a house that was Medieval in spirit, and he began a manufacturing business with friends. Eventually, Morris ran it on his own, and the patterns have never been out of production since. They are still appropriate for modern interiors furnished in the Arts and Crafts style. An example of Morris' work appears in FIGURE 5.22. The pencil lines of the grid format formulate the repetition for Morris' complex painted motifs.

LAYOUT

In addition to the choice of motif, a pattern is determined by its layout. Layout refers to the placement of one motif relative to another. It considers the distance between the motifs as well as the direction of the first motif in relation to the second. Many arrangement decisions have their origin in the grid structure. As changes are made to the grid, so are they made to the placement of the motif, thereby changing the character of the pattern.

In some layouts or arrangements, motifs may vary in direction. The case where one or more motifs are placed "right side up" is called a **one-way** design (FIGURE 5.23A). A **two way** has motifs placed both up and down in a design (FIGURE 5.23B). A **four way** shows motifs placed up and down as well as left and right in the same design (FIGURE 5.23C). Motifs occur in all directions in a **tossed** design (FIGURE 5.23D).

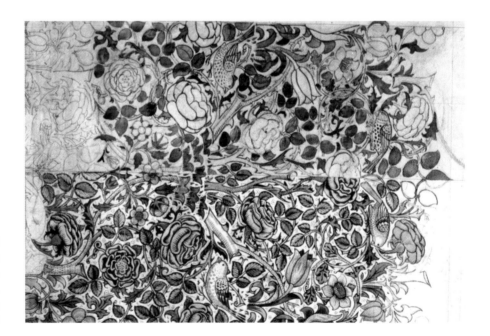

5.22 William Morris developed this floral pattern in the style of the Arts and Crafts movement in 1883.
© V&A IMAGES, VICTORIA AND ALBERT MUSEUM

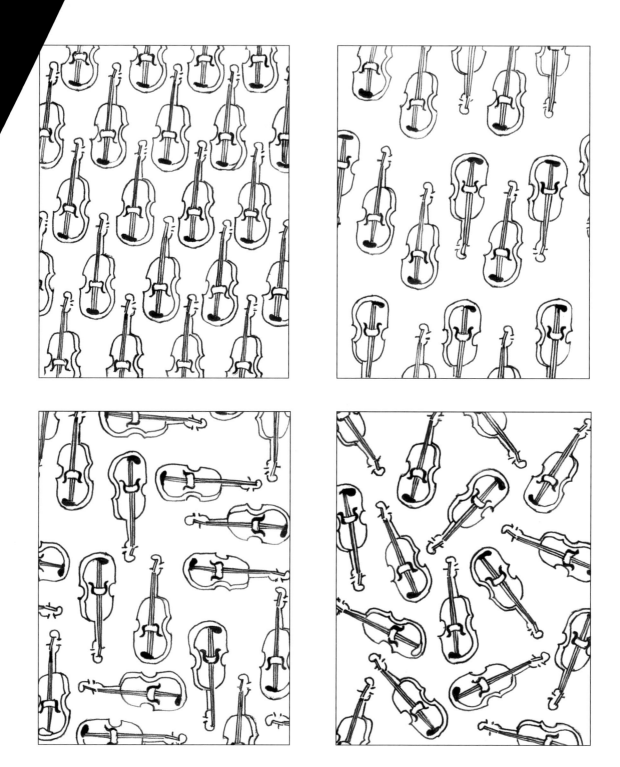

TOP LEFT: 5.23A   A one-way layout for a printed pattern. ILLUSTRATION BY JANICE GREENBERG ELLINWOOD

TOP RIGHT: 5.23B   A two-way layout for a printed pattern. ILLUSTRATION BY JANICE GREENBERG ELLINWOOD

BOTTOM LEFT: 5.23C   A four-way layout for a printed pattern. ILLUSTRATION BY JANICE GREENBERG ELLINWOOD

BOTTOM RIGHT: 5.23D   Tossed layout for a printed pattern. ILLUSTRATION BY JANICE GREENBERG ELLINWOOD

Another consideration in the arrangement of a pattern is **coverage**. When motifs are highly concentrated, with little space between them, the design is described as **tight** or **packed.** Conversely, if there is a lot of distance between motifs, the layout is described as **open** or **spaced.**

The most common type is the set layout, which is based upon an invisible grid where the motifs are arranged in the squares. For printed patterns, the squares of the grids may change to rectangles or triangles, with the motif repeating in rows. This arrangement is appropriate for all types of motifs but is often used for conversational and abstract patterns. The woven tartan plaids are also based on a grid or sett, where the colored bars of varying widths repeat in the same sequence both horizontally and vertically.

TYPES OF LAYOUTS

A **random layout** features motifs in a scattered or seemingly random arrangement where they are placed in all directions. It is also referred to as a tossed or **all-over layout**. Despite its randomness, the layout is planned so that the pattern provides balance and harmony and may repeat itself in an aesthetically pleasing fashion.

A **stripe layout** organizes its pattern in colored bands, sometimes alternating with rows of motifs, a typical arrangement for documentary designs. Bands may run vertically or horizontally and even in diagonal formats.

A **plaid layout** offers intersecting lines or bands of color. A woven structure features them only in vertical and horizontal directions, but a planned print may provide them at a 45-degree angle, yielding a plaid on the diagonal. Designers may obtain the same effect by draping a woven stripe or plaid on the bias.

A **border print** contrasts a border pattern with one that covers the remainder of the fabric or the **field**. The border runs along the edge, or **selvage**, of the fabric. It may vary in its width, and hence, its proportion to the field. The coordination of the motifs in the border and in the field is always an interesting attribute of the pattern. A border print is often used for women's apparel, as in the printed fashion by Italian designer Emilio Pucci (1914–1992) shown in FIGURE 5.24. Pucci became distinctive for his signature prints in the 1960s. The patterns, which were inspired by heraldic banners, had a random quality, with motifs featured at a larger scale than what was fashionable previously. They were excitingly vibrant and colorful, yet implemented in comfortable and wrinkle-resistant fabrics. His company was revived after his death in the 1990s, producing the design featured in Chapter 4 (FIGURE 4.17), among others.

5.24 Model Susan Murray wears a distinctive border printed garment by Emilio Pucci in 1970.
HENRY CLARKE © 1970
CONDÉ NAST PUBLICATIONS

An **engineered design** is similar in nature to a border print with one major exception. Instead of running along the length of the fabric, it is engineered for a particular area or shape, signifying an important relationship between the pattern and the garment. It may fit simply the front of a skirt, on one side of a blouse bodice, or the center back of a robe. It is the same process used for the designing and printing of scarves. The motifs for a square specifically emphasize the corners, and for an oblong rectangle, they adorn the ends.

A **croquis** is the artwork that features the textile designer's communication of an original design, complete with main motif(s) and colors. From that stage, the design must be "put into repeat." A **repeat** is the adaptation of the design to the industry printing process. This ensures that the pattern is not interrupted as it accommodates yards of fabric. The design must repeat both horizontally and vertically. The repeat is created after the croquis has been accepted.

PATTERNS AND THE FASHION INDUSTRY

Like many other elements of design, pattern is influenced by the chang **trends** in the fashion industry. In fact, there are periods when the consum is not interested in wearing a pattern at all. Conversely, there are time when patterns are the rage and consumption of them peak. At these times, all kinds of motifs may become popular, or one style of pattern may supersede the others. For instance, when menswear looks in women's fashions highlight pinstripes and tattersall, floral patterns have little appeal. However, couture designers may drive trends in pattern by launching a new, innovative idea. In 2008, the house of Balenciaga featured floral motifs at an unusually large scale in its fashions.

Season is also an influence on pattern. Some motifs are traditionally acceptable at specific times of the year. For instance, plaids, herringbone, checks, small geometrics, foulards, paisleys, and stripes have expected appeal during the fall and winter seasons, while floral and conversational motifs, often with great range of colors, have longer life during spring and summer.

Women's apparel and accessories are ideal receptacles for patterns. Dresses, sportswear, swimwear, sleepwear, loungewear, outerwear, and evening wear all sport them when fashion trends and season are supportive. Patterns also find their way on to handbags, footwear, scarves, and shawls.

Patterns are also used in ways that emphasize the uniqueness of a fashion house or brand. Businesses often utilize their logo as a repeating motif in a pattern, as in the case of Louis Vuitton. The pattern itself may carry a distinctive association with a company, like Burberry's distinctive plaid, the quilting on a Chanel bag, or the equestrienne motifs used by Hermès. Sometimes a company purchases a croquis with the guarantee that the pattern is exclusive to it for the season. This is common in the sleepwear industry, but it often occurs with sportswear as well. Companies are also founded on the appeal of distinctive patterns. While this historically was the case for Liberty of London or the romantic country prints of Laura Ashley, it also was for American company Lily Pulitzer, which features bright, coastal patterns. Companies such as these may feature patterns that are designed as **collections** or **coordinates**. A collection is a group of patterns that relate to each other by a common theme. The theme may originate from a historical source, a geographic location or region, a holiday, a type of floral or style, and so on. Coordinates refer to a group of patterns designed to coordinate with one another. Examples include a multifloral with foliage or a conversational pattern with a textured background. The patterns may differ in scale or spacing, however, making one appropriate for a blouse and another for a skirt. Whichever approach is tackled, it is clear that pattern is an element that has an exciting role in the design of fashion.

KEY TERMS

abstract	folk	realistic
all-over layout	foulard	repeat
arrangement	four way	resist
Arts and Crafts movement	geometric	rotary screen printing
Art Deco	gingham	screen printing
Art Nouveau	grid	season
batik	herringbone	selvage
border print	houndstooth	set layout
botanical	ikat	sett
brocade	imagination	source
calico	interpretation	spaced
chintz	jacquard	stencil
collection	layout	stripe layout
conversational	Liberty	stylize
coordinates	man-made objects	symbolism
coverage	motif	Symbolism movement
Country French	natural objects	tartan
croquis	one way	tattersall
damask	open	tie-dyeing
direct printing	packed	tight
discharge printing	paisley	Toile de Jouy
documentary	patchwork	tossed
embroidery	pattern	traditional
engineered design	plaid layout	trapunto
eyelet	Pop Art movement	trends
field	quilting	two way
floral	random layout	warp printing

PROJECTS

1. Keeping in mind your previous learning from Chapter 3 about positive and negative space, the notan theory, create a black and white asymmetrical motif for duplication later into different layouts. Your motif may be abstract or realistic. In your sketchbook, evolve four to six designs, using black marker. Choose the most effective from the group for the following steps.

2. The second step involves the creation of a grid to use as a guide. The pro of duplicating your motif into different layouts may employ your col puter's graphic software, a black and white copier, or hand efforts, using light box and tracing paper. If using practical materials, create the grid in pencil on tracing paper. Most types of graphic software include a grid as a guide. If rendering by hand, use squares that are three inches by three inches as a maximum size, creating a full grid at the dimensions of twelve inches by twelve inches. That allows four motifs in each of four rows. Using white Bristol as a background for hand materials and white copy paper for copier or computer, insert your motif into each square. Render it with black marker or use cut black construction paper, if attempting the project by hand. Be certain to erase the grid guidelines on your final product. The result is a one way layout using your motif (FIGURE 5.25A).

5.25A One-way layout in grid format.
ILLUSTRATION BY
JANICE GREENBERG ELLINWOOD

3. Create a second grid using the same methods and at the same dimensions as the first. Insert the same motif in each square again, but this time, flip or reverse the image in every other block. Remember to erase the grid guidelines. As a result, the second pattern employs a two way layout (FIGURE 5.25B).

4. This time create a shift or drop grid by moving alternate rows of the grid from side to side, resulting in a brick format. Insert the motif into each

block, although in some of the cases, only half of the image will fit, implying a continuous pattern that runs off the page, like the pattern on wrapping paper that you have cut to wrap a gift. On the final product, remember to take out the grid guidelines. In the class critique, compare the three patterns created. Which of the three is the most visually successful? Why? (FIGURE 5.25C)

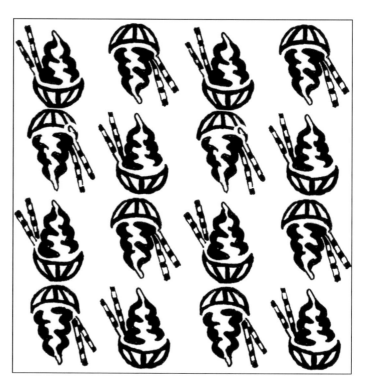

5.25B Two-way layout in grid format.
ILLUSTRATION BY
JANICE GREENBERG ELLINWOOD

5.25C Brick layout in shift or drop-grid format.
ILLUSTRATION BY
JANICE GREENBERG ELLINWOOD

REFERENCES   Clausen, H. (2003). *A short history of camouflage uniforms.* Retrieved Ma
31, 2009, from http://camo.henrikc.dk/history.asp.

Davis, M. L. (1996). *Visual design in dress* (3rd ed.).Upper Saddle River, NJ:
Prentice Hall.

Faiers, J. (2008). *Tartan.* Oxford: Berg.

Fisher, R., & Wolfthal, D. (1987). *Textile print design.* New York: Fairchild
Books.

Joyce, C. (1982). *Designing for printed textiles: A guide to studio and freelance
work.* Upper Saddle River, NJ: Prentice Hall.

Honnef, K. (1990). *Andy Warhol, 1928 – 1987: Commerce into art.* Köln:
Benedikt Taschen.

Lacroix, C., Mauriès, P., & Saillard, O. (2007). *Christian Lacroix: Histoires de
mode.* Paris: Les Arts Décoratifs.

Martin, R. (1997). *Gianni Versace.* New York: The Metropolitan Museum of
Art.

Martin, R. (1997). *Versace.* New York: Universe Publishing and Vendome
Press.

McShine, K. (Ed.). (1989). *Andy Warhol: A retrospective.* New York: The
Museum of Modern Art.

Parry, L. (1994). *William Morris textiles.* New York: Crescent Books.

Stegemeyer, A. (2004). *Who's who in fashion* (4th ed.). New York: Fairchild
Books.

Stewart, M. (2008). *Launching the imagination: A comprehensive guide to
basic design* (3rd ed.). New York: McGraw-Hill.

Stoops, J., & Samuelson, J. (1983). *Design dialogue.* Worcester, MA: Davis
Publications.

Van De Lemme, A. (n.d.). (1986). *A guide to Art Deco style.* Seacaucus,
New Jersey: Quintet Publishing.

| # COLOR AND VALUE

Color is the first element in fashion to have visual impact, often before the silhouette, look, or details can be assessed. It attracts the shoppers' eyes as they enter a store and directs their path to the fixture or display unit that features it, even though only the sleeve and side of the garment may be apparent.

A seemingly infinite number of colors are available to the fashion designer. These originate in nature, as the American painter Georgia O'Keeffe (1887–1986) demonstrated through her iconic flowers, skulls, and landscapes (FIGURES 6.1A AND B). The perception of color is actually more complex than one might presume. It is both an external occurrence and an internal sensation. The traditional explanation of color refers to the manner in which the sensation of light is transmitted to the brain through the eye, originating from **electromagnetic waves** that radiate from a light source and reflect on a surface. Artists, designers, and chemists are more concerned with color in **dyes** and **pigments**. Moreover, color has the potential to influence mood and carry cultural significance.

This chapter focuses on theories regarding color and its relationship to light and to pigment, as well as **color temperature** and the ways in which colors interact with each other. We will examine the variables that influence the perception of color and its **value**, which refers to the degree of its lightness or darkness. (In Chapter 7, "Color and Industry," we will look at the fashion and textile industries, the psychological influence of color, and its cultural significance.)

COLOR AND LIGHT

Color is perceived in the presence of light. That is evident from the experience of moving about the bedroom in the middle of the night. Edges of forms may present themselves in the darkness, but the colors of the blanket or bedside lamp do not. When light is strong, colors appear more intense, like they are under the sunlight in a tropical climate. A rainbow organizes its colors in a particular order or **spectrum**, including red, orange, yellow, green, blue, blue-violet, and violet. "Indigo" is often the term used for blue-violet in the spectrum.

The recognition of this order is credited to the physicist and mathematician Sir Isaac Newton (1642–1727) and the experiments he conducted in the seventeenth century. Newton placed a glass prism in front of a ray of daylight as it entered a darkened room. The prism caused the white light to bend, or refract, breaking it down into the spectrum of colors described above (FIGURE 6.2). Each of these is thought to distinguish itself to the human eye, because of a different range of **wavelengths** of radiant energy. Hence, it is considered the **visible spectrum**. A wavelength is the distance between the crests in a wave of energy. Red, for instance, has the longest distance in wavelengths, while violet has the shortest.

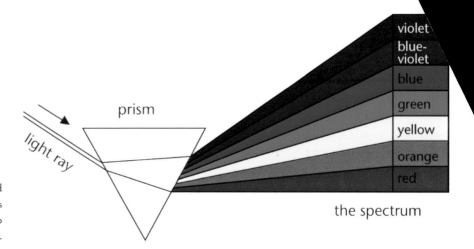

the spectrum

6.2 Sir Isaac Newton discovered that a glass prism enables a light ray to break into the visible spectrum.

Both physicists and artists have developed theories regarding the combination of colors in light. These theories are particularly relevant to individuals who work as lighting designers, videographers, and Web site designers. They are also meaningful to theater costumers, whose work is seen under lighting, and to producers of fashion shows, for the same reason. They understand that the dynamic of working with colored light rays is called **additive color**. That means the more they are mixed with other colors, the lighter they become. The basic or **primary colors** of light, those that cannot be mixed by combining any other colors, are red, green, and blue. (That is also from where the computer screen's term "RGB" originates.) When combined together in equal amounts, the result is white light. However, when these colors of light overlap in varying amounts, other interesting colors form, and these are called **secondary colors**. The overlapping of red and blue creates magenta. Red and green make yellow, while green and blue produce cyan (FIGURE 6.3).

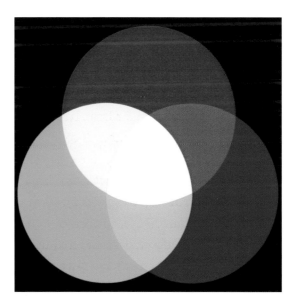

6.3 When the primary colors of light—red, green, and blue—intersect, they create the secondary colors of magenta, yellow, and cyan. All of these additive primaries create white light.

White light contains all colors of the visible spectrum in equal amounts. When it hits a surface, two possible actions result. Either it is reflected in sharp, white highlights, which the fashion designer experiences with the use of sequins, beads, satin, or vinyl. The layperson sees it when observing the dance of sunlight on water. In most other scenarios, some of the white light penetrates the surface of an object, and it absorbs all of the wavelengths except one. That is the color that is perceived when the unabsorbed wavelength is reflected to the viewer's eye. The surface of a Red Delicious apple, for instance, absorbs all wavelengths except those that cause the sensation of red. An object with no pigmentation appears white. When a surface absorbs almost all of the wavelengths, and few are reflected, the object looks black. The process of experiencing these sensations through reflected light is called **subtractive color**. When creating fashion, the designer is primarily concerned with the color(s) reflected to the eye or the pigment or dye of the fabric.

COLOR AND PIGMENT

Theories about pigments originate from a desire to organize colors and their relationships in order to predict and maximize their visual effects. Consider all of the individuals to whom that is important—painters, printmakers, jewelers, sculptors, illustrators, textile designers, floral designers, architects, landscape architects, interior designers, visual merchandisers, as well as fashion designers. Before we survey these theories, let's look at a few color terms.

Hue is the general term or family name of a color, which is determined by its wavelength on the light spectrum or its corresponding sensation based on its location on the organizational chart called the **color wheel**. (A description of color wheels follows this listing of color terminology.) Value is the darkness or lightness of a hue. This refers to the lightest form of the hue, gained by adding white to it, the darkest form, which results from adding black, and all of the scale in between. Adding white to the hue produces its **tint**. Adding black creates its **shade**. **Intensity** or **saturation** refers to the range of brightness to dullness of a hue. Colors in their purest, most brilliant state are at maximum saturation. To the extent they are grayed means they are in low saturation. **Chroma** is synonymous with saturation, a measure of a hue's purity or brilliance. A surface or object with an identifiable hue is described as **chromatic**. Those without it, such as white, gray, or black, are **achromatic**. The term is also used for surfaces that are transparent but is more often interchangeable with the word **neutral**. Neutrals have special significance to the fashion designer. In not having hue, neutrals are presumed to present harmony with each other and/or with an color. As a result, they are prized for their versatility in a wardrobe, and th are considered appropriate for a range of occasions. Neutrals are also dis cussed in Chapter 7, "Color and Industry." As previously mentioned, primary colors are those that cannot be mixed by any others. In any method of color organization, they combine to form secondary colors, which, in turn, combine with one another to produce **tertiary colors.**

A SPECTRUM OF THEORIES

In addition to the work of Sir Isaac Newton, theories about color date back to the Greek philosophers and to the Renaissance artist and scientist Leonardo da Vinci. Many other theories developed from the eighteenth century to the present. One of these is the system of color that is the most relevant for fashion design. Several fashion books refer to it as the **standard color wheel.** Most students are introduced to it at the elementary level of education, so it is familiar. Bear in mind that it is built on the reasoning of several theorists; that is why it is so user-friendly and reliable.

Sir David Brewster (1781–1868), an English physicist who was the inventor of the kaleidoscope, laid the groundwork for the system while examining the work of Newton. He believed that the light spectrum was actually composed of three individual types of light—red, blue, and yellow—that he called primary colors. Although this belief was not held in high regard, Brewster is credited with the perception that three properly chosen colors of light, when mixed in careful proportions, are all that are necessary to reproduce all color sensation.

German painter Phillip Otto Runge (1777–1810) wrote a book on his theory of color for pigments, which organized 12 hues around what he identified as three primary colors: red, blue, and yellow. He arranged them in the form of a sphere, leading to the first three-dimensional color model.

Louis Prang (1824–1909) knew color from other perspectives. As a boy, he learned to dye fabric. When he migrated from Germany to the United States, he worked as a wood engraver, lithographer, color printer, and publisher. He is even acknowledged as the originator of the Christmas card. Prang wrote extensively on color, and his teachings had a profound effect on American art education. His color wheel featured 12 hues, which included primary, secondary, and "intermediate" colors, along with their shades and tints.

Johannes Itten, the painter and originator of the preliminary course at the Bauhaus who was discussed in Chapter 1, taught both color and design and published books on color. He created a "star" of color for his preliminary course, which was a flattened version of Runge's sphere. It too encompassed 12 colors around the three primary colors of red, blue, and yellow. From this organization evolved Itten's wheel, in which he placed yellow at the top, because it is the brightest hue and the closest to white light. In the center, Itten placed a triangle featuring the primary colors and surrounded by the secondary colors of green, violet, and orange (FIGURE 6.4).

It is clear that the Standard Color Wheel resulted from many theorists and applications. One other color wheel, sometimes referred to as the Process or Light Wheel, is a twenty-first-century invention that is not directly relevant to fashion. It is a 12-hue color wheel that features the primary colors of red, green, and blue, like the primary light colors. The secondary colors are magenta, cyan, and yellow. This system is relevant for the computer applications used in the work of the graphic designer.

THE MUNSELL "COLOR TREE"

There is one other color system to consider: the Munsell Wheel or color tree, named for professor and artist Albert Munsell (1858–1918). Munsell attempted to integrate hues with intervals of values. For that the system is noteworthy. Munsell featured five "principal" colors that he based on nature—yellow, red, green, blue, and purple. These choices were also based on the color interaction of **afterimage**, which is discussed later in this chapter. Munsell organized the color wheel into a tree form where intervals of value, measuring lightness and darkness, are placed along the trunk or vertical axis. Any color along the trunk is a neutral, while the branches or horizontal intervals measure the saturation of a hue. That places the purest

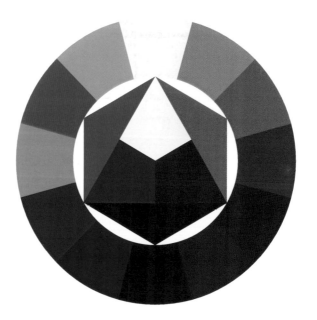

6.4 Johannes Itten's Color Wheel—12 colors around the primary colors of red, blue, and yellow—is basically the Standard Color Wheel used today. Note the primary and secondary colors featured in the center.

form of each hue at the outside edge. This system is used for dye manuturing for yarn and fabric coloration, as well as industry production interior design and cosmetics (FIGURE 6.5).

USING COLOR SCHEMES

The ingenious function of a color system is that it offers a guide for discovering the color combinations, schemes, or relationships that should have the greatest visual impact. The Standard Color Wheel does that for the fashion designer. The placement of a hue on the color wheel indicates the most workable color schemes. The fashion design student should remember, however, that each hue on the color wheel represents a color family, and the success of that hue in combination with any other is true for any shade, tint, or intensity of it. The dynamics of blue, in the purity of the way in which it is perceived on the Standard Color Wheel, denotes the same presumptions for robin's egg blue, deck blue, or navy blue.

The simplest is the **monochromatic** color scheme, where a garment design rests on one hue (FIGURE 6.6A). It might be the color of the entire garment, or one part of it, or the dominant color of a pattern, where the others are achromatic or neutral. Or the design may combine different values of the same hue. One predominant color may seem boring, but the consumer finds it easy to wear.

The next simplest is called **tone on tone** and involves two hues that lie next to each other on the color wheel (FIGURE 6.6B). These are harmonious because they have a portion of the same hue in common.

6.5 The Munsell Color Wheel, or "Tree," integrates five principle hues with intervals of values.
SCIENCE MUSEUM/SCIENCE AND PICTURE LIBRARY

Adjacent hues on the color wheel create an **analogous** color scheme (FIGURE 6.6C). Usually there are three hues, but sometimes as many as five. Often the combination is recognized in nature. Yellow, yellow-orange, orange, and red-orange simulate the imagery of autumn leaves or fire.

A **complementary** color scheme contains two hues that are opposites on the color wheel (FIGURE 6.6D). Of these, the most familiar are red and green, because they are often featured in Christmas decorations. They are especially effective for that purpose because opposites intensify each other when placed in proximity. On the contrary, red and green in their purest forms may seem overbearing for clothing, especially in the case where one color lies above the waist and the other below. The lesson, then, is to use them in smaller doses or in varying tints, shades, or intensities. There is an interesting result when opposite pigments are combined, as in the case of paint. In equal doses, they result in gray, so adding an opposite hue in smaller degrees can make a color more grayed. In actual practice, the paint combination may look more like brown or taupe. When a designer is illustrating a garment design, the performance of color in paint, pencils, pastels, or markers is important. However, in a garment, the question of combining colors comes up when two different-colored yarns are used that are woven or knitted in the same fabric structure. Red and green yarns used equally in the same structure would construct a gray fabric.

Cultivating complementary colors in a design brings a wider range of color possibilities than those that result from adjacent hues. A **split complementary** color scheme uses one hue and the two on either side of its complement (FIGURE 6.6E). More variation occurs from using tints, shades, and intensities of these hues. A **double complementary** scheme consists of two colors on either side of a hue and the two on either side of its complement (FIGURE 6.6F).

A color scheme featuring three hues equidistant on the color wheel is a **triad** (FIGURE 6.6G). The most familiar triadic color scheme includes the three primary colors—red, blue, and yellow. They were beloved by the Bauhaus in the 1920s. They are often chosen for the toys, environments, and clothing for young children. They are also reminiscent of the circus.

The final color scheme in the list is known either as a **tetrad** or a **double split-complement** (FIGURE 6.6H). It refers to four colors that are equidistant on the color wheel. The layout of the combination forms a rectangle. This is the most complex of all the color relationships. It works more successfully if the colors are not used in equal proportions.

Selecting a color scheme or story is an important step in the creation of any successful art or design product. The painter Claude Monet and his

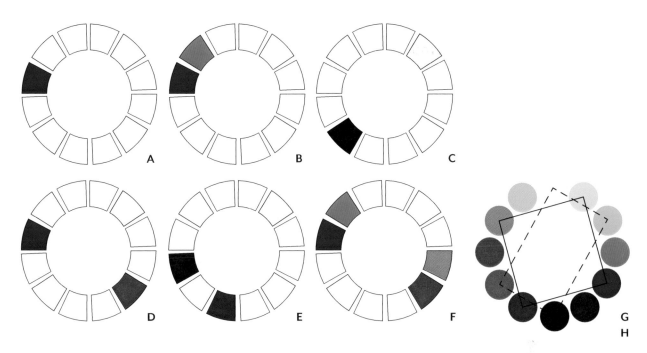

A

B

C

D

E

F

G
H

colleague Impressionist painters, Auguste Renoir (1841–1919), Camille Pissarro (1830–1903), and Alfred Sisley (1839–1899), among others, omitted the color black from their paint palettes. At the time, there was continuing research in optics and the theory of complementary colors was new. They reasoned that shadows were not black but had color, so they employed a color's complement for them, because the complement offered the contrast that best featured a color's brightness (FIGURE 6.7). Conversely, the

6.7 In *The Greenhouse*, by Auguste Renoir, the color palette omits black and employs complementary colors to provide contrast.
VISUAL ARTS LIBRARY/ART RESOURCE, NY

6.8 The color scheme in *Two Women from Tahiti* (1892) by Paul Gauguin is high-toned and packed with emotion.

movement of painting called Fauvism, which featured painters such as Paul Gauguin (1848–1903), Henri Matisse (1869–1954), and André Derain (1880–1954), used colors that were described as unnatural and violent. The high-toned colors were meant to reflect emotion, rather than reality. "Les Fauves" is French for "the wild beasts" (FIGURE 6.8).

COLOR TEMPERATURE

The Standard Color Wheel organizes hues by color temperature, another valuable indicator for color choice. Color temperature is experienced from interaction with nature. Colors that are **warm**—those that are yellow-based, oranges and reds to violets—occupy half of the color wheel and convey associations with the sun or fire. When hit with light, they actually feel warmer. Those that occupy the opposite side of the color wheel, blues and greens, are **cool**, summoning thoughts of sky, grass, foliage, and water. These visually recede by comparison to the warm hues.

All designers develop a sensitivity for, knowledge of, and ability to manipulate color. The Italian fashion designer Roberto Capucci (1930–) has been a master of both color and form (BOX 6.1).

COLOR INTERACTIONS

The experience of working with color teaches that its final form is not always predictable. That is because there are both environmental and optical factors that affect the perception of it. A stylist, as a result, may try dif-

ferent color accessories with a fashion in order to discover which mak[
biggest impact in a photo shoot. A painter sometimes mixes a color on ,
palette only to find it looks different on the canvas.

SIMULTANEOUS CONTRAST

One example of this phenomenon is called **simultaneous contrast**. In short, this means that a color looks different when placed in proximity to another color. This is the reason, for example, that complementary colors appear to intensify one another. Their similarities decrease and their dissimilarities increase (FIGURE 6.9). This observation is credited originally to the French chemist Michel Eugène Chevreul (1786–1889), the director of the dye house for Gobelins tapestries in Paris during the early nineteenth century. He was asked to determine why some of the colors appeared differently in the Gobelins tapestries. With his expertise in dyestuffs and tints, he determined that the colors looked different because of the colors they were placed beside. He published his findings in *The Principles of Harmony and Contrast of Colors* in 1839. The timing was critical, because that knowledge inspired both the Impressionist and Post-Impressionist painters to think carefully about what color brushstrokes were placed in proximity. The painter Josef Albers (1888–1976) experimented with this concept in a series of paintings entitled *Homage to the Square*, in which he placed varying hues within square formats (FIGURE 6.10).

BELOW LEFT
6.9 Simultaneous contrast means that colors look different depending on what other colors are placed in proximity.
ILLUSTRATION BY ERIN FITZSIMMONS

BELOW RIGHT
6.10 Josef Albers' painting series *Homage to the Square* (1960–1964) explores the visual effects of simultaneous contrast.
ALBERS FOUNDATION/ART RESOURCE, NY

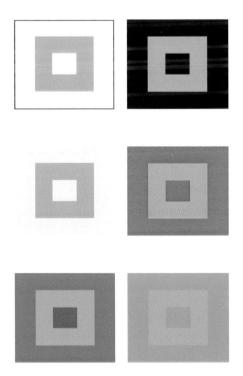

BOX 6.1

ROBERTO CAPUCCI

IN ITALY, ROBERTO Capucci is considered a legendary fashion designer, and something of a wunderkind, because he opened his fashion house there at the age of 21. Nevertheless, he preferred to call himself a researcher. He was born in Rome in 1930 and obtained an education at the Academy of Fine Arts. He wanted to be a set designer, costume designer, or an architect, but instead developed a life as a couturièr. He presented his first collections in Florence in 1951 and opened a Paris salon in 1962. It was not long before Capucci discovered that he preferred freedom from the ruling fashion trends and the demands of the fashion calendar. Unlike his contemporaries, he eventually delivered one collection annually in different towns and mostly in museums. A collection was the product of his research.

That was appropriate, because his concept of haute couture was as an art form, inspired by the fashions of the 1950s. He thought of fashion as architecture within which the body inhabits. He measured the success of each design by the elements of line, texture, volume, and color, without forgetting their relationship to the human figure. He gained inspiration from his garden, which instilled in him a sense of balance, proportion, harmony, and color.

For one collection he prepared as many as 1,200 sketches, drawn in black and white, so his selections were made without the benefit of color. Ironically, the choice of color contributed to his sense of perfection. He might reproduce up to 172 shades of one color for a particular dress. That dress might require four months of work and 200 yards of fabric.

His architectural or sculptural dresses were geometric in feeling. The linear and planar qualities referred to crystalline structures, while the curvilinear volumes resembled floral forms. He manipulated fabrics with pleating or cut them into mosaics. A botanist might see the designs as flowers, while a mathematician would appreciate their geometry. A historian would identify them as soft suits of armor, but a painter would admire his choice of color.

The colors were the result of his inspirations, which ranged from the flight of a colorful bird during an African safari to the simple peeling of an orange. In some instances, Capucci would limit himself to just black and white, so the absence of color would emphasize line and space. More typically, his color choices were described as phantasmagoric or iridescent.

In one garment he would include the green of an emerald, the green of a new leaf, the green of the sea, the green of an apple, and the green of a glass bottle. Or he would pair a cool color with a warm one, always considering whether the color was inside or outside of the dress, whether it was part of the body's form or part of the outer wrapping. He used a variety of color schemes—monochromatic, complementary, analogous, or warm with cool, sometimes interspersed with a neutral (FIGURE BOX 6.1A–C).

THE BEZOLD EFFECT

Rug designer Wilhelm von Bezold (1837–1907) discovered another color interaction, which is now called the **Bezold Effect.** In rug designs using a few colors, he found that by changing just one, he created a completely different visual product (FIGURE 6.11). This is especially exciting for fashion and textile designers. With the change of just one color, a fabric print or pattern produces a completely new product for the consumer.

SUCCESSIVE CONTRAST

Chevreul reported another optical phenomenon that was also identified by the German poet Johann Wolfgang von Goethe (1749–1832). Goethe's observations were meant to be a response to Newton's, but he concentrated on the behavior of the eye instead of light. He was the first to suggest that shadows had color. Chevreul identified Goethe's idea as **successive contrast**. In the simplest terms, they observed that if one stares at a color for a long time and looks away, the complementary color appears in an afterglow. There is a physiological reason for this occurrence. The human eye contains two different layers of cells—rods, which record lightness and darkness, and cones, which distinguish hues. These serve as photoreceptors in the retina. The cones can register only one color in a complementary pair at a time, a function referred to as **opponent theory**. Staring at a color for a length of time fatigues the cones, which then revert to seeing the color's complement. The contemporary term for Chevreul's idea is called afterimage. The painter Jasper Johns (1930–) played with this concept in a series of paintings called *Flags* (FIGURE 6.12). If the viewer stares at the dot in the center of the flag for a period of time, and then shifts to the dot in the rectangle below, the American flag appears in its characteristic red, white, and blue, the complements of the colors in Johns' painted flag.

6.11 Changing one color in a multicolor design changes its entire appearance.
ILLUSTRATIONS BY ERIN FITZSIMMONS

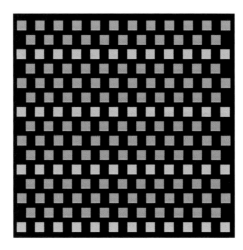

6.12 Jasper Johns explored the theory of successive contrast in his art series called *Flags* (1968). Staring at the flag image for a while and then switching to the dot in the rectangle below should create the image of the American flag in its characteristic colors.

ORPHISM, OR "SIMULTANEISM"

There was a movement in both painting and fashion that expanded upon Chevreul's theory of simultaneous contrast. The movement originated with the painter Robert Delaunay (1885–1941) and his wife Sonia Terk Delaunay (1885–1979), who was a painter, clothing designer, and textile designer. It was called **Orphism**, but Robert preferred **simultaneity** (or simultaneism). The former term was named for the Greek god Orpheus and meant that movement, light, and rhythm are more important than the presentation of an object. The reference to Orpheus was to music, because his paintings encompassed so many colorful harmonies. Both Robert and Sonia were influenced by the systematic placement of color practiced by the Impressionist painters and the bold, saturated colors used by the Post-Impressionist and Fauve painters. In addition, they were friends with the prominent couturièr Paul Poiret, discussed in Chapter 3, who freed women from the corset and originated the hobble skirt. In exploring colors and the effect of those beside them, their paintings, clothing, and textile designs demonstrated animation caused by simultaneous contrasts within a design, attracting the eye in different directions and causing a sense of rhythm and movement. In addition, the contrasting and juxtaposed colors in geometric shapes suggested new and different shapes (FIGURES 6.13A AND B).

OTHER PHENOMENA OF COLOR PERCEPTION

Another variable that influences the perception of color is the size of the colored area. A huge expanse of color appears brighter than a small one. The smaller the area, the more the color dulls and the edges lose their sharpness.

Colors change their appearance according to the lighting under which they are perceived. Claude Monet changed the colors he used to paint *La Cathédral de Rouen*, according to the time of day, as discussed in Chapter 4 (FIGURES 4.16A AND B). That is because the angle of the sun's rays changes, while clouds and atmospheric particles cause light refraction. Regarding the interior, incandescent lighting can look yellow, while florescent light has a blue cast. Artists, designers, and even consumers prefer natural light, in order to see colors in their purest form.

Color perception is also dependent on the qualities of the surface from which it is reflected.

BELOW LEFT
6.13A This painting by Robert Delaunay reflects his philosophy of simultaneous contrasts that began the movement of Orphism or use of simultaneity.
ERICH LESSING/ART RESOURCE

BELOW RIGHT
6.13B Sonia Terk Delaunay's simultaneous dress in wool, silk, velvet and fur from 1913 explores the use of simultaneity in fashion.
ILLUSTRATION BY JANICE GREENBERG ELLINWOOD

A smooth, shiny surface, which has maximum light reflection, mak[es] color appear lighter. The fashion designer explores this quality when choo[s]ing satin or taffeta fabrics or metallic yarns. Conversely, a rough or porou[s] texture, like the loopy bouclé knit or tweed, makes colors look darker.

Most people are not acutely sensitive to color changes. They learn color from experience, and it remains in their visual memory. A house looks white whether viewed at daybreak or sunset. This phenomenon is called **color constancy**. It is a method by which the brain preserves well-being, so familiar objects are consistently recognized.

VALUE AND ITS PERCEPTION

As previously discussed, value refers to lightness and darkness. It is perhaps easier to understand how value affects a hue than how value itself influences perception. Adding white to a hue forms a tint and adding black makes a shade, but how does one comprehend value itself? The potential gradations between white and black on a gray scale are infinite, but there is a limit to the number that humans can distinguish. In this vibrant, highly technological world, how does one conceive of value? It was easier before color was a possibility in photography, television, and film. Value was all that the viewer saw in old photographs, early films, and television.

One way to think of value is in terms of relativity, by comparing one value to another. **Low-key values** refer to the middle gray values to black. **High-key values** are those from white to the middle grays. A **value scale** gives the concept a context, as one tone is viewed against the next (FIGURE 6.14). **Contrast** is critical; it is the amount of difference in values. **High contrast** draws attention and provides clarity. **Low contrast** contributes variety in a subtle manner.

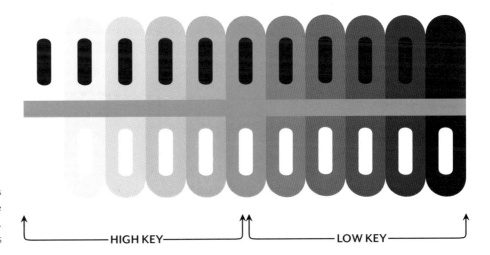

6.14 The value scale shows all of the values possible in a scale from white to black.
ILLUSTRATION BY ERIN FITZSIMMONS

HIGH KEY — LOW KEY

VALUE AND PERCEPTION

Here are some of the influences that value has on perception: Light values advance and enlarge, while dark values recede. That means they can be manipulated to create the illusion of slimming or expanding the human figure.

Value affects apparent density. Dark values have greater visual weight. Because of our sense of gravity, there is greater visual comfort with darker values placed close to the ground. A dark top over a light bottom may seem top-heavy.

Light values juxtaposed with dark values push each other apart. A white top over a dark skirt tends to break up the body and therefore is more appropriate for a tall figure.

Extreme value contrast distracts from hues; they are more evident in the presence of subtle contrast. As a result, consider using high contrast in apparel with neutrals and low contrast with fashion colors.

The astute fashion designer has a command of both color and value. That contributes to both the flattery of the figure and the success of each design.

KEY TERMS

achromatic	electromagnetic waves	simultaneity
additive color	high contrast	simultaneous contrast
afterimage	high-key values	split complementary
analogous	hue	spectrum
Bezold Effect	intensity	standard color wheel
chroma	low contrast	subtractive color
color	low-key values	tertiary colors
color constancy	monochromatic	tetrad
color temperature	neutral	tint
color wheel	opponent theory	tone on tone
complementary	Orphism	triad
contrast	pigment	value
cool	primary colors	value scale
double complementary	saturation	visible spectrum
double split-complement	secondary colors	warm
dye	shade	wavelength

PROJECTS

1. **COLOR EXERCISES.** These are short-handed exercises for students to obs⟨e⟩ some of the color theories discussed in the chapter. Required supplies: thre⟨e⟩ by five-inch index cards or Bristol board or mat board cut to the same dimension; balls of yarn in a number of colors (these may be shared among students in the classroom). For each exercise, yarn is wrapped around the card strand by strand. The products are evaluated from a distance.

   A. Monochromatic color scheme—Wrap yarn in four shades of the same hue around the index card or board in equally sized stripes.

   B. Analogous color scheme—Choose three to five colors that lie adjacent to one another on the Standard Color Wheel. Wrap the colors of yarn around the index card or board in stripes of equal widths.

   C. Complementary color scheme—Wrap yarns of two complementary colors on the Standard Color Wheel around the index card or board, alternating every other strand. What color is perceived from the final product at a distance?

   D. Split complementary color scheme—Choose one hue on the Standard Color Wheel and the two on each side of the color's complement. Wrap the three hues of yarn around the index card or board in stripes of equal width.

   E. Bezold Effect—Return to the product you made for a, b, or d. Create the same striped product, replacing one of the colors with a new one. Compare the two products. Are they significantly different? Consider whether this is also an example of simultaneous contrast.

2. **MASTER PAINTER'S COLOR SCHEME.** Find a reproduction of a favorite master painting. Choose three to four colors in the painting and match them with 1-inch squares of Color-aid paper, gouache paint, markers, or colored pencil. Obtain an exact match. Mount the reproduction on white board, leaving an adequate margin around the reproduction. Adhere the three or four squares in the lower right margin, just below the reproduction. The colors identified represent the scheme chosen by the master painter.

3. **FASHION FEATURING MASTER PAINTER'S COLOR SCHEME.** Design a garment using the three to four colors that the master painter used in the

reproduction. Draw at least five versions in your sketchpad before deciding on the best of the group. Create a larger version on Bristol board. Show colors by using cut Color-aid paper, markers, or gouache paint, adhering to the exact match. If you are using colored pencils, choose drawing paper for the final form of the design and mount it on white Bristol board.

REFERENCES

Albers, J. (1975). *Interaction of color.* New Haven, CT: Yale University Press.

Albritton, A. (2005). "She has a body on her dress": Sonia Delaunay-Terk's first simultaneous dress, 1913. *Dress* 32, 3–13.

Bauzano, G. (Ed.). (2001). *Roberto Capucci: Timeless creativity.* Milan: Skira.

Boker, S. M. *Brewster.* (1995, February 12). Retrieved June 1, 2009, from http://people.virginia.edu/~smb3u/ColorVision2/node6.html.

Capucci. *DellModa.* (2009, March 25). Retrieved March 25, 2009, from http://dellamoda.it/fashion_dictionary/c/capucci.php.

Cunningham, R. (1994). *The magic garment: Principles of costume design.* Long Grove, IL: Waveland Press.

Davis, M. L. (1996). *Visual design in dress* (3rd ed.). Upper Saddle River, NJ: Prentice Hall.

Feisner, E. A. (2001). *Color studies.* New York: Fairchild Publications.

Louis Prang 1824–1909. Retrieved June 1, 2009, from www.emotionscards.com/museum/louisprang.htm.

Florida State University. Sir David Brewster. Science, optics and you: Pioneers in optics. *Molecular Expressions.* Retrieved June 1, 2009, from http://micro.magnet.fsu.edu/optics/timeline/people/brewster.html.

Ocvirk, O. G., Stinson, R., Wigg, P., Bone, R., & Cayton, D. (2002). *Art fundamentals* (9th ed). New York: McGraw-Hill.

Roberto Capucci. (n.d.) *Fashion Encyclopedia.* Retrieved March 25, 2009, from http://www.fashion encyclopedia.com/Bo-Ch/Capucci-Roberto.html.

Roberts, W. (2003–2008). Brewster's kaleidoscope, op art, and interactive moiré resonances. *Principles of Nature.* Retrieved June 1, 2009, from www.principlesofnature.net/connections_between_art_and_science/brewster_kaleidoscope_op_art_and_interactive_moire_resonances.htm.

Florida State University. Sir David Brewster. Science, optics and you: Pic neers in optics. *Molecular Expressions.* Retrieved June 1, 2009, from http://micro.magnet.fsu.edu/optics/timeline/people/brewster.html.

Stewart, M. (2008). *Launching the imagination: A comprehensive guide to basic design* (3rd ed.). New York: McGraw-Hill.

Zelanski, P., & Fisher, M. P. (1989). *Color. Upper Saddle River,* NJ: Prentice Hall.

CHAPTER 7

COLOR AND INDUSTRY

OBJECTIVES

To explain the factors that influence change in fashion colors

To enumerate the color concerns of designers for mass fashion, such as the personal coloring of consumers, customers' desire for self-expression, color psychology, symbolism, and cultural meaning

To examine how designers of high fashion have chosen colors for their collections

Just one trip to the shopping mall highlights the assortment of colors available in apparel at one time. How is that possible? Who chooses the colors? Do designers favor certain ones? Which are the preferred colors of customers? Do their preferences change?

In an effort to answer these questions, this chapter explains how changes in the technology of dying fabrics have an effect on color, how the fashion industry attempts to forecast in advance which colors the consumer will prefer, and how designers of mass fashion use this information in their work, along with a consideration of customers' personal coloring and the psychology of color. Finally, this chapter enumerates how designers of high-end apparel choose colors for their collections.

COLOR AND DYES

Color is added to a garment through the fiber, yarn, fabric, or complete product, depending on the desired effect, the quality, and the end use. **Dyes** are molecules that bond with the fiber, yarn, or fabric with the aid of a carrier, like water, for penetration. They have great color strength, much more than pigment. Just a small amount is necessary to color fabric. Most dyes bond chemically so that they sufficiently penetrate the fiber instead of staying solely on the surface, which is the case with pigment. Maximum dye penetration is achieved at the fiber stage, called **fiber dyeing**. Because a yarn is a smaller entity than fabric yardage, dyeing at the yarn stage (**yarn dyeing**) is more effective than **piece dyeing**, which refers to dyeing the fabric. **Product dyeing**, once the garment is formed, is the least effective method. The absorption of dyes occurs easiest between loose fibers, especially in those that are known for their absorbency, like cotton. Despite its filament form, silk also takes dyes especially well. Color is added to manmade fibers at the initial stage of production, which ensures that they are **colorfast**.

The designer may desire a particular color property, for instance, the brilliant shade of a colored silk, a fiber-speckled tweed, a contrasting yarn-dyed plaid, or a piece of cloth that bears the dye in an **ombre** effect,

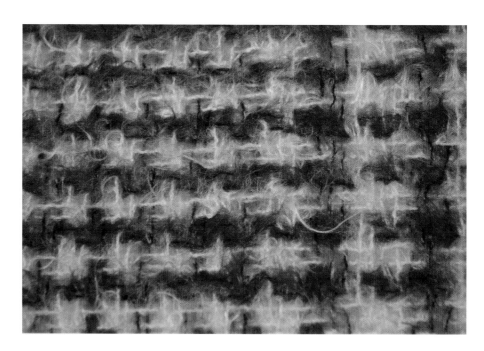

meaning from the darkest value of a hue to its tint to white. The artistic
decision of choosing a space-dyed mohair worsted wool tweed, like Chanel
used in her suit jackets, is much like the effect that pointillist painter Paul
Signac (1863–1935) achieved using dotted brushstrokes of different colors in
a painting (FIGURES 7.1A AND B).

History instructs that certain colors define a particular period in fashio. These are often tied to the fabrics and dyes that were available. Many eighteenth-century costumes in current museum collections feature colorful silks that were worn by the upper classes in red, blue, and yellow. In the early nineteenth century, advancements in **bleaching** methods made white, most often in cotton, the sought-after color. **Aniline dye** was created accidentally from coal in 1856 by the English chemist William Henry Perkin (1838–1907), who was in the process of searching for a cure for malaria. The first dye was mauve, which actually caused a color more like a vivid purple with fuchsia tones. Purple was historically associated with royalty, since the dye was so expensive. Because of Perkin's discovery, it was suddenly available at an affordable price, so it became very popular.

The zeal for the color was further promoted by Empress Eugénie of France's Second Empire, a fashion leader of the day. When she advised Queen Victoria to wear the color to her daughter's wedding in 1858, its desirability was sealed. Eventually the bright purple bore tones of ultramarine blue. Examples of it in attire are evident in the portraits painted of the day. Fashions of the color were pictured in the work of Impressionists Claude Monet and Auguste Renoir.

The discovery of aniline dyes stimulated the growth of the chemical industry, coinciding with improvements made to the sewing machine. At first, chemical dyes were not colorfast, but with improvements, they replaced natural dyes with colors not accessible previously, such as alizarin black and methyl purple. The Impressionist painters were experimenting with chemically synthesized inorganic pigments. They discovered that the fashions of the time were a wonderful venue to feature the new palette colors of mauve and bright blue. Paintings and literature of the day also illustrated a desire for black for both wealthy and working-class women, because it was considered practical and glamorous (FIGURE 7.2). Coco Chanel recognized its potential in the 1920s, and its desirability has continued to present day. Although once thought appropriate only for mourning, black communicates professionalism, offers versatility, and flatters the figure.

Conversely, during the period of World War II, there were shortages of dyes. Only 15 shades for textiles were available to apparel manufacturers. Women wore beige and gray, and *Vogue* recommended colorful accessories to complement black and white outfits.

7.2 Auguste Renoir's painting *The Umbrellas* (1881–1886) pictures women in the fashionable colors of the day—black and a purplish blue.
© NATIONAL GALLERY, LONDON/ ART RESOURCE, NY

In the 1950s, the early versions of manufactured fibers like nylon and polyester, with their limited absorbency, supported the trend for pastel colors. Today the fashion industry researches the anticipated acceptance of color choices well in advance of the consumer's opportunity to purchase.

COLOR FORECASTING

Color is so significant to the sale of fashion that all levels of the industry involved in its mass production seek predictions about it. Those who produce the fibers and the dyes must know the appropriate colors two years before the retail sale season. Then the information is dispersed to the fabric producers, converters, apparel manufacturers, and trade publications.

Other industries are just as interested in color, such as cosmetics, home nishings, and the automotive industry.

COLOR ADVISORY ASSOCIATIONS

There are principal **color advisory associations** in a number of countries. The Color Association, which originated in 1915, operates in the United States, and the British Textile Group, including representatives of fiber companies, fashion services, retailers, and textile firms, is in the United Kingdom. Others in Europe include the Deutsche Mode Institut (Germany) and the Institute da Moda Espagnol (Spain). Thirteen European and Asian member countries report their color palettes to Intercolor, an international nonprofit organization representing China, Finland, France, Great Britain, Germany, Hungary, Italy, Japan, Korea, Portugal, Switzerland, and Turkey. In addition, there are profit-making **fashion and color reporting services**—some that are small and focus specifically on color and others that report trends more broadly across several classifications of apparel.

Color advisory associations meet at conferences twice per year in order to define and summarize their perception of the trends. They dispense that information in the form of dyed yarns or fabric swatches. Fiber companies also conduct color research. They circulate written color forecasts to their customers.

7.3 Fashionable colors in the home furnishings of particular twentieth-century decades ultimately became obsolete until the period was considered retroactively fashionable again.
COURTESY OF BIG CHILL

SOCIAL AND CULTURAL INTERPRETATION

Color forecasting involves the analysis and interpretation of social and cultural events, the economy, and certain market sectors in order to make predictions, which are based on forecasters' insight and experience, as well as mathematics. Forecasters do not dictate colors but identify to the best of their ability what the consumer is ready to consume. Research confirms that they tire of sameness and are stimulated by something new. By the same token, colors can eventually saturate the market until they become obsolete. This phenomenon is often observed in the home furnishings market (FIGURE 7.3). In the 1950s it took seven years for colors to move from the higher price points to the lowest until they were no longer in demand. Today the process takes two to three years.

FORECAST SPECTRUMS

Color forecasters formulate their ideas in a **color spectrum**. Two or three are provided for a **season**. Each spectrum has a theme, which makes the color tones comprehensible and determines color names, which are chosen to underscore their novelty. One theme in recent years is living "green" or in a manner that protects the environment. However, the most recent color signal for green living has changed ironically to blue. In order to indicate the association, the names for blue indicate it connection with water, like ocean blue.

FASHION CYCLES AND COLOR

Some presumptions about color are based on experience. For instance, there are seven-year cycles between warm-toned and cool-toned colors, while there is a longer time, up to 25 years, between intense, multicolored fashions and subdued neutrals. Some color families have a longer fashion cycle, while others last for a shorter time. During economic prosperity consumers like bright colors, and they choose darker ones when times are not good.

In areas of climatic change, season plays a role in color choice. Darker colors—such as dark green, berry, dark blue, brown, black—are more important to varying degrees in autumn and winter. This is very pragmatic, since dark clothing does not soil as easily as light. Conversely, spring and summer seasons bring pastel tones and feature white.

COLOR COMBINATIONS

Contrary to previous periods, there are no rules regarding the wearing of color combinations. It was once thought that red could not be worn with pink or blue with green. Redheaded women could not wear red, and white shoes were allowed only from June through August. Shoes, gloves, and hats all had to match an ensemble. Today designers thrill to unexpected combinations of colors and patterns.

Neutral colors have an especially significant role in fashion. As explained in Chapter 6, neutrals are achromatic or without a hue. In other words, they are not found on the color wheel. Such colors are black, brown, beige, tan, gray, off-white, and white. Neutrals are thought to harmonize with all hues and with each other, so they are an important part of building a wardrobe. Neutrals are represented in every season, although fashion research may place more importance on one over another. Like black, the other neutrals can communicate professionalism and even glamour. Some women wear neutral apparel only.

One shade of a particular hue on the color wheel performs gene
like a neutral. That is **indigo**, a dark blue, and the dye used originally .
jeans. In today's lifestyle, indigo harmonizes with other hues, and denim ›
considered a basic in the wardrobe.

DESIGNING FOR MASS FASHION

A fashion color palette for ready-to-wear usually includes from 4 to 10 colors. A few, sometimes the more basic or neutral, make up the main part of the color story, while the other fashion-forward ones are used as accents or within prints. Contrasts and dramatic tones draw attention to the wearer, while low contrasts are more placid. Here is a good opportunity to remember that light colors move forward visually, while dark ones recede. Color is an important element, like line and shape, to flatter the figure.

The designer is usually limited to the colors of the fabrics that have been manufactured for a season. These include the basic, seasonal colors and those that are the result of fashion forecasting. The designer will have conducted research in order to know which those are. Typically, there are between 6 and 18 months before the line of apparel reaches the retail selling floor. The current trend is to commit to color choice as late as possible, in order to make the best hypothesis on what the consumer will purchase. That might indicate product dyeing as the method of choice, so single-shade garments can be styled ahead of time. Computer use also increases the speed of the dyeing process, because it induces quicker design preparation and better color matching.

COLOR-MATCHING SYSTEMS

There is also a need for the designer's colors to match with others used in the industry. That is how a consumer can shop along a mall and find coordinating garments in different stores. There are a number of standardized commercial **color-matching systems**. The best-known ones are the SCOTDIC (Standard Color of Textile Dictionnaire Internationale de la Couleur) system and the Pantone Professional Color System. Both use a method of measuring colors according to hue, value, and chroma, according to the Munsell Color Wheel. SCOTDIC covers dye colors for cotton, polyester, and wool. The cotton system consists of 2,300 colors, the polyester one includes 2,468, while the wool has 1,100. Pantone uses a six-digit numbering system that indicates the color's location on the color wheel and relates its value to black and white and also its intensity. The Pantone system relates to computer colors, markers, and papers, so that it is easy to illustrate the design and its exact color.

COLOR AND THE CONSUMER

When choosing colors, the designer stays aware of the consumer's concerns. For example, perhaps the consumer wants colors that harmonize with his or her **personal coloring**.

PERSONAL COLORING

Personal coloring indicates the composite of skin, hair, and eye colors. Of the three, skin serves as the immediate background to colored apparel. Skin tone is determined by the hemoglobin, carotene, and melanin in the skin. There is a great range of pigment (brown) intensity in melanin. Variation in skin color is largely due to genetics. For many years, **wardrobe consultants** have advised the consumer to look for an undertone in skin or gum color that is either cool (blue) or warm (yellow). This tone is viewed with the colors of hair and eyes (considered just an accent) and then applied to the theory derived from the standard color wheel and discussed in Chapter 6. The recommended colors are those that have a place in the color combinations that result from the hue's placement on the color wheel. A consumer learns the best apparel colors from experience as well, whenever a compliment is made on his or her appearance. Designers and retailers also discover which colors are the best for their target markets based on prior selling. For instance, yellow and green can reflect color back onto the skin, having a less flattering effect. Beige and pale pink are often difficult to wear because they wash out skin tone.

PERSONAL EXPRESSION

Consumers also select colors as a vehicle for **self-expression**, and at other times, to reflect a desirable **image** in a social group. Self-expression means the decision is made primarily on aesthetics and may involve experimentation. Image rests on the opinions of others. Do individuals perceive the wearer in the proper role? Vocation may define role, as in the case of a business executive, lawyer, or college administrator, or the wearer may seek the position of fashion leader in the social group. As a result, consumers are often aware of color psychology and symbolism, as well as their cultural meanings.

As discussed previously, black has a range of meanings, which makes it, in fact, a popular color. While it is the color of mourning in Western cultures, it is also used for formal occasions (noted in the expression "**black tie**"). Ironically, it is considered dignified, professional, and appropriate for the workplace but is also perceived as sexy and even mysterious (FIGURE 7.4). Although it has been the color of rebellion, representing the punks

7.4 The woman in John Singer Sargent's portrait from 1883–1884, *Madame X*, was considered seductive and mysterious.

© THE METROPOLITAN MUSEUM OF ART/ART RESOURCE, NY

and the Goths, it has become a **staple** in the wardrobe. Considered elegant by designers, some women find it stark for the complexion. Its sophistication makes it inappropriate for children, so wearing it is a rite of passage.

Blue is one of the preferred colors in a full range of values by both men and women. Its historic associations are peace, honor, trust, loyalty, solitude, cold, and heaven. It is appropriate for formal occasions and for the office. Its association with sky and water makes it appropriate for clothing with nautical trims, like the U.S. Navy uniform. In its palest form, it represents the male gender in children's apparel.

Green has many associations—living "green," medicine, wealth, luck, envy, youth and inexperience, nature and life, and the indication to move forward on a traffic light. It is a color that does not harmonize with all complexions.

Orange is also difficult to wear for some people but has gained in its popularity in recent years. It is revitalizing and means warmth, cheer, youthfulness, vigor, and excitement. Some people are not comfortable with its intensity.

Pink means femininity for many consumers. It is associated with sweetness and affection and symbolizes the female gender in children's apparel. However, it is accepted in small doses today for men's apparel as well.

Historically, purple was the color of royalty. It communicates stateliness, drama, and spiritual awareness. It appears in the wardrobe as a fashion color and is well liked in a range of values.

Red has both positive and negative associations. As the color of blood, it signified executioners. Because red lights hung at the doors of brothels in France, it symbolized prostitution. Although it tells traffic to stop, red is associated with aggression and passion. It is on the flags of several countries. It also means love, desire, speed, power, danger, life, obsession, and strength. It stimulates both mental and physical energy. Some women are uncomfortable wearing red because it attracts too much attention.

White is the color of mourning in Eastern cultures. It also means joy, purity, innocence, cleanliness, spirituality, and winter. In Western cultures, it is the color choice for bridal apparel. As a neutral, it is a staple in the wardrobe. Designers have often professed the versatility of a white blouse.

Yellow also carries negative and positive associations. It represents cowardice, fear, treachery, and ill health. Psychologically, it can stimulate nerves, so the consumer may tire of it before other colors. But its brightness conjures sunlight, warmth, and cheerfulness. It is used to symbolize infancy when the gender is not known. However, it is a difficult color to wear, because of its dissonance with skin colors having cool undertones.

Brown is a bit atypical in this roster for colors. In its earthiness, it brings a sense of casualness. It generally lacks sophistication and excitement. As a neutral, however, it can be a staple in the wardrobe.

To what extent are the high-end designers mindful of the psychological, symbolic, and cultural meanings of colors when they put together their collections? The answer varies, but these concerns are seldom the top priority of the high-end designer.

THE DESIGNER AND COLOR

Designers of the highest price apparel are most interested in making an artistic statement in their collections. The type of artistic statement varies with the designer and the period within which he or she works. Regarding color, inspirations may arrive in a number of ways.

Sometimes a designer chooses a **signature color**, one that defines the house's image and the continuing collections. Elsa Schiaparelli (1890–1940) was a prime example. She made innovative and whimsical fashions, which are discussed in Chapter 9, "Emphasis." Her favorite color was a brilliant pink that she described as "shocking" (FIGURE 7.5). In fact, that was the name of her famous fragrance, which was packaged in a bottle designed like a dressmaker's mannequin form. Valentino (1932–) used red for his signature color and included a red garment in every collection (BOX 7.1).

Although not literally considered her signature color, Coco Chanel is credited with the origin of a highly recognized design defined by a color. Her "little black dress," with a color originally lifted from menswear, became an iconic fashion, which has been further promoted by subsequent designers. One noteworthy example is the dress for actress Audrey Hepburn in the movie *Breakfast at Tiffany's* designed by Hubert de Givenchy (1927–) in 1961 (FIGURE 7.6).

7.5 Elsa Schiaparelli displayed her signature color in this evening dress from spring/summer 1953.
© V&A IMAGES, VICTORIA AND ALBERT MUSEUM

When an **art movement** inspires a designer, it determines the colors chosen for a collection. Yves Saint Laurent often designed his fashions from art. Chapter 2 described the group of dresses he based on the paintings of Piet Mondrian, so they featured red, blue, yellow, black, and white (FIGURE 2.4). Other themes for his designs were discussed in Chapter 4. The Pop Art movement of the 1960s was identified among them. Elsa Schiaparelli based some of her designs on the Surrealist movement of painting and the artist Salvador Dali. They are discussed further in Chapter 9, "Emphasis." Paul Poiret, the first couturièr of the twentieth century, had many interests, including Orientalism, Diaghilev's Ballets Russes, and the brilliant, emotional colors used by the Fauves painters. He captured them in several designs (FIGURE 7.7).

BOX 7.1

ALENTINO GARAVANI

VALENTINO GARAVANI WAS born in Voghera, Italy, and expressed an interest in fashion during his primary school years. He moved to Paris with the support of his parents, where he studied, at the age of 17, at the Ecole des Beaux-Arts and the L'École de la Couture Parisienne. In 1952, he capitalized on a fashion design competition award from the Wool Secretariat by obtaining a job with the couturièr Jean Dessès (1904–1970). From Dessès, Valentino learned the importance of precise draping and to work in a unique style, rather than to set the new fashion trends. From there he spent two years serving as design assistant to Guy Laroche (1923–1990).

Valentino returned to Italy in 1959, where he opened his own couture house in Rome. He met Giancarlo Giammetti, who subsequently became his business partner. His international debut occurred in 1962 in Florence, which was then the Italian fashion capital. By 1968 he opened his first boutique in Paris and showed his ready-to-wear collections there beginning in 1975. During this process, Valentino attracted important clients, including Jacqueline Kennedy Onassis, Elizabeth Taylor, Audrey Hepburn, Veruschka, and Princess Margaret.

His collections always featured his unique style. He showed a red design in every collection, which the fashion world came to know as "Valentino red." The unique trademark color was inspired by a trip to the Barcelona opera in the 1950s, where Valentino spotted a woman dressed entirely in red in the audience (FIGURE BOX 7.1).

His spring–summer 1968 collection was considered a pivotal one. He featured the color white only, varying its texture in crisply tailored suits, stockings embroidered with lace patterns, trimmings of reembroidered lace, soutache braid, pearls, and ostrich feathers. He was the first designer to use a monogram as a decorative pattern in his clothes and accessories, a "V" that originated in 1965. In other collections he featured animal prints of leopard, giraffe, crocodile, and zebra, leather appliqué, sequin and bead embroidery, and roses made from tulle.

Valentino's designs defined femininity. He used expert draping in delicate fabrics like chiffon and details such as bows, scallops, ruffles, complex pleating, lace insets, and frilled edges.

Valentino sold his company in 1998, but his impact on the fashion industry continued through his designing and other venues. He made a cameo appearance in the film *The Devil Wears Prada* in 2006. There was an extravagant, retrospective 45th anniversary fashion show and exhibit of his designs in Rome in 2007. A documentary of how he worked was filmed from 2005 to 2007. *Valentino: The Last Emperor* premiered at the 2008 Venice International Film Festival and was the highest-grossing documentary in 2009.

7.6 Holly Golightly, played by
Audrey Hepburn in the 1961 film
Breakfast at Tiffany's, wears a
black dress designed by
Hubert de Givenchy.
COURTESY EVERETT COLLECTION

Designers are also inspired by a **culture**, **subculture**, or **historic period**, so they can determine the colors of a collection. The very theatrical John Galliano featured voluminous organza ball gowns overlaid with Masai beadwork corsets and collars from Africa in his initial collection for Christian Dior in 1997 (FIGURE 7.8). Jean Paul Gaultier has typically referenced ethnic cultures and subcultures in his collections. Two examples, featuring soft hues in pleasing combinations, are pictured in FIGURES 7.9A AND B. The collections of Vivienne Westwood are rich with references to the punk movement and a variety of historic periods (BOX 7.2).

Designers may choose color with the desire to feature the garment's **construction**. This was the case with the construction innovator, Madeleine Vionnet. Her pioneering approach of cutting fabric on the bias was discussed in Chapter 1. In addition to causing the fabric to drape

against the body, Vionnet's approach placed gathers, seams, and other elements of construction at interesting angles and in unusual places. They were therefore an important part of her designs but could disappear in fabric of too dark a value. As a result, she chose white, beige, soft pastels, and gradations of single colors. With black or other dark fabrics, she juxtaposed textures, like the dull and lustrous sides of satin-back crepe or used velvet running in different directions, creating the illusion of a difference in color (FIGURE 7.10).

The designer may also choose colors that emphasize one of the other elements of design, like **texture**, as described in the last paragraph, or **silhouette**. When a light color value is chosen, the viewer can get lost in the surface richness of the material. With black or the darkest value of another hue, the general silhouette is emphasized (FIGURE 7.11).

ABOVE LEFT
7.8 John Galliano was inspired by the Masai tribe of Africa in this design from his initial collection in 1997.
CONDÉ NAST ARCHIVE

ABOVE RIGHT
7.9A Jean Paul Gaultier drew from cultural inspiration to design this blue and white jacket from 1994.
PIERRE VAUTHEY/CORBIS SYGMA

RIGHT
7.9B More cultural inspiration stimulated Jean Paul Gaultier to choose these unusual color combinations in his fall–winter 1994–1995 collection.
© THE METROPOLITAN MUSEUM OF ART/ART RESOURCE, NY

ABOVE
7.10 Madeleine Vionnet's
light-colored dress from 1920
features all of the construction
elements of her design.
© THE METROPOLITAN MUSEUM
OF ART/ART RESOURCE, NY

RIGHT
7.11 Silhouette is the defining
element in Yohji Yamamoto's
bustled design from fall–winter
1986–1987, thanks to the
emphasis on black and red.
NICK KNIGHT/YOHJI YAMAMOTO/
TRUNK ARCHIVE

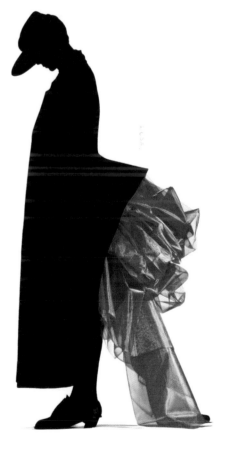

KEY TERMS

aniline dye	culture	product dyeing
art movement	dye	season
black tie	fashion reporting service	self-expression
bleaching	fiber dyeing	signature color
color advisory association	historic period	silhouette
colorfast	image	staple
color forecasting	indigo	subculture
color-matching system	neutral	texture
color reporting service	ombre	wardrobe consultant
color spectrum	personal coloring	yarn dyeing
construction	piece dyeing	

PROJECTS

1. Research the fashion colors for the upcoming season. Use Internet and print sources from fiber producers and trade associations, as well as the Web sites listed under "References."

2. Match papers in a variety of textures to the colors anticipated for the coming season. Use Color-aid paper, magazine paper, hand-made papers, scrapbooking papers, tissue paper, and so on.

3. Adhere your assortment of papers to a sheet of Bristol and arrange them in a pleasing collage. The collage will set the color mood for the upcoming season. Use a brush and white glue or glue stick for the adhesive. Consider whether to use paper shapes with ripped or cut edges. Hint: Be certain to use different textures for the same color.

REFERENCES

Davis, M., & Jacobs, R. (2006, September). Jean Paul Gaultier: Celebrating 30 years at Bergdorf Goodman. *Fashion Windows.* Retrieved June 21, 2009, from http://www.fashionwindows.com/windows3/2006/0606.asp.

Davis, M. L. (1996). *Visual design in dress* (3rd ed.). Upper Saddle River, NJ: Prentice Hall.

Farrell-Beck, J., & Parsons, J. (2007). *20th Century Dress in the United States.* New York: Fairchild Books.

Field, J. (2006). Bernat Klein's couture tweeds, color and fabric innovation, 1960–1980. *Dress,* 33, 41–56.

Frings, G. S. (1999). *Fashion from Fiber to Consumer* (6th ed.). Upper Sa River, NJ: Prentice Hall.

Frankel, S. (2001). *Visionaries: Interviews with fashion designers.* London: V&A Publications.

Fukai, A., & Thompson, P. W., Tsukamoto, Y., Bloemink, B., Lévi-Strauss, C., Font, L., Imbert, C., Kobayashi, Y., & Cardon, D. (2004). *Fashion in colors.* New York: Assouline Publishing.

Hunter, V. (2007). *The ultimate fashion study guide: The design process.* Los Angeles: Hunter Publishing.

Jackson, C. (1980). *Color me beautiful: Discover your natural beauty through the colors that make you look great and feel fabulous!* New York: Ballantine Books.

Jones, S. J. (2005). *Fashion design* (2nd ed.). London: Laurence King Publishing.

Kadolph, S. J. (2007). *Textiles* (10th ed.). Upper Saddle River, NJ: Pearson Education.

Miglietti, F. A. (2006). *Fashion statements: Interviews with fashion designers.* Milan: Skira.

Museum of London. (2000). *Vivienne Westwood: A London fashion.* London: Philip Wilson Publishers.

Parmal, P. A., Grumbach, D., Ward, S., & Whitley, L. D. (2004). *Fashion Show, Paris Style.* Boston: MFA Publications.

Rawsthorn, A. (2007, July 8). The red story. *New York Times.* Retrieved on June 10, 2009, from http://www.nytimes.com/2007/07/08/magazine/08Style-t.html.

Stegemeyer, A. (2004). *Who's who in fashion* (4th ed.). New York: Fairchild Books.

BOX 7.2

VIVIENNE /ESTWOOD

VIVIENNE WESTWOOD ORIGINALLY made her reputation as an antiestablishment designer. Born Vivienne Isabel Swire in Derbyshire, England, in 1941, her father was a munitions worker and her mother was a textile weaver. Her mother named her for the actress Vivienne Leigh. When she was 17, her parents bought a post office and she moved to Middlesex. She worked in a factory, went to school for teaching, and married Derek West-wood, from whom she was divorced in three years. At that time she met Malcolm McLaren, leader of the Sex Pistols. They opened a shop on London's King's Road and then another in the West End.

They were inspired by London Street life—fetishism and Punk rock. Most of West-wood's clothing was black, the color of protest. The shops were filled with black leather jackets, bossed sweaters, and teddy boy clothes. Rubber clothes, leather and vinyl acces-sories, chains, and T-shirts added to the assortment. The King's Road store changed its name many times until it was finally retitled World's End. It became one of London's land-marks, identified by a large clock that signals the hour backward. By the 1980s, the Punk era had waned, and Westwood embarked upon the career for which she is known.

A DESIGNER AS "STUDENT OF HISTORY"

Historical periods have always inspired her, especially the ones that convey stories of outlaws. Her first fashion show in London featured a collection termed "Pirate," and the designs exemplified the stereotype with the creative use of fabrics and colors. Subsequent collections followed, such as the New Romantic movement, Savages, and Buffalo Girls. Color was her means of putting the Punk period behind her.

Westwood was a true student of history, taking her inspiration from the art, history, and costume she explored in museums. She tried to evoke history in her designs in order to stimulate her audience to reflect on it and to technically capture the resources of the past into the mass production of the present. On her historical journey, she has adopted the corset and bustle in a variety of forms, the checks and stripes of menswear, the tartans of Scotland, and the pastels of Rococo paintings. In her slashed red voile dress of 1991, Westwood turned to Tudor portraiture and the seventeenth-century practice of slashing fabrics (FIGURE BOX 7.2A). The nylon lace jacket and layered skirt of 1993 was a bit reminiscent of the Pirate collection. The jacket featured a floral print and was lined in blue organdy, while the skirt was cut in graduated lengths to feature multicolored layers of tulle (FIGURE BOX 7.2B). In her 1996 collection, she drew from eighteenth-century fashions and the portrayal of the sack-back gowns in Watteau's paintings. Here the design features the pastel tones of the era (FIGURE BOX 7.2C).

A "WIZARD OF CUT"

From her examination of literature, art, history, and costume, Westwood has become a wizard of cut with a respect for the traditional methods of construction. She has taught at the Vienna Academy of Applied Arts and the Berliner Hochschule der Künste. Her designs continue to demonstrate her intrigue with the power of clothes to control the body. Westwood shows her designs in both Paris and London.

THE PRINCIPLES OF DESIGN

OPPOSITE
ILLUSTRATION BY
JANICE GREENBERG ELLINWOOD

CHAPTER 8

BALANCE

OBJECTIVES

To define the types of balance that designers apply to fashion

To examine how the principle of balance relates to three-dimensional design

To understand how a designer creates original fashions while staying aware of balance in the process

THIS CHAPTER OF the book begins Part II, "The Principles of Design." In Chapter 1, the elements of design were likened to the ingredients used in a cooking recipe. The principles are the manner in which the elements combine in order to obtain a tasty—or in this case, an aesthetically pleasing—final product.

For instance, a white sauce uses two tablespoons butter, two tablespoons flour, a cup of hot milk or cream, along with salt and pepper to taste. Is there another way to make it? There probably is an alternative, but if the final goal is a dish that uses pasta, vegetables, and other ingredients, why take the time to experiment, especially if there is a risk to the ultimate taste or consistency? After the dish has been successfully completed several times is a better time to experiment.

The same is true for the principles of design. They are tried-and-true guidelines for success. Use them reliably before pioneering an original approach.

This chapter explains how to apply the principle of **balance** to a fashion design, analyzing the term **visual weight** with a consciousness of the force of **gravity**. It defines the types of balance, including **horizontal balance**, **vertical balance**, **formal balance**, **informal balance**, **radial balance**, and **balance of all-over pattern**. In the process, it discusses **symmetry**, **approximate symmetry**, **asymmetry**, and how balance is considered in relation to three dimensions.

THE BASICS OF BALANCE

Balance is the sense of evenly distributed weight, resulting in the overall feeling of stability. There is nothing as disconcerting as feeling off balance, so one can comprehend how equilibrium contributes to the completeness or unity of a design.

Weight, however, is perceived visually. Variations in the use of the elements, such as the darkness of a value, the depth of a texture, the size and placement of a shape, the orientation or width of a line, and the brightness of a color contribute to the interpretation of weight. Visual weight also denotes the relative importance of an element in the design.

OPPOSITE
Vera Wang's spring 2011 bridal show.
COURTESY OF WWD/ GEORGE CHINSEE

179

Balance works visually as it would with a pair of scales. Items of equal weight balance evenly. If a box on one side of the scale weighs more than the box on the other, one must change something with the lighter box in order to compensate. Perhaps the addition of a second small box would even the distribution. Alternatively, the lighter box might move closer to the fulcrum in order to achieve balance.

Any discussion of balance must take gravity into consideration. Everyone lives with the sense that gravitational force pulls toward the earth, and therefore, gravity interacts with all of experience. Fashion, architecture, and art all present themselves with the orientation of a top, sides, and a bottom. So the elements provoking greater weight appear most appropriate in the bottom area of a design.

HORIZONTAL AND VERTICAL BALANCE

There are two approaches most commonly utilized to determine weight distribution—horizontal balance and vertical balance.

HORIZONTAL BALANCE

To determine horizontal balance, draw an imaginary vertical line down the center of a fashion and examine each side. How do the elements—the values, shapes, lines, textures, patterns, and colors—occur? Are they evenly distributed? Some kind of evenly weighted distribution is necessary to create a sense of stability in the design.

Formal Balance. When each element on one side of the line has a counterpart on the other, the result is called formal balance. Formal balance provides a sense of dignity, restraint, conservatism, and of course, formality. Take, for example, the design of the Pantheon in Rome (FIGURE 8.1). With its imposing vertical columns and triangular pediment, the viewer understands that it is an imposing and significant monument. Compare it to the pleated evening gown designed by Halston (1932–1990). (SEE FIGURE 8.2.) Its consistently draped, silk chiffon pleats, and halter-styled, plunging neckline resemble one fluted column. It too has a sense of weighted formality. Halston designed it with a companion double-tiered cape, styled like a Greek himation. Both the gown and the temple depend greatly on vertical lines to emphasize their appeal.

Informal Balance. When the elements on either side of the imaginary vertical line achieve equality in weight but with variety in line, shape, value, texture, or color, it is called informal balance. An example is the informality of

RIGHT
8.1 The Pantheon in Rome is an example of formal balance in architecture.
COURTESY ISTOCKPHOTO

BELOW
8.2 Halston's evening gown from 1974 is reminiscent of a fluted Greek column.
© THE METROPOLITAN MUSEUM OF ART/ART RESOURCE, NY

the Queen Anne style of architecture, which was antithetical to the classicism of Greek architecture (FIGURE 8.3). Queen Anne was a style prevalent in England and America in the late nineteenth century during the reign of Queen Victoria. In contrast to the simple Greek columns, it offered an abundance of architectural elements, such as steeply pitched, patterned roofs, forward-facing gables, porches, and windows, all of which organize themselves with a variety of lines, shapes, and textures on either side of a centerline. The 1922 fashion shown in FIGURE 8.4 by Madeleine Vionnet also has informal balance. What makes it unique is the use of the soft, organic fabric folds and silhouette combined with the straight vertical and horizontal lines on the garment's surface.

VERTICAL BALANCE

The goal of vertical balance is for the top of the garment to balance the bottom, yielding the perception that the figure rests on the ground firmly without appearing top-heavy or weighted down. To determine if that is the case, draw an imaginary line horizontally through the middle of the figure. A comparison of two designs by Hubert de Givenchy helps to explore this

8.3 Queen Anne architecture, with all of its towers, turrets, and porches, is a style that features informal balance.
© JEFF GREENBERG/ THE IMAGE WORKS

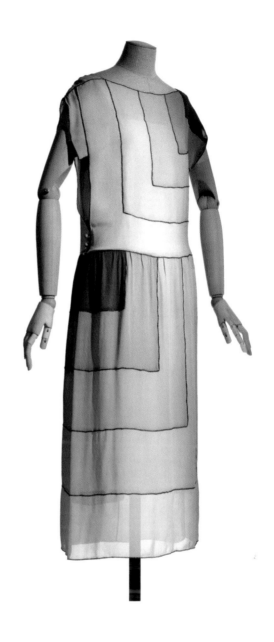

8.4 Madeleine Vionnet's dress from 1922 is an example of informal balance.
BARBARA WOOLWORTH MILLER, MUSEE DE LA MODE ET DU TEXTILE, COLLECTION U.A.F.C.

concept. The first is an evening gown from 1985 with a gold-trimmed black velvet bodice and a cream satin full skirt (FIGURE 8.5A). Bearing in mind that black, the darkest value, has more visual weight than lighter ones, the bodice makes up a significantly smaller part of the gown. As a result, the long, full cream skirt is required to balance the black bodice. In the second case, consider the evening separates that Givenchy designed in 1952 (FIGURE 8.5B). This time the skirt is black and the blouse white. The skirt is full-length, but slim, tapered, and body skimming. The white blouse provides adequate balance; although it is shorter in length, the portrait collar and full sleeves add the width that is visually necessary. In Givenchy's prolific career, he was a master at creating balance in his simple, elegant designs (BOX 8.1).

RIGHT

8.5A The long cream skirt on Givenchy's evening dress from 1985 balances the black bodice because it has a dark value.

ILLUSTRATION BY JANICE GREENBERG ELLINWOOD

BELOW

8.5B The center figure wears Givenchy's slim black evening skirt, which is balanced by the width of the white blouse with portrait collar and full sleeves.

NAT FARBMAN/TIME LIFE PICTURES/GETTY IMAGES

SYMMETRY AND ASYMMETRY

Symmetry indicates a strict adherence to the elements on either side o. median line, such as shape, size, line, value, texture, color, and arrangeme For example, the Pantheon exhibits obvious symmetry. The Walt Disne, Concert Hall in Los Angeles does not.

SYMMETRY

There are many approaches to attaining symmetry. One is the use of repetition, as in the case of the columns of the Pantheon and the pleats in Halston's gown. A second is the creation of a dominant centerpiece that is flanked by smaller parts on either side. Fashion designers use this method masterfully, because the figure is logically the dominant centerpiece. For example, Karl Lagerfeld's couture design for Chanel from fall 2008 features dimensional forms flanking the figure, almost as if he had used the Japanese paper-folding craft of origami (FIGURE 8.6). A third approach is the

(Text continued on page 190.)

8.6 The symmetry in this Chanel couture design by Karl Lagerfeld for fall 2008 is caused by the dimensional forms that flank the skirt.
COURTESY OF WWD/ GIOVANNI GIANNONI

BOX 8.1

UBERT DE GIVENCHY

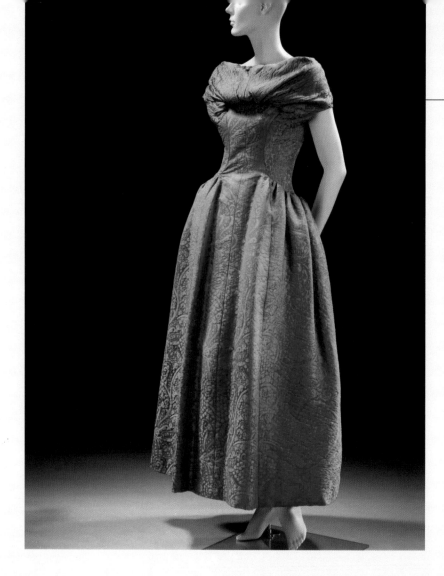

HUBERT DE GIVENCHY was born in Beauvais, France, in 1927. At the age of ten, he visited the fashion pavilion at the International Exhibition in Paris. From that time, he expressed an interest in fashion. After World War II, he studied at the Beaux-Arts School in Paris. He went to work for the designer Jacques Fath (1912–1954) in 1945. Later he worked for Lucien Lelong (1889–1958), where he met Lelong's assistants, Christian Dior and Pierre Balmain (1914–1982). There was also a stint under Elsa Schiaparelli.

Then in 1952, at the age of 25, Givenchy opened his own fashion house. His first collection was notable for evening wear designed as interchangeable separates. He also used inexpensive men's shirting for it, from which his "Bettina" blouse was born, named for a famous model of the day. The high-necked, full blouse with ruffled sleeves became a classic.

Givenchy was recognized for refined, simple styles, elegant fabrics, and bold colors. A silk matelasse brocade evening dress from 1955 was typical (FIGURE BOX 8.1A). The design had architectural symmetry, yet softness, and bridged the opulence of haute couture with youthful styling.

He dressed impressive women of the day, including Jacqueline Kennedy, the Duchess of Windsor, Princess Caroline of Monaco, Greta Garbo, and Audrey Hepburn, who was his muse for most of his career.

He met Audrey Hepburn in 1954, when she had the idea that the costumes in the movie *Sabrina*, in which she starred, should include authentic haute couture and she obtained director Billy Wilder's agreement. Givenchy was busy preparing a collection and was expecting his visitor to be the actress Katharine Hepburn! As a result, he directed

Audrey to choose designs from his new collection. In *Sabrina* she wore an exquisite white organdy gown embroidered with black and white flowers (FIGURE BOX 8.1B). It became the envied fashion of the day. The design used shape and pattern to define its symmetry. The only award *Sabrina* achieved was for costumes, which went to the assigned costume designer Edith Head, even though many designs were Givenchy's. Audrey Hepburn apologized profusely for the error and never allowed the mistake to happen again. His designs also appeared in *Love in the Afternoon* (1957), *Funny Face* (1957), *Breakfast at Tiffany's* (1961), and *Charade* (1963). Audrey Hepburn had the privilege of wearing Givenchy's designs in her private life as well, including the memorable gown from *Sabrina*. The design also influenced the work of future designers, such as Keren Craig and Georgina Chapman, the designers for Marchesa. Their spring 2009 evening wear design transformed the fabric and pattern into a memorable asymmetrical version (FIGURE BOX 8.1C).

In addition to his work for Hepburn, Givenchy designed the cream silk gown with embroidered bodice that First Lady Jacqueline Kennedy wore on her first state visit to France in 1961. Ironically, there was another Givenchy dress in which Mrs. Kennedy was highly photographed. It was the one she wore to her husband's funeral in 1963.

Since his interest in fashion began, Givenchy valued the work of Cristóbal Balenciaga. They had an opportunity to meet in 1953, which evolved into a long-term friendship. Givenchy eventually moved his design house across the street from Balenciaga's in 1959.

They communicated regularly, even critiquing each other's sketches and collections. Givenchy's appreciation for Balenciaga's talent is easy to recognize in his architectural black evening dress from 1980 (FIGURE BOX 8.1D). The bodice and full sleeves balance the sumptuous full skirt. The romantic design coincided with Princess Diana's marriage to Prince Charles. Her wedding gown, designed by David and Elizabeth Emmanuel (1952–, 1953–, respectively), featured similar sleeves and skirt.

Givenchy's simple and often symmetrical designs were a favorite of ready-to-wear manufacturers who sought to interpret them. He understood that women sought less fussy, easy-to-wear clothes, although he never sacrificed his trademark elegance. He designed his last couture collection in July 1995, when his house was purchased by LVMH.

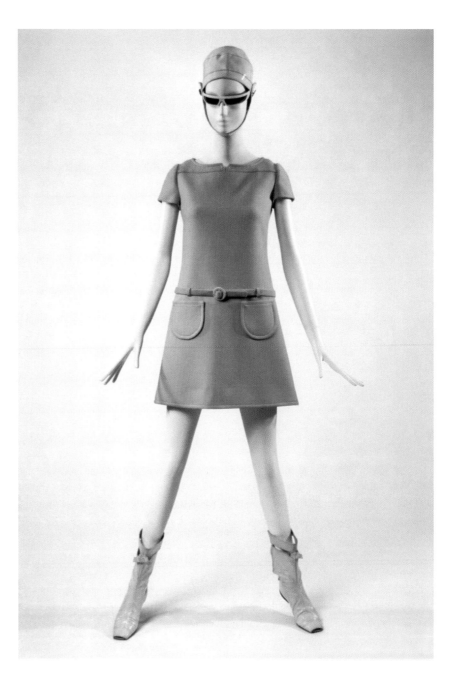

8.7 The symmetry in André Courrèges' design from 1968 is caused by mirroring the details of one side on to the other.
© THE MUSEUM AT FIT

(Text continued from page 185.)

creation of a mirror image on the other side of the median line. The A-line shift dress designed by André Courrèges (1923–) in 1968 is an example of that (FIGURE 8.7). The design is less formal than Halston's gown because of the diagonal edges of the silhouette and the curved pockets.

APPROXIMATE SYMMETRY

The main detriment to the use of symmetry is the possibility of boredom. All elements in the design are expected, since they are the same on either side of the centerline. When there is a desire for formal balance, yet the need for a small difference in order to make the design more dynamic, artists are said to employ approximate symmetry. The same distribution of elements occurs on both sides of the design, in order to assure its balance, with a slight change. Hussein Chalayan's (1970–) "Airplane" dress for spring–summer 2000 is an appropriate example (FIGURE 8.8). It was innovative in its materials of Fiberglas and resin cast in a mold. Its flaps are mechanically operable and open to reveal pink tulle. At first glance, the design appears symmetrical, and it certainly has flanks that set off a centerpiece, the A-line silhouette. A close examination of its arrangement of seams and the small flap on one side of the bodice underscores that its symmetry is only approximate. Stephen Burrows' (1943–) calf-length A-line dress from 1970 is a distinctive example in that color is the element that makes the symmetry approximate (FIGURE 8.9). On either side of the front zipper, which is positioned like a centerline, the shapes, lines, and arrangement appear exactly the same. A close examination reveals that one pocket is red and the other pink and that the stripes at the ends of the sleeves vary in number and in colors.

8.8 Hussein Chalayan's "Airplane" dress is an example of approximate symmetry.
© THE METROPOLITAN MUSEUM OF ART/ART RESOURCE, NY

8.9 The use of color is an important reason why Stephen Burrows' A-length dress has approximate symmetry.
© THE MUSEUM AT FIT

ASYMMETRY

Asymmetry is the true antidote to the boredom of symmetry. Asymmet[ric] balance is also called **occult balance**. Asymmetrical designs are different [on] either side of the median but still convey the feeling of equally distributed weight due to the decisions regarding shape, line, color, value, pattern, size, arrangement, or construction. Hence, the differences or contrasts in the design are controlled in order to achieve that goal. The result offers the potential for real surprise, but at the very least, a design that is more lively, dramatic, casual, complex, or flamboyant. Another design by Karl Lagerfeld for Chanel is a wonderful example (FIGURE 8.10). It has already been established that the classic designs associated with Coco Chanel, like the Chanel suit, exhibit symmetry, so his design from spring–summer 2000 presents the unexpected. The cut of the jacket, the row of buttons, and the collar all create asymmetry in what would otherwise be a traditional evening suit.

8.10 This evening suit by Karl Lagerfeld for Chanel (spring–summer 2000) features an asymmetrical jacket.
COURTESY OF WWD

Asymmetry sometimes constitutes a fashion trend. At those times, it is exemplified in hemlines, dresses, skirts, blouses, jackets, sweaters, and even eyeglasses and automobiles. A garment may have a sleeve on one side, for example, but not on the other. However, there are other concerns about asymmetry besides aesthetic decision making. When one side of a garment is different from the other, the process of mass production may become more costly.

The student of fashion design must have keen observational skills. It is necessary to detect symmetry, approximate symmetry, and asymmetry before using them in original designs. Those observational skills must transfer to the process of making patterns as well. As one might expect, a pattern for one side of a garment will differ from the other if the design is asymmetrical.

OTHER TYPES OF BALANCE

Radial balance is a system of arrangement that occurs around a central point. When implemented, the eye rotates circularly in the direction of radials, until a distribution of weight is sensed throughout the design. Radial balance may occur symmetrically or asymmetrically. Christian Dior's "Eventail" cocktail dress of the 1950s implements symmetrical radiation from a piece of fan-pleated fabric at the midriff (FIGURE 8.11). The

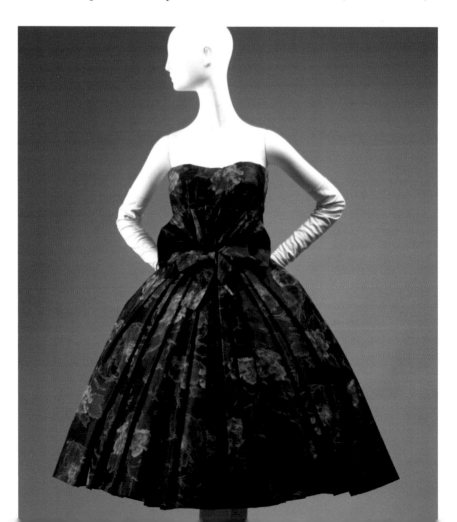

8.11 The pleating of the fan at the midriff and the skirt causes this cocktail dress by Christian Dior to have radial balance.
© THE METROPOLITAN MUSEUM OF ART/ART RESOURCE, NY

8.12 The radial balance caused by
the draping in this evening dress
by Alix Grès is asymmetrical.

GEORGE HOYNINGEN-HUENÉ © 1933
CONDÉ NAST PUBLICATIONS

radials continue into the full skirt via similar pleating. By comparison, the radial balance is asymmetrical from the waistline, following folds of fabric in the cleverly draped "Grecian" evening dress from 1938 by Alix Grès (FIG-URE 8.12). In these cases, radial balance occurs through pleats and folds, but a designer might also use seams, appliqué, embroidery, surface pattern, or other methods.

Balance of all-over pattern is another vehicle for the distribution of visual weight. The existence of a regularly spaced pattern is an arrangement that leads the eye throughout the design and is especially effective within a simple silhouette. Givenchy's 1963 evening gown of cotton lace re-embroidered with coral-colored beads and coral pieces is an excellent example due to its minimalist silhouette (FIGURE 8.13). It is a tribute to the designer's ability to balance extravagance with a minimalist design.

Balance is considered a bit differently in relation to three-dimensional form, as in the way fashion relates to the human figure. The distribution of weight is not only considered from top to bottom but with the dimension of depth from multiple views. As the garment envelopes the body, a design allows for symmetrical balance, asymmetrical balance, or radial balance. Symmetrical and radial are more formal than asymmetrical balance. Symmetrical balance implies equal distribution of weight around the figure from all views. Radial balance is spherical with the distribution of weight originating at the center.

However, asymmetrical balance is the most common because it gives fashion designers the greatest latitude for artistic expression. Take, for instance, Rei Kawakubo's 1997 gingham dress discussed in Chapter 3, in which the addition of lumps challenged the feminine ideal. Examine it

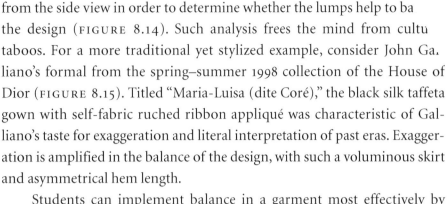

from the side view in order to determine whether the lumps help to ba the design (FIGURE 8.14). Such analysis frees the mind from cultu taboos. For a more traditional yet stylized example, consider John Ga. liano's formal from the spring–summer 1998 collection of the House of Dior (FIGURE 8.15). Titled "Maria-Luisa (dite Coré)," the black silk taffeta gown with self-fabric ruched ribbon appliqué was characteristic of Galliano's taste for exaggeration and literal interpretation of past eras. Exaggeration is amplified in the balance of the design, with such a voluminous skirt and asymmetrical hem length.

Students can implement balance in a garment most effectively by using a mannequin, a half-scale mannequin, or a doll in the design process. In Chapter 1 we learned that Madeleine Vionnet utilized a wooden mannequin on a swiveling stool in order to determine her designs. This is not an old-fashioned method. Jason Wu (1982–), the Taiwan-born designer of First Lady Michelle Obama's inaugural gown, expressed his design ideas by using dolls as mannequins at the age of nine (Wilson, 2009, ST1). Ironically, he started his label with savings from the job of freelance designer, and then creative director, for a line of designer dolls called Fashion Royalty that is manufactured by Integrity Toys. Today his evening dresses are sold at top New York City stores such as Bergdorf Goodman. The examples of Kawakubo's and Galliano's designs, as well as Vionnet's and Wu's methods, illustrate the creativity designers invest in their work, while staying mindful of the principle of balance.

approximate symmetry	gravity	symmetry
asymmetry	horizontal balance	vertical balance
balance	informal balance	visual weight
balance of all-over pattern	occult balance	
formal balance	radial balance	

PROJECTS

1. Find a photograph of a symmetrical fashion design that is visually stimulating. Using colored pencils or colored markers and your sketchbook, create four asymmetrical versions of that design. Which of the four is the strongest? Why?

2. Try the opposite challenge. Find a photograph of an asymmetrical fashion design that is visually stimulating. Using colored pencils or colored markers and your sketchbook, create four symmetrical versions of the design. Which of the four is the strongest? Why?

3. Using a half-scale mannequin form, choose materials such as fiberfill and cut cardboard shapes to "build out" volume and drape fabric on top. Tie ribbon, lacing, or cording around sections of your "experimental" garment in order to finish the design and hold the support materials in place. Do the voluminous sections balance each other from varying points of view?

REFERENCES

All about Givenchy. (2009). *eSSORTMENT.* Retrieved June 27, 2009, from http://www.essortment.com/lifestyle/givench_smkb.htm.

Asymmetrical design: Boom in clothes that are not symmetrical. (2005, January 12). *Trends in Japan, Fashion.* Retrieved on June 30, 2009, from http://web-japan.org/trends/fashion/fas050112.html.

Chambers, B. G. (1951). *Color and design: Fashion in men's and women's clothing and home furnishings.* Englewood Cliffs, NJ: Prentice Hall.

Cunningham, R. (1994). *The magic garment: Principles of costume design.* Long Grove, IL: Waveland Press.

Davis, M. L. (1996). *Visual design in dress* (3rd ed.). Upper Saddle River, NJ: Prentice Hall.

Hubert de Givenchy. (n.d.). *Fashion Encyclopedia.* Retrieved June 27, 2009, from http://www.fashionencyclopedia.com/Fr-Gu/Givenchy-Hubert-de.html.

Hubert de Givenchy and Audrey Hepburn. (n.d.) *Famous Women and Beauty.* Retrieved July 2, 2009, from http://www.famous-women-an beauty.com/hubert-de-givenchy.html.

Kirke, B. (1998). *Madeleine Vionnet.* San Francisco: Chronicle Books.

Krenz, C. (2000). *Audrey: A life in pictures.* New York: Metro Books.

Martin, R., & Koda, H. (1996). *Christian Dior.* New York: The Metropolitan Museum of Art.

Mears, P. (2007). *Madame Grès: Sphinx of fashion.* New York: Fashion Institute of Technology.

Ocvirk, O. G., Stinson, R. E., Wigg, P. R., Bone, R. O., & Cayton, D. L. (2002). *Art fundamentals: Theory and practice* (9th ed.). New York: McGraw-Hill.

Steele, V. (2006). *Fifty years of fashion: New Look to now.* New Haven, CT: Yale University Press.

Stewart, M. (2008). *Launching the imagination: A comprehensive guide to basic design* (3rd ed.). New York: McGraw-Hill.

Wilson, E. (2009, January 23).The spotlight finds Jason Wu. *New York Times.* Retrieved September 24, 2009, from www.nytimes.com/2009/01/25/fashion/25WU.html.

| # EMPHASIS

THE FASHION DESIGNER'S talent is the ability to direct the viewer's eye to the garment and then guide it throughout the entire design, so that it is fully regarded and, ultimately, appreciated. This is why the principles of design are so important. Their use enhances the designer's effectiveness at attracting the eye. The location where the eye first settles on the garment is called **emphasis**. The practiced designer knows a host of approaches to place and create it. As a result, the focus on this chapter is on one designer—Elsa Schiaparelli—in order to demonstrate that expertise.

This chapter more fully defines emphasis and underscores its importance in relation to the human figure. In this chapter, we look at the designer's considerations when choosing its location and how that has been influenced during historic periods. Finally, we consider ways in which the elements of design may enhance the implementation of emphasis.

EMPHASIS DEFINED

Emphasis is what the designer wants the viewer to see. It is the center of attraction or the area of greatest visual importance. It is the point of initial eye contact on the design. Therefore, it is also referred to as the **focal point** or the **point of emphasis**. It is specifically selected and visually stressed. With emphasis, all areas in the rest of the design are subordinate or supportive. As a result, when the eye scans the arrangement, it is able to rank the various parts of the design in their importance.

Do all garments have a point of emphasis? Most do, but there are some exceptions. Without it, the danger is a sense of disorganization. The implementation of emphasis offers a reliable road to an aesthetically pleasing design. One exception, however, is the simultaneous dress designed by Sonia Terk Delaunay (FIGURE 6.13B). Both she and her husband, the painter Robert Delaunay, explored the theory of simultaneous contrast in their exploration of color. Robert preferred the term "simultaneity" to define this philosophy. In Sonia's dress design, the contrasts of shape and color occur concurrently, attracting the eye simultaneously to different locations. This results not in one area of emphasis, but in a sense of vibration or movement called rhythm, a topic further discussed in Chapter 10, "Rhythm."

EMPHASIS AND THE FIGURE

When emphasis attracts attention to a location on the garment, it cannot help but attract it to that area of the human figure. This gives it even greater meaning. Designers are sometimes innovative or experimental about the choice of location. More often, they draw attention to a physically attractive portion of the body. In so doing, they diminish physical attributes that may be considered unattractive. Clothes should make the wearer more attractive, and so designers seek to flatter the wearer.

Emphasis may also have social considerations. **James Laver** (1899–1975), the late curator of the Victoria and Albert Museum, developed theories about fashion from a desire to date images accurately through the clothing depicted in them. He was a proponent of three theories: the **Utility Principle**—that people dress for concerns such as warmth and comfort; the **Hierarchical Principle**—that people dress to indicate position in society; and the **Seduction Principle**—that people dress to attract others. Today some fashion historians feel that these oversimplify the reasons for fashion change, but in discussing emphasis, attention must focus on the third one. Also referred to as the **sex appeal theory**, it has gained additional notice as the **theory of the shifting erogenous zone**. In other words, the

9.1 Cleavage is an erotic zone of eighteenth century apparel as pictured in the portrait of Marquise de Pompadour (1756) by Francois Boucher.
BILDARCHIV PREUSSICHER KULTURBESITZ/ART RESOURCE, NY

9.2 The dress exposes the shoulders in this portrait of Empress Eugenie (1855) by Franz Xaver Winterhalter.
REUNION DES MUSEES NATIONAUX/ART RESOURCE, NY

human body can be so desirable that one cannot take it all in at once but must concentrate on one part at a time. These are the erotic "zones" or sexually secondary characteristics, such as the breasts, hips, derriere, or even the legs, feet, back, shoulders, or waist. The challenge, then, is that, as interest in one of these parts fluctuates, the fashion industry must anticipate and place the focus elsewhere on apparel. An examination of historic periods highlights the part of the body of special focus during that period. That is evident either by selective exposure, concealment, or visual emphasis. For instance, in the portrait of the Marquise de Pompadour in 1756 by Francois Boucher (1703–1770), the elaborate costume, with the emphasis on the ribbons of her bodice, nevertheless reveals her cleavage (FIGURE 9.1). The portrait of the Empress Eugenie of 1855 by Franz Xaver Winterhalter (1805–1873) exposes her shoulders (FIGURE 9.2). The detailed costume painter

James Jacques Joseph Tissot (1836–1902) portrayed both the concealment and the added volume of the bustle to convey emphasis on the derriere in *Too Early*, painted in 1873 (FIGURE 9.3).

The astute fashion designer is able to create a garment that features any part of the body or garment. The location is the result of aesthetic decision making, but it also depends on social concerns, such as prevailing trends as well as the needs of the client. To illustrate the concept of emphasis, this chapter focuses on the work of one legendary designer whose work illustrates the range of decisions a designer can make regarding emphasis— Elsa Schiaparelli (BOX 9.1).

THE FACE

The face is a significant part of the body, because it establishes identity and contributes to the ideal of beauty. Women commonly use cosmetics to perfect facial features. Looking into others' eyes is a means of making a connection with them. As a result, designers often place emphasis in a location that directs attention to the face, such as collars and necklines. Schiaparelli's hand-knitted "jumper" from 1927 is a great example (FIGURE BOX 9.1A). A

9.3 The nineteenth-century bustle places emphasis on the derriere as depicted in this 1873 genre painting, *Too Early*, by James Jacques Joseph Tissot.
HIP/ART RESOURCE, NY

geometric bow of contrasting value is knitted into the design at the n
causing a trompe l'oeil (discussed in Chapter 4) effect that draws attenti
to the face. Schiaparelli herself wore this design to a luncheon and receive
numerous orders for it. It also inspired other designers, including Yves
Saint Laurent, who placed a bow at the neck on an evening suit by use of an
appliqué.

IMPLEMENTING EMPHASIS

There are several approaches to implementing emphasis on a design. Examples of these include isolation, isolation through anomaly, contrast, placement, repetition, and radiation.

ISOLATION

One approach is called emphasis by **isolation**. A shape that stands by itself, for instance, is bound to attract attention. Add to that the premise of **anomaly** and the capacity to draw attention is even greater. Anomaly means a deviation from the norm. Someone who visits the seashore on a summer day in a fur-trimmed coat is an anomaly. In relation to fashion, it is interesting to further explore Schiaparelli's designs. Her coat from 1937 is an example of both emphasis by isolation and anomaly (FIGURE BOX 9.1G). Emphasis is employed via the applied pink roses located on the upper back. Value, shape, and texture are the elements that draw the eye to the area. Note the interesting placement for a focal point; locating the decoration on the front of the coat is far more expected. There are a myriad of ways to utilize design elements to cause emphasis by isolation. Isolating one motif separately from an all-over pattern is one method. A particular construction detail—ruching, pleating, smocking—used in one area against a plane of flat fabric is another.

CONTRAST

Contrast is also an approach to implement emphasis. The eye easily perceives two types of arrangement—similarities and differences. Contrast is when two forces operate in opposition, causing a significant difference. In fashion design, these forces may involve any of the design elements—value, shape, line, texture, color, space, or pattern—as well as scale, which is the comparison of an exaggerated proportion to human proportion, and which will be discussed in Chapter 11, "Proportion." The focal point on Schiaparelli's dinner jacket from 1940 is at the bottom (or hip area), thanks to the contrast in value and pattern of the gold embroidery against the black fabric (FIGURE 9.4). On her dinner dress from 1934, she contrasts the

(Text continued on page 210.)

BOX 9.1

ELSA
IAPARELLI

BY COMPARISON TO her contemporaries, most notably Coco Chanel, Elsa Schiaparelli thought of dressmaking not as a profession but as an art.

Schiaparelli was born in Rome in 1890, where her father worked as a scholar of Oriental literature and languages and headed a library. As a child, she dressed up in bustled dresses and studied illustrated books and illuminated manuscripts in her father's library. That was her first opportunity to appreciate bright pink, the color that later became her signature (see Chapter 7). As a young woman, she published some poetry and articles on music. Then she married and moved to the United States, where she became friends with artists such as photographers Edward Steichen and Man Ray and the painter Marcel Duchamp. When her husband left her in 1920, she moved with her daughter to Paris, another community rich with artists and writers.

Through a friend she met Paul Poiret, and he took her under his wing, inviting her to his parties, supplying her with coats and gowns, and introducing her to the world of haute couture. She began working as a freelance designer and spent about a year in the employment of another designer, before she was ready to strike out on her own.

In 1927 Elsa launched a collection under her own name with knitted sweaters of novel designs. The triumph of her first collection was a black and white pullover sweater with a trompe l'oeil bowknot (FIGURE BOX 9.1A). The design was heralded both by *Vogue* and in the United States. An Armenian woman knitted the sweater for her, using an unusual stitch that was quite durable. Two colors were blended into one yarn, producing a tweedlike effect.

By 1928 she moved her business to a new location and expanded her collection of coats, skirts, and sweaters to include bathing suits, beach pajamas, and crocheted berets. Sweaters continued as the key item until the early 1930s, when they were replaced with distinctively designed blouses.

Schiaparelli experimented with new fabrics and notions, and they became her hallmarks. She used a rubberized silk and wool mixture for a raincoat and black vinyl trim for an aviator's costume. She featured zippers not only as front closures but also on shoulder seams, side seams, sleeves, and pockets. She designed a divided skirt, which was considered quite controversial at the time, as well as a separate top held in place with a tab between the legs, a forerunner of the bodysuit.

RIGHT
FIGURE BOX 9.1A The black-and-white pullover sweater with trompe l'oeil bowknot was the hit of Elsa Schiaparelli's first collection. The white bow draws the eye to the face.
© V&A IMAGES, VICTORIA AND ALBERT MUSEUM

OPPOSITE
FIGURE BOX 9.1B Salvador Dali uses the theme of the "chest of drawers" in *La Giraffe enflammee* from 1935.
BRIDGEMAN-GIRAUDON/ ART RESOURCE, NY

By 1932, after adding evening dresses, Schiaparelli expanded her design space. Most of her clothing featured contrasts, such as black and white, dull and shiny surfaces, thick and thin fabrics, and unusual contrasting colors. Her architectural, neat lines, with angles replacing feminine curves, drew the eye to the shoulders. She was primarily associated with that silhouette. The variety of approaches she used to emphasize the shoulders was remarkable. She used padding, fur "macaroons," circular fagot-stitched bands, and "shoulder trays," which were fluted bands of fabric mounted from shoulder to elbow.

By 1933 she added a London branch to her business and moved to a larger Paris location in 1935. To celebrate her success, Elsa designed cotton and silk fabrics printed with her own press clippings.

Schiaparelli was famous for her collaboration with the Surrealist painter Salvador Dali, and later, with the artist Jean Cocteau. Surrealism, drawing heavily on the theories of Sigmund Freud and the art movement of Dadaism, was a twentieth-century movement of artists and writers who used fantastic images and incongruous juxtapositions in order to express unconscious thoughts and dreams. It was meant as a rejection against the rationalistic thought that had guided European culture and politics and had culminated in World War I. For example, Dali used the theme of a "chest" of drawers in his paintings, and in her 1936–1937 collection, Schiaparelli designed Surrealist suits, in which the pockets were meant to simulate bureau drawers (FIGURE BOX 9.1B AND C). Other designs that came

out of their collaboration included her lobster dress, while Dali designed a telephone with a plastic lobster enveloping the receiver (FIGURE BOX 9.1D AND E). Possibly the most famous product was a black felt hat in the shape of a high-heeled shoe with a shocking pink heel, also available in all black (FIGURE BOX 9.1F). Her collaboration with Jean Cocteau resulted in a mirror image embroidered onto the back of a blue silk evening coat (FIGURE BOX 9.1G). It is a reference to the Surrealistic belief that more than one possible meaning may be attached to the same image. The two faces in profile can also be viewed as a rose-filled vase. There was also Surrealistic influence in her circus collection of 1938, which featured circus-inspired motifs in its embroidery, hats, handbags, fabric prints, and day and evening ensembles.

When the Germans invaded France in 1939, Schiaparelli spent most of her time in the United States. She was the first European designer to receive the prestigious Neiman Marcus Award for Distinguished Service in the Field of Fashion. She reopened her couture house in 1945. Although her designs were received well in the press, they never regained their initial popularity, and she closed the business in 1954. She went on to consult with many businesses and lived in Tunisia and Paris until her death in 1973.

LEFT
FIGURE BOX 9.1C Schiaparelli showed pockets in her suit jacket meant to simulate bureau drawers.
THE PHILADELPHIA MUSEUM OF ART/ART RESOURCE, NY

RIGHT
FIGURE BOX 9.1D Schiaparelli implements emphasis by her placement of the lobster on her famous dress from 1937.
THE PHILADELPHIA MUSEUM OF ART/ART RESOURCE, NY

RIGHT
9.1E The Surrealist telephone with lobster handle was created by Salvador Dali in 1936.
TATE, LONDON/ART RESOURCE, NY

BOTTOM LEFT
9.1F This black felt high-heeled shoe hat was a Schiaparelli design from 1937–1938.
© THE METROPOLITAN MUSEUM OF ART/ART RESOURCE, NY

BOTTOM RIGHT
9.1G The evening coat is a collaboration between Schiaparelli and Jean Cocteau. The pink roses on the back of the shoulders create emphasis, and the embroidered profiles are also perceived as a vase for the roses.
© V&A IMAGES, VICTORIA AND ALBERT MUSEUM

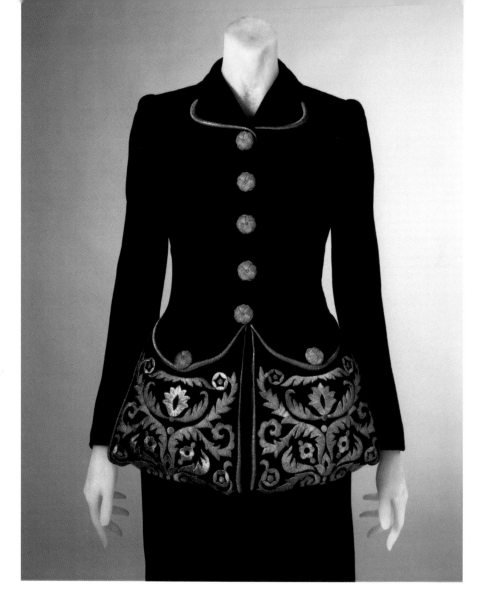

9.4 The focal point on Schiaparelli's dinner jacket of 1940 is created by the gilded metallic thread embroidery embellishing the bottom section that covers the hips.
THE PHILADELPHIA MUSEUM OF ART/ART RESOURCE, NY

(Text continued from page 205.)

space behind the cutout shapes against the silhouette (FIGURE 9.5). The texture of the seal collar juxtaposed with the flat wool fabric creates emphasis on her jacket from 1931–1932 (FIGURE 9.6).

There are many other ways to create emphasis through contrast. Designers can choose to use any assertive or unusual shape; sharp, bold lines; shiny, reflective surfaces; warm colors or bright intensities. The juxtaposition of these bold statements with their opposites is certain to attract the eye.

PLACEMENT

Placement is another method to establish emphasis. Every part of the design has the potential to distinguish it. The designer knows that placement alone can increase the importance of a selected shape. Schiaparelli used this technique in a unique manner with the placement of her lobster motif on the front of the skirt of her famous dress (FIGURE BOX 9.1D). In art, placement is reinforced by the power of **centricity** and **eccentricity**.

RIGHT
9.5 The cutouts on Schiaparelli's dinner dress (1934) attract the eye.
© THE METROPOLITAN MUSEUM OF ART/ART RESOURCE, NY

BELOW
9.6 The seal collar on Schiaparelli's jacket from 1931–1932 creates emphasis because it juxtaposes the texture of the fur against flat fabric.
THE PHILADELPHIA MUSEUM OF ART/ART RESOURCE, NY

Centricity theorizes that there is a compositional center that, when emphasized, causes compressive compositional force, leading the eye further into the design. Often the artist utilizes **optical center**, which is a bit higher than the actual center. Translating the theory for fashion, the designer must consider how optical center corresponds to the figure. For a traditional bell-shaped gown, it might hit at the center-front waist. However, a different silhouette warrants more consideration. Eccentricity refers to the effect if emphasis is located closer to the outside edge(s) of the composition, causing expansive compositional force. That pushes the visual energy to the outside of the composition.

REPETITION

Repetition may also express emphasis. The idea is that something important is worth repeating. The repetition of line creates emphasis on the bustle-

9.7 Repetition of line creates emphasis on this bustle-backed evening dress from 1939 by Elsa Schiaparelli.
THE PHILADELPHIA MUSEUM OF ART/ART RESOURCE, NY

backed evening gown designed by Elsa Schiaparelli in 1939 (FIGURE 9./ addition to line, repetition of shape or color may also signal emphasis.

RADIATION

Radiation, or the use of a sun-like or wheel-shaped form, may establish emphasis by drawing the eye to its center. Schiaparelli used this technique in her cape from 1938 called "Apollo of Versailles" (FIGURE 9.8). The design is embroidered in gold on black velvet and was inspired by the Neptune Fountain in Paris at the Parc de Versailles. A similar vehicle for creating emphasis is called **concentricity**. It means that a circular shape also draws the eye to the center. In addition to embroidery, circular shapes may result from other techniques such as seams, hand painting, quilting, and appliqué.

9.8 The radiation on the embroidered motif of the "Apollo of Versailles" cape (1938) by Elsa Schiaparelli creates emphasis.
© THE METROPOLITAN MUSEUM OF ART/ART RESOURCE, NY

STRUCTURAL DETAILS

Of course, all of the vehicles for implementing emphasis may result from structural efforts, such as the edges of pattern parts, the clever manipulation of draped folds, unusual closures, or the particular placement of seams. In Schiaparelli's gown from 1938, the folds at center front catch the eye even before it surveys the fabric's bold stripes (FIGURE 9.9). She used **trapunto quilting** techniques in her unorthodox "skeleton" dress, also from 1938 (FIGURES 9.10A AND B). Its black silk crepe is so constricted that it forms a second skin, upon which Schiaparelli suggested enormous "bones" by stitching their outline through two layers of fabric and then inserting cotton wadding to cause their relief from the surface. The repetition of the "ribs" on the front of the garment attract the eye, while the elongated "spine" performs the same function on the back. Applied trims and the use of jewels may also define emphasis. An opulent dinner jacket by Schiaparelli from 1935 is a superlative example (FIGURE 9.11). The placement of

9.9 The folds at center front on this 1938 evening gown by Elsa Schiaparelli attracts the eye even before its bold stripes.
COURTESY OF WWD

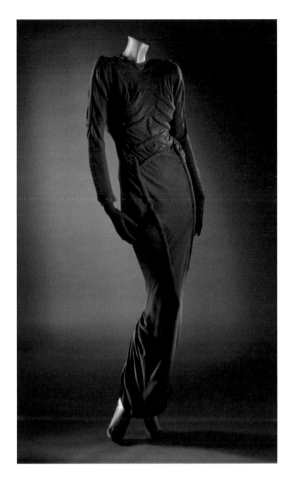

ABOVE

9.10A AND B Trapunto quilting suggests the bone structure on Schiaparelli's "Skeleton Dress" from 1938, causing the repetition of the ribs to attract the eye on the front and the spine to do the same on the back.

© V&A IMAGES, VICTORIA AND ALBERT MUSEUM

RIGHT

9.11 The embellishment of mirrors set into gold embroidered frames brings emphasis to the breasts on this dinner jacket (1935) by Elsa Schiaparelli.

© THE METROPOLITAN MUSEUM OF ART/ART RESOURCE, NY

small rectangular mirrors set into gold embroidered frames called attention to the breasts. The elaborate design recalled the mirror-paneled doors and decorations at the *Salon de la Guerre* and the *Salon de la Paix* (Salons of War and Peace) on either side of the *Galerie des Glaces* (Hall of Mirrors) at the Palace of Versailles.

Emphasis is powerful; premeditation and careful handling are demanded. So is the necessity to make all other features of the fashion subordinate. According to Mary Stewart in *Launching the Imagination: A Comprehensive Guide to Basic Design,* the balance that occurs when emphasis occupies 20 percent of the compositional space with 80 percent accounting for the rest is especially effective. However, fashion designers might question the existence of a hard-and-fast rule.

KEY TERMS

anomaly	Hierarchical Principle	repetition
centricity	isolation	Seduction Principle
concentricity	James Laver	sex appeal theory
contrast	optical center	theory of the shifting
eccentricity	placement	erogenous zone
emphasis	point of emphasis	trapunto quilting
focal point	radiation	Utility Principle

PROJECTS

1. Locate six photographs of garments from magazines, catalogues, or other sources. Circle the point of emphasis for each garment with marker. Identify and discuss with the class the approach the designer used for developing emphasis.

2. Create a collage on Bristol board using solid and printed papers of up to three hues. Use white glue applied with a brush or a glue stick for the adhesive. By cutting, ripping, folding, and positioning paper shapes, feature a focal point on the collage without allowing any other area to compete for equal attention. Critique the collage with the rest of the class in order to determine your success with the task.

3. Trace the back or front of a fashion figure dressed in leotards or swimsuit or "borrow" a croquis figure used by designers to make flat technical sketches. Use it as the base for a collage meant to simulate a garment. Choose a focal

point, staying mindful of the part of the body it will feature. Choose solid printed papers of up to three hues and white glue and brush or glue stick ı the adhesive. By cutting, ripping, folding, and positioning paper shapes, feature the focal point without allowing any other part of the design to compete for visual attention. Do this process twice, featuring a different part of the body each time. Which of the two products is the more successful? Why? What approach did you use to implement emphasis on your design?

REFERENCES

Blum, D. E. (2003). *Shocking! The art and fashion of Elsa Schiaparelli.* Philadelphia: Philadelphia Museum of Art.

Brainard, S. (1998). *A design manual* (2nd ed.) Upper Saddle River, NJ: Prentice Hall.

Cunningham, R. (1994). *The magic garment: Principles of costume design.* Long Grove, IL: Waveland Press.

Davis, M. L. (1996). *Visual design in dress* (3rd ed). Upper Saddle River, NJ: Prentice Hall.

Laver, J. (1959, January 1). Fashion: A detective story. Retrieved July 7, 2009, from http://www.gbacg.org/costume-resources/original/articles/ LaverFashion.pdf.

Steele, V. (1985). *Fashion and eroticism: Ideals of beauty from the Victorian era to the Jazz Age.* New York: Oxford University Press.

Stegemeyer, A. (2004). *Who's who in Fashion* (4th ed.). New York: Fairchild Books.

Stewart, M. (2008). *Launching the imagination: A comprehensive guide to basic design* (3rd ed.). New York: McGraw-Hill.

Stoops, J., & Samuelson, J. (1983). *Design dialogue.* Worcester, MA: Davis Publications.

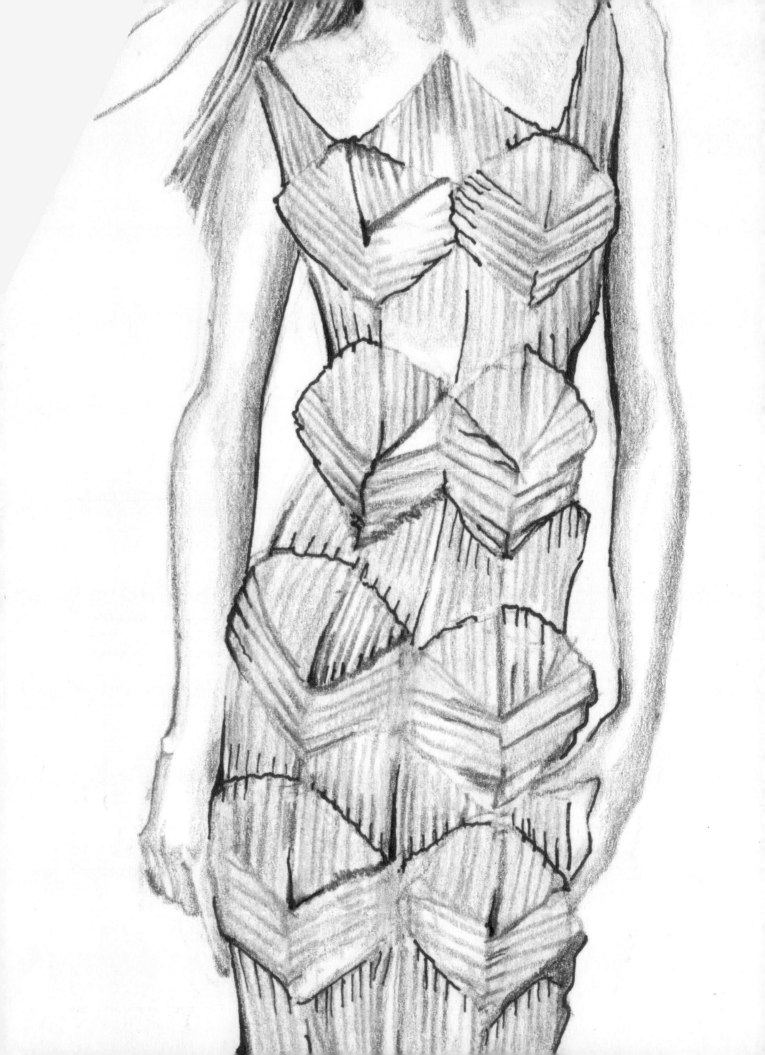

CHAPTER 10

RHYTHM

To define rhythm by using examples of art and fashion

To show how design elements may be organized to portray rhythm

To illustrate the structural methods designers use to implement rhythm in fashion

THE PREVIOUS CHAPTER conveyed the importance of emphasis, the initial point of eye contact, to the design. How do fashion designers ensure that the viewer will see the rest of the garment after that?

Like all other artists and designers, they employ **rhythm**, a term that may sound humorous at first because it is more commonly associated with music. When a musical rhythm is heard, what happens? People begin to tap their feet, snap their fingers, or clap their hands. Musical rhythm stimulates **movement**. In fact, that is what happens with design too.

When the fashion designer implements rhythm, it moves the eye from the point of contact throughout the rest of the design. So it is the movement of the eye that is of primary concern. Some contemporary theorists use the term "movement" in its place, but rhythm is the original one used by the artists of the Bauhaus. Rhythm has also been defined as a recurrence of movement.

This chapter reviews the elements of design and their relationship to rhythm. It enumerates the structural parts of the garment and how they relate to rhythm. Then it covers many devices that fashion designers use to implement rhythm in their garments.

VISUAL PATHWAYS

What kind of movements does the eye make when surveying a design? Are they quick and abrupt or smooth and flowing? Is the process brief or does it take some time? Is it an enjoyable opportunity or is it taxing? The answer lies in the contemplation of art.

Consider the Japanese woodblock print called *The Great Wave of Kanagawa* (1830–1832) by Katsushika Hokusai (FIGURE 10.1). The eye rests at first on the top of the wave in the upper-left-hand side of the piece, and then it follows the swirling waters. It veritably rides downward slowly and then crests—definitely an enjoyable experience. Conversely, study *Squares Arranged According to the Laws of Chance* (1917) by Jean Arp (FIGURE 10.2). The eye jumps from one rectangle to another in short, staccato movements. So there is a variety in the process of viewing a design, from smooth, calm

OPPOSITE
ILLUSTRATION BY
JANICE GREENBERG ELLINWOOD

10.1 The rhythm reflects the feeling of the waves in *The Great Wave of Kanagawa* (1830–1832) by Katsushika Hokusai.
© THE METROPOLITAN MUSEUM OF ART/ART RESOURCE, NY

10.2 The eye moves in short, staccato steps in *Squares Arranged According to the Laws of Chance* (1917) by Jean Arp.
© THE MUSEUM OF MODERN ART/LICENSED BY SCALA/ART RESOURCE, NY

movements to jerky, and from brief to extended.. Some say that a longed development to a climax is preferable, but probably only to an opmum point.

RHYTHM AND THE ELEMENTS OF DESIGN

The most intriguing aspect of rhythm—as well as balance, emphasis, and in fact, all principles of design—is that it results from the creative decisions made by the fashion designer, who is in complete control of what the viewer sees. How does that happen? Like the artist, the designer has the elements of design at his or her immediate disposal, and they may be combined differently every time. These are **line**, **shape**, **form**, **space**, **color**, **value**, **pattern**, and **light**.

Line leads the eye as a consequence of its visual path, its thickness, and its direction—whether straight, curved, zigzag, scallop, or broken. The eye moves speedily along a straight line and undulates according to a curve or a wave. Jagged lines stimulate jerky vibrations, scallops are lilting, and broken lines cause staccato movements. The designer harnesses the counterpart quality when choosing the type of line. Frank Stella used straight, parallel lines that uniformly bend into angles in *Mas o Menos* ("More or Less") (1964) (FIGURE 10.3). The eye takes a quick, slippery ride from one plane to another. Hokusai's *Bullfinch on a Cherry Tree Branch* (1834) features a

10.3 Parallel lines take the eye for a slippery ride in *Mas o Menos* (1965) by Frank Stella.
CNAC/MNAM/DIST. REUNION DES MUSEES NATIONAUX/ART RESOURCE, NY

10.4 The curved line in *Bullfinch on a Cherry Tree Branch* (1834) by Katsushika Hokusai allows the eye to survey the entire format of the picture.
REUNION DES MUSEES NATIONAUX/ART RESOURCE, NY

curvy line that, as the eye travels down it, enables the viewer to survey the entire format of the print (FIGURE 10.4).

Shapes take on the same traits as lines, depending on whether their edges are angular or curved. But eye movement also depends on the placement of shapes, as evident from the rectangles in Arp's painting. Some facilitate easier transitions from one to the next, especially interspersed paisley or teardrop shapes.

The relationship of space to rhythm is subtle. The existence of space between motifs or shapes allows the eye to come to rest. Too much space slows the eye's movement and may result in boredom.

Colors contribute to rhythm when strong intensities catch the eye. They are especially effective when viewed in a spectrum or sequence, as is the case in Frank Stella's *Single Concentric Squares* from 1974 (FIGURE 10.5). The color sequence is mirrored on each side of the square, which leads the eye to the center.

Dark values also attract the eye. When interspersed with mid-light values, the eye jumps among the darker ones. Artists know how arrange them effectively in paintings and drawings.

In an all-over pattern, the viewer's eye moves from motif to motif. It logical for a fashion designer to take advantage of that dynamic with a printed fabric. Henri Matisse created the effect in *Polynesia, the Sky* (1946), using gouache-heightened cutouts mounted on canvas (FIGURE 10.6).

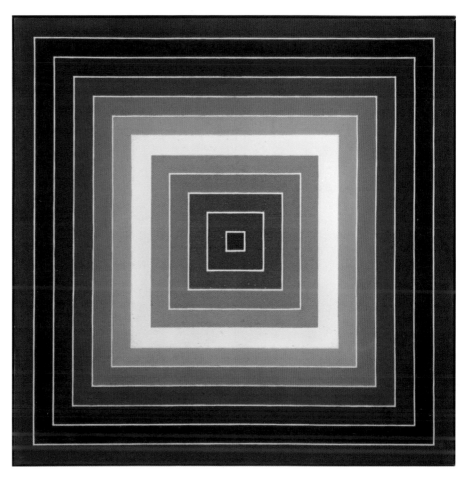

THE STRUCTURAL EXPRESSION OF RHYTHM

Armed with the elements of design, the painter turns next to the medium, whether watercolors, acrylics, or oils, and the fashion designer does the same thing. Instead of paints, the primary medium is fabric, but the elements of construction are also required in order to turn the flat piece of fabric into a garment. The structure of the fabric itself, whether woven or knitted, may exhibit elements of design such as line, shape, color, value, pattern, and of course, **texture**. Treatments to the fabric surface, like printing, also feature them. So fabric type and pattern contribute to the garment's rhythm.

As designers select the components of construction, they consider which will move the viewer's eye throughout the design, such as seams, darts, edges of pattern parts, draped folds, pleats, tucks, gathers, and shirring, as well as tiers, flounces, smocking, and decorative trims. The painter picks a particular paintbrush, paint stroke, or application; the fashion designer chooses techniques such as pleating, draping, seaming, or a combination therein.

KINDS OF RHYTHM

Designers put a variety of methods to work to create rhythm. These include **repetition**, **progression**, **sequencing**, **parallelism**, **alternation**, the **grid**, **broken rhythm**, **transition**, **all-over pattern**, and **radiation**.

REPETITION

Repetition is the repeating of a design element. As a vehicle for emphasis, repetition means that something important is reinforced visually when repeated in a concentrated area. Its purpose in relation to rhythm is to move the eye throughout the entire design. Line is one of the most popular elements chosen for repetition. As discussed in Chapter 2, line may take different forms in a garment. In Claire McCardell's red Asian-inspired dress of 1950, the point of emphasis was the obi sash, and the pleating carried the eye both up to the shoulders and down to the hem (FIGURE 10.7). Norman Norell (1900–1972) placed emphasis on the white bow of his black dress and then drew the eye toward the hem via the implied line of white button closures (FIGURE 10.8). A pattern on the surface of fabric or in the structure of a weave or knit may also feature repetition of line. Madame Grès conveyed line through the draped folds of her 1979 gown, placing emphasis on the concentricity of the cowl neckline and expressing rhythm through those that fall to the hem (FIGURE 10.9, page 226). Grès was such a master of draping that she expertly manipulated rhythm through her cleverly placed folds (BOX 10.1).

Repetition of other elements, such as shape or color, also may create rhythm. Even a construction detail can repeat. One of the wittiest examples is the jacket designed by Viktor & Rolf (Viktor Horsting, Rolf Snoeren; both 1969–) from 2002 in which the collar and bow are repeated five times (FIGURE 10.10, page 227).

PROGRESSION

Progression is another vehicle for the implementation of rhythm. Also called **gradation**, it refers to a sequence of adjacent units that change in steps from one to the next. Christian Dior used this approach more than once, but significantly in his "Junon" ball gown, from fall–winter 1949 (FIGURE 10.11, page 232). Dior used the overlapping feathers of a peacock's tail for his inspiration. The petal-shaped tiers of the skirt increase in size from the layer beneath the waist to the one at the hem. Another example is Madeleine Vionnet's evening dress from 1939 in which the "bow" motif graduates in size from those nearest the waistline to the ones at the hem

Draped folds carry the eye from the cowl to the hem in this evening dress (1979) by Madame Grès.
ILLUSTRATION BY
JANICE GREENBERG ELLINWOOD

(FIGURE 10.12, page 233). The placement of the motifs is also significant. More space occurs around the smaller motifs, which flank the center of the bodice and draw the eye down a line to the brick repeat in the skirt.

SEQUENCING

Sequencing is a similar arrangement, where one unit follows another in a particular order, but in this case, in regular succession, as in Stella's *Single Concentric Squares.* This rhythmic device especially lends itself to the vertical or horizontal repeat of multicolored striping or embroidery.

10.10 Multiple collars and bows lead the eye down the jacket (2002), which is innovatively designed by Viktor & Rolf.
COURTESY OF WWD/ GIOVANNI GIANNONI

PARALLELISM

Parallelism utilizes equidistant units on the same plane, as in the case of Stella's *Mas a Menos*. In that piece, the eye easily follows equidistant lines that continue in the same direction and angle. Parallelism also works with shapes and space. Claire McCardell's later version of her "Popover" dress (1950), in red and purple silk faille, exemplified the advantages of

(*Text continued on page 232.*)

BOX 10.1

ᴀME GRÈS

MADAME GRÈS WAS born Germaine Barton in Paris in 1903. Her wealthy Parisian family schooled her in the arts, but when she desired a career first as a ballerina and then as a sculptor, they discouraged her. Her obvious interest in the figure persisted, and she hoped to express it through work in haute couture. First, she worked as a hatmaker and then apprenticed herself to a couture house named Premet. It was there, where they cultivated geometric patterns embellished with appliqué, beading, and fringe, that she learned her dressmaking skills.

Under the name Alix Barton, she began a small business for selling her dress proto-types to merchants who sold them in Europe and exported them to the United States. Although her draped dresses are considered her greatest contribution to fashion history, Grès' first-known designs were sport clothes, and she made them as late as the 1980s.

She then experimented with day dresses, using a silk jersey that was woven specifically for her. Her approach to draping in the 1920s and 1930s appeared to simulate attire of the classic periods. Despite the variety of art movements that prevailed at the time—Cubism, Expressionism, Fauvism, and Surrealism—historians reason that a renewed classicism blossomed concurrently. Others thought that her designs reflected a love for classical sculpture, but her explanation was different. They were a response simply to the feel of the fabric, which fell into place by itself and required no understructure. One memorable result is pictured in FIGURE 8.12, where the clever, asymmetrical draping appears at odds with the symmetry of ancient Greek attire. The example is a good illustration, however, of Grès' use of drapery for rhythm, where the folds travel from the top of the bustline down to the floor. The design also testified that, by comparison to Madeleine Vionnet's draped designs, Grès' was a tribute to the body and the movement of the cloth.

In 1934, she moved the business to a new location that bore only her first name, Alix. She presented her designs at the *Exposition Universelle* in Paris in 1937, where she won first prize for Haute Couture. Subsequently, she had difficulty with her silent partners, and when she left the business, she lost the copyright to her name. Hence, she adopted the name Grès, an anagram of her husband's name, Serge Czerefkov, by spelling his first name backward.

In 1942 she opened her new business under that name and continued to design dresses with unique draping (FIGURE BOX 10.1A). But under the German occupation, her

business was subsequently closed, either as a result of showing red, white, and blue evening gowns thought to be a nationalistic statement for France or because she was purchasing fabric on the black market. Grès' designs utilized a lot of yardage, and she did not like the imposed wartime restrictions.

After the war, her draping changed. It no longer adhered to a classical interpretation. She began to use fluting or fine crystal pleating, which created an overt rhythm by virtue of the increased repetition. She used a finely woven gauzelike material, which was less dense and weighty than silk jersey. She eventually added an understructure to her dresses. Corsets were prevalent in the work of her peers during the 1950s, and a foundation was required in order to implement the designs that featured the crystal pleating. It effectively moved the eye around the garment and its undulations flattered the human form, like the horizontally pleated bodice in FIGURE BOX 10.1B. Alternatively, she enabled the pleating to define the breasts and rib cage or travel diagonally from one shoulder to the waist and then down to the hem (FIGURE BOX 10.1C AND D).

Madame Grès always draped the fabric herself, originally on wooden mannequins, and later in life, on a live model. She limited the seams in order to better feature the figure. She directed the flow of the folds with her hands and stitched them into place. She cut, pinned, and basted the pattern and then handed the work to her staff. She was known to wear out three pairs of scissors for each collection. One garment might necessitate 300 hours before completion.

She dressed many famous women of the time—Jacqueline Kennedy, the Duchess of Windsor, and actresses such as Grace Kelly, Greta Garbo, and Vivien Leigh. For Madame Grès, clothing was an art in which she valued form and composition over color and ornamentation. She died obscurely in 1993.

10.11 The petal shapes in the skirt of Christian Dior's "Junon" ball gown (1949) progress in size.
© THE METROPOLITAN MUSEUM OF ART/ART RESOURCE, NY

(Text continued from page 227.)

parallelism (FIGURE 10.13, page 234). The eye follows the equidistant stripes as they cross the bustline and continue horizontally down the skirt.

ALTERNATION

Striping is a pattern that features another rhythmic device called alternation. That is the term for a sequence of two units that change back and forth, like the red and purple stripes in McCardell's dress. In addition to color, shapes, patterns, or textures may alternate. Issey Miyake designed an ingenious example of alternation in his dress from 1991 (FIGURE 10.14, page 234). The rounded leaf shapes at the bustline implement emphasis from which the eye is drawn to the hem via alternating shapes in his signature pleated fabric.

10.12 The bows in Madeleine Vionnet's evening dress from 1939 graduate in size, drawing the eye from the bodice to the hem.
© THE METROPOLITAN MUSEUM OF ART/ART RESOURCE, NY

THE GRID

The grid is another arrangement that implements rhythm. The vertical and horizontal lines create a tension that suggests stillness and formality. Those feelings are definitely conveyed in Yves Saint Laurent's "Mondrian" dresses, another version of which is pictured in FIGURE 10.15, page 235. In this one, the main vertical line is placed center front, transporting the eye from neckline to hem, while the horizontal lines enable the viewer to peruse the periphery, which includes both the red and yellow blocks.

BROKEN RHYTHM

Theorists believe that rhythm functions effectively even when it is broken, leading to a device called broken rhythm. That is what happens when a

10.15 In this "Mondrian" dress by Yves Saint Laurent, the grid format implements rhythm.
© REUTERS/CORBIS

pattern is interrupted, as is the case in another of Matisse's works, *Parrot and Siren* (FIGURE 10.16, page 236). The viewer sees an all-over pattern and anticipates its consistency. The interruption actually draws the eye to itself. This is a common approach that is used in graphic design, especially in posters, cover art, and print ads. Christian Dior employed broken rhythm when he chose to taper off the all-over applied pattern of embroidered gold thread, sequins, and pearls on his "Bosphore" evening dress of midnight velvet (FIGURE 10.17, page 236). He was known to implement this practice in other patterned evening dresses.

TRANSITION

Transition is the term used when an element's change is so subtle that it is difficult to notice, but it nevertheless keeps the eye moving along the design. Examples of transition include a "U" neckline with a curve that actually flattens as it crosses the bustline, a black shawl collar that continues into piping along a jacket's edge, or a skirt that hugs the waist and hip, only to fall away from the body at the thigh.

ALL-OVER PATTERN

An all-over pattern is another vehicle to establish rhythm. The eye automatically moves from motif to motif, as it does in the simply structured "Baby Doll" minidress designed by André Courrèges in 1967 (FIGURE 10.18). Its pattern consists of appliquéd pink satin flowers with centers of iridescent paillettes.

RADIATION

Radiation is the final rhythmic device listed in this chapter, and it is a marvelously effective one. In the last chapter, the term was discussed in relation to emphasis. Where there is a wheel-shaped form, emphasis begins at the center. So, in relation to rhythm, the eye moves outward, along the radials, from the center. Construction elements, surface pattern, and seaming all may implement radiation in a garment. Christian Dior's "Eventail" cocktail dress, pictured in FIGURE 8.11, dramatizes the effect. The point of emphasis is the bow at the waist. The pleats in the fan-shaped fabric above the bow carry the eye up into the bodice, and the pleats below the bow direct it throughout the skirt. Through her expert craft of draping, Madame Grès implemented radiation in many of her designs, but notably at the bustline in her black wool jersey day dress from 1942 (FIGURE BOX 10.1A, page 228).

It is clear that the knowledgeable fashion designer orchestrates a design with a sense of balance, a point of emphasis, and a vehicle for rhythm. Imagine how those concerns influence the selection of fabric, color, texture, and construction techniques.

KEY TERMS

all-over pattern	line	sequencing
alternation	movement	shape
broken rhythm	parallelism	space
color	pattern	texture
form	progression	transition
gradation	radiation	value
grid	repetition	
light	rhythm	

PROJECTS

1. Choose six photographs of garments and circle with marker the area on each in which rhythm is implemented. Discuss with the class the type of rhythm presented and what elements are utilized.

2. Using markers, draw in your sketchbook four different garment designs that portray balance, emphasis, and rhythm, using the following elements in each version: rectangle, vertical line, and two values of the color green. Which is the best solution? Why?

3. With markers, draw in your sketchbook four different garment designs that portray balance, emphasis, and rhythm, using the following elements in each version: circle, line, a neutral, and a warm hue. Which is the best solution? Why?

REFERENCES

Benaim, L. (2003). *Grès*. New York: Assouline Publishing.

Brainard, S. (1998). *A design manual* (2nd ed.). Upper Saddle River, NJ: Prentice Hall.

Cunningham, R. (1994). *The magic garment: Principles of costume design.* Long Grove, IL: Waveland Press.

Dantzic, C. M. (1990). *Design dimensions: An introduction to the visual surface.* Englewood Cliffs, NJ: Prentice Hall.

Davis, M. L. (1996). *Visual design in dress* (3rd ed.). Upper Saddle River, Prentice Hall.

De Pietri, S., & Leventon, M. (1989). *New Look to now: French haute couture 1947–1987.* New York: Rizzoli.

Fukai, A. (2004). *Fashion in colors.* New York: Assouline Publishing.

Martin, R., & Koda, H. (1996). *Christian Dior.* New York: The Metropolitan Museum of Art.

Martinez, B., & Block, J. (1995). *Visual forces: An introduction to design* (2nd ed.). Upper Saddle River, NJ: Prentice Hall.

Mears, P. (2007). *Madame Grès: Sphinx of fashion.* New York: Fashion Institute of Technology.

Milbank, C. R. (1985). *Couture: The great designers.* New York: Stewart, Tabori & Chang.

Steele, V. (1991). *Women of fashion: Twentieth century designers.* New York: Rizzoli.

Steele, V. (2006). *Fifty years of fashion: New Look to now.* New Haven, CT: Yale University Press.

Stegemeyer, A. (2004). *Who's who in fashion* (4th ed.). New York: Fairchild Publications.

Stoops, J., & Samuelson, J. (1983). *Design dialogue.* Worcester, MA: Davis Publications.

| PROPORTION

OBJECTIVES

To relate proportion to
the human figure

To understand ideal proportion
from the disciplines of science,
mathematics, and art history

To define scale by comparison
to proportion

To explore proportion in relation
to fashion and discover what
proportional arrangements
designers have chosen

PROPORTION AND THE FIGURE

IN ADDITION TO balance, emphasis, and rhythm, the fashion designer uses another principle of design as a guide, and that is **proportion**. Proportion lives subconsciously in every mind and is of primary concern to all artists and types of designers. Simply put, it is the result of the comparative relationships of distances, **sizes**, amounts, degrees, or **parts** to the whole (e.g., the garment design, for the fashion designer). These comparative relationships are considered within one part of the design, among different parts of the design, between one part and the entire design, or between the design and its environment.

This chapter relates proportion to the human figure, examines its meaning in science and mathematics, and explores the possibility of an ideal proportion. It also defines **scale** by comparison to proportion and discusses the benefits of proportional arrangement to the design of apparel.

Proportion has its roots in organic forms, most importantly in the sizes and arrangements of the parts of the human figure. That is why it is a concept that everyone understands. The system of proportion of the human figure is the most familiar. Conversely, it helps to define the term **out of proportion**, a concept found in Amedeo Modigliani's painting style. His *Portrait of a Polish Woman* (1919) is typical, in its rendering of the elongated neck, which is considered "out of proportion" by comparison to the average human figure (FIGURE 11.1). The human figure is also the norm for the architect, who must figure the size of doors and height of ceilings, for instance, as well as the artist of representational subject matter.

The length of the head is used as the measurement for the rest of the human figure. The Western standard for the average body height is 7 heads tall. For fashion illustration, the figure is lengthened to between 8 and 10½ heads, in an effort to picture an ideal. That height enables the figure to appear thinner, and the longer leg provides more space to display the garment. It is important, however, for the fashion designer to think in terms of real human proportion, so that original designs fit and flatter the customer.

1.1 The neck in Modigliani's *rait of a Polish Woman* (1919) is out of proportion by comparison to an actual human figure.

THE PHILADELPHIA MUSEUM OF ART/ART RESOURCE, NY

ORGANIC PROPORTION

For scientists, proportion comes from a reference other than the human figure. They relate it to the atoms that make up the cells of plants and animals. Their DNA automatically and regularly forms spirals that result from a set of fixed geometric proportions. These spirals are evidence that bodily existence rests on geometric relationships. They underscore the importance of weighing shapes in relation to one another. Spirals are regularly repeated in other forms of nature that are easily identified by the naked eye (FIGURE 11.2A AND B).

RIGHT
11.2A Spirals are a geometric proportion found often in nature, such as this nautilus shell.
COURTESY OF ISTOCKPHOTO

BELOW
11.2B Pinecones are constructed in spirals.
COURTESY OF ISTOCKPHOTO

Mathematicians have attempted to define "good" proportion by expressing numerous ratios. In their work, they use the following terms. **Part** is an amount that is less than the whole that can be separated from the whole either physically or in the imagination. **Portion** is one of a number of equal parts into which the whole is divided. **Size** is the magnitude or quantitative degree in relation to a particular standard of measurement. **Ratio** is a comparison of two quantities. "One to two" (1:2) means that a group has two parts, but only one is of concern. **Fraction** is a mathematical expression of a ratio. For instance, the ratio mentioned above is also expressed as ½.

THE GOLDEN MEAN

Philosophers, mathematicians, scientists, and artists all search for the ideal proportion, expressed as a numerical standard, in order to identify beauty. Originally the Egyptians attempted to set up laws of proportion. The Greeks, however, believed that mathematics was the controlling force of the universe. The Greek mathematician Euclid determined the **golden mean**, also referred to as the **golden section**. From it he believed in "the moderation of all things," or a place between two extremes, which is both a sound life philosophy as well as an interesting prescription for good design. The golden mean stated that a small part relates to a larger part as the larger part relates to the whole. In mathematics, the same idea occurs when a line is divided into what is called the mean and the extreme, or when line AB is sectioned at point C, AC is the same ratio to AB as CB is to AC (FIGURE 11.3). It is also expressed as AC:AB = CB:AC.

The Greeks applied this ratio in both architecture and sculpture. In sculpture, they related it to components of the human figure. The Greek sculptor Polykleitos (450–420 BC) wrote a treatise on the ideal system of proportions for sculpture, which is now lost. He demonstrated this philosophy in the sculpture of a spear bearer. A marble copy of a bronze by Polykleitos or his follower, without the spear or the lower arms, is pictured in FIGURE 11.4. If the figure was estimated at 7½ heads tall, the distance from the top of the head to the chest was considered to be one-quarter of the height.

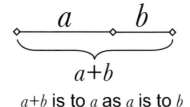

11.3 The geometric interpretation of the golden mean.

$a+b$ is to a as a is to b

11.4 Using the golden mean, for a figure measuring 7½ heads tall, like this copy of a sculpture by Polykleitos or his follower, the distance from the top of the head to the chest is about ¼ of the height.
BILDARCHIV PREUSSICHER KULTURBESITZ/ART RESOURCE, NY

Using the golden mean, the ratio between the mean and the extreme has the numerical value of .6180. That means any new unit must be that much smaller or larger than the original one, creating a new ratio of 1 to 1.6180. The Greeks applied this concept to geometry in order to create the most beautifully proportioned rectangle.

THE FIBONACCI SERIES

Subsequent generations have built on the golden mean. A medieval mathematician, Leonardo Fibonacci (1170–1250), discovered a series of numbers that demonstrates the increasing ratio of 1 to 1.6180. The sequence adds together the two previous numbers to arrive at each new number: 0, 1, 1, 2, 3, 5, 8, 13, 21, 34, 56, and so on. It is called the Fibonacci Series, which would work with any beginning number, and was published in the *Book of Abacus* in 1202. Scientists have discovered that the plotting of these numbers on a horizontal and vertical axis creates the spiral that occurs in nature like the examples in FIGURES 11.2A AND B. The picture of the nautilus shell in FIGURE 11.5 is, in effect, the complete Fibonacci spiral. For an example of ideal proportion, examine how much of the shell is occupied by pattern by comparison to the part that is not.

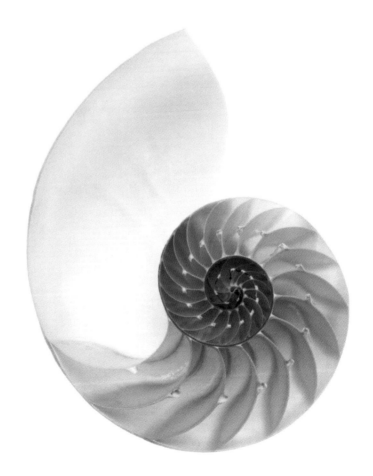

11.5 The complete nautilus shell represents the shape that results from plotting the Fibonacci series on a horizontal and vertical axis. It is considered to be ideal proportion.
COURTESY OF ISTOCKPHOTO

John Ruskin, artist and art critic of the nineteenth century, prot[…] against the golden mean. He felt, like many of today's artists and crit[…] that there is no one ideal of proportion that is appropriate for every situa[…]tion. The most important lesson of the golden mean is that diversity and uneven intervals in size and amount relationships are more visually interesting than those that are too similar. Regularity or equality causes boredom, while differences create contrast. Some proportional relationships, however, are generally viewed as pleasing: two-thirds to one-third or two-fifths to three-fifths.

SCALE

Scale is the term used when size proportions are compared to human size. Exaggerated proportions attract attention, because they are different from the norm. They are more aggressive and advancing. Note the effect obtained by Claes Oldenburg and Coosje van Bruggen with their fountain-sculpture *Spoonbridge and Cherry* (1985), which places a large-scale spoon and cherry against the Minneapolis cityscape (FIGURE 11.6).

In fashion, scale is a consideration for silhouette, decorative shapes, motifs, pattern, accessories, and hem length. The traditional view is to adjust scale to the whole of the garment and to the body as a whole. There are exceptions, however. Designer Yohji Yamamoto has explored scale in his Paris collections (BOX 11.1).

(Text continued on page 252.)

11.6 In *Spoonbridge and Cherry* (a fountain), by Claes Oldenburg and Coosje van Bruggen (1985–1988), from the Minneapolis Sculpture Garden, the scale of every day items has been vastly increased.
CLAES OLDENBURG AND COOSJE VAN BRUGGEN, SPOONBRIDGE AND CHERRY, 1985–1988, ALUMINUM, STAINLESS STEEL, PAINT, 354x618x162", COLLECTION WALKER ART CENTER, MINNEAPOLIS, GIFT OF FREDERICK R. WEISMAN IN HONOR OF HIS PARENTS, WILLIAM AND MARY WEISMAN, 1988 © CLAES OLDENBURG AND COSSJE VAN BRUGGEN

BOX 11.1
YOHJI
AMAMOTO

RIGHT
FIGURE BOX 11.1A Yohji
Yamamoto left the characteristics
of deconstruction behind with this
"Secret Dress" designed for his
spring–summer 1999 collection.
COURTESY OF FAIRCHILD ARCHIVE

OPPOSITE
FIGURE BOX 11.1B Yamamoto
used scale for artistic comment
when he showed this enormous
gown and hat in his fall–winter
1998-'99 collection.
COURTESY OF WWD

YOHJI YAMAMOTO IS known for fashion that makes a unique artistic statement, totally his own, which melds Japanese design with Western dressmaking traditions. He was born in Yokohama, Japan, in 1943 and was raised by his seamstress mother. He first studied law at Keio University, graduating in 1966, before he studied fashion for two years at Bunka College of Fashion in Tokyo. In 1968 he won a scholarship to study in Paris. He returned to Japan in 1970 and began his first ready-to-wear company in 1972. He presented his first collection in Paris in 1981, which garnished great reaction.

Like Issey Miyake and Rei Kawakubo, he was exploring new ways of dressing that omitted the traditional idea of displaying the female figure. His work showed a sensibility for deconstruction, with unfinished and haphazard construction as well as distressed fabrics. All the garments were black, a color traditionally associated in Japanese culture with the farmer and the spirit of the *samurai*. They featured asymmetrical shapes and voluminous layers, odd flaps and pockets, lopsided collars, and uneven hems. He believed that beauty was better expressed with a variety of textured materials than by applied decoration.

Yamamoto had a great love of soft fabric. He placed the heaviest part of it at the collarbone and then draped his complex layered and wrapped silhouettes. He used stiff fabrics for tailored garments that he cut up and reassembled. His knitwear was a vehicle for innovative construction that would curl up and distort, confusing inside with outside.

He developed a customer following of architects, artists, and writers. They were nicknamed *karasuzoku,* which translated into "members of the crow tribe." Black was considered a statement of antifashion and was identified with the Punk movement.

His distinguishable approach was altered in his 1999 wedding dress collection. It still featured the masculine tailored suits and white shirts for which he had built a reputation,

but his gowns blended the romance of traditional couture with his unique construction methods (FIGURE BOX 11.1A).

It was during the fall–winter 1998–1999 collection that Yamamoto first played with the concept of scale. He showed an enormous hat and a gown so large that it spilled off the runway and swept across the front rows of the audience (FIGURE BOX 11.1B).

His spring–summer 2006 collection showcased garments of exaggerated and blown-out proportions. This time they were his signature black suits and white shirts, with huge collars, cravats, and cuffs. The inspiration came from a Parisian period from the late 1920s when women empowered themselves by dressing like men. He continued to work at that scale for his fall–winter 2006–2007 collection, with supersized suits that sported false hanging sleeves (FIGURE BOX 11.1C AND D).

With his artistic ideas, Yohji Yamamoto has reached the pinnacle of success. He has businesses in Tokyo, Paris, and New York with earnings of more than a hundred million dollars per year. He creates costumes for ballet and opera, and he is the only Japanese fashion designer to receive the Chevalier de l'Ordre des Arts et des Lettres.

RIGHT
FIGURE BOX 11.1C Scale was important again in Yamamoto's fall/winter 2006–'07 collection.
COURTESY OF WWD/ GIOVANNI GIANNONI

OPPOSITE
FIGURE BOX 11.1D Yamamoto's suits in his fall/winter 2006–'07 collection were supersized, some with false sleeves.
COURTESY OF WWD/ GIOVANNI GIANNONI

PROPORTION AND THE DESIGN OF FASHION

The fashion designer is in charge of the choosing of potential proportional relationships in apparel, although there are some guideposts. For instance, the astute designer is aware of the proportional ratios that have been successful historically. In addition, pleasing proportions are culturally influenced. The designer is undoubtedly influenced by his or her own culture, as has been the case with noted Japanese designers. The cultural background of the clients is another consideration. The designer of mass apparel chooses the proportional relationships that please the target customer for a particular season. Those proportions should also flatter the figure type that is characteristic of that market.

The use of proportion facilitates figure flattery. The proportions of clothing must relate to the human figure. When designers reorganize the dimensions of the figure with a new silhouette and subdivide the internal space into a new visual arrangement of shapes and spaces, the result is a different perception of the figure, one that has the potential to conceal any flaws. The new proportion may affect the existing ideal of beauty. In order to obtain this result, the designer must master figure proportions. Observing the figure, sketching the figure, and design experience all contribute to that competency.

The comparative relationships of proportion for fashion include, first of all, those within one part of the design, such as the length and width of a skirt. Secondly, designers compare parts, like the bodice with the skirt or the sleeve to the bodice. They may also correlate a part to the whole, as in the comparison of the length of the bodice with the length of the entire garment. When designers compare the whole to the environment, they are actually relating the garment to the figure.

It is easiest to begin the discussion about proportion by comparing shapes within the design. Shape inevitably has proportion. In many cases, a space within the design has dimensions too, such as the midriff of a two-piece swimsuit or the one revealed by a cropped top and skirt. All the elements play a role in relation to proportion. Comparing the length of seams is an example related to line. The intensities or the values of colors are often compared, as is the light reflection or tactile quality of textures or the scale of patterns.

The history of Western dress is a great source for understanding proportion. Even a focus on the twentieth century is instructive. For example, examine the lengths and shapes of the bodice and skirt in the evening dress designed under the influence of Paul Poiret, dated approximately 1916 (FIGURE 11.7). What is the ratio between them? Look, by comparison, at the length of the bodice and skirt in the 1920s evening dress by Coco Chanel

(FIGURE 11.8). Where has the waistline moved by 1955, in the
Muguets" (Lilies of the Valley) evening gown by Givenchy (FIGURE 11.
What is the ratio of the tunic to the pants in the 1970s evening ensemble b
American designer Bill Blass (1922–2002) (FIGURE 11.10)?

    Proportion is one of the most important principles of design. Fashion
designers often credit their successes to a mastery of that principle as well as
a profound understanding of the proportions of the human body.

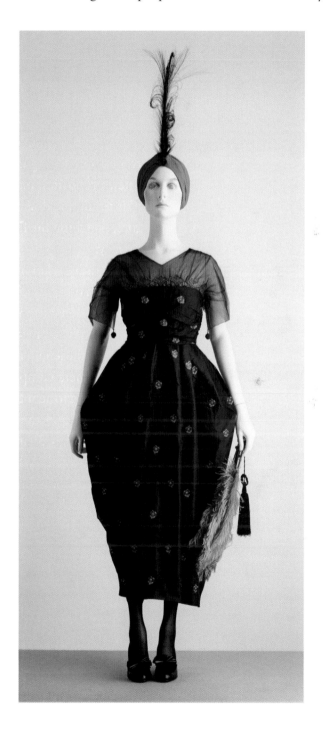

11.7 Compare the lengths of the
bodice and skirt in order to
determine the proportion in this
evening dress from around 1916
under the influence of Paul Poiret.

ABOVE

11.8 Compare the length of the bodice from neckline to dropped waist to the length of the skirt in this evening dress designed by Coco Chanel in the late 1920s.

© THE METROPOLITAN MUSEUM OF ART/ART RESOURCE, NY

RIGHT

11.9 The length of the bodice is far shorter than the skirt in this evening dress entitled "Les Muguets" (Lilies of the Valley), by Givenchy in 1955.

© V&A IMAGES, VICTORIA AND ALBERT MUSEUM

11.10 The tunic represents a long shape balanced against what is revealed of the pant in this evening ensemble designed by Bill Blass in the 1970s.

BILL BLASS (AMERICAN, 1922–2002), ENSEMBLE (EVENING JACKET AND PANTS), 1980s, FRENCH SILK AND LUREX BROCADE, PHOTO BY KEN HOWIE, COLLECTION OF PHOENIX ART MUSEUM, GIFT OF MRS. HUGH DOWNS

KEY TERMS

fraction	out of proportion	ratio
golden mean	parts	scale
golden section	portion	sizes

PROJECTS

1. Select six photographs of garments. Use marker to circle the proportional parts for each example. Figure the ratio of each proportional part. Present your analysis to the class.

2. Research costume of the twentieth century. Make a copy of a garment from each decade. Use marker to circle the proportional part for each one. Figure the ratio of each proportional part in each case. Present your analysis to the class.

3. In your sketchbook, draw four vertical rectangles of the same size. Using black fine-tipped marker, divide each one horizontally in one or two places, so that each rectangle is different. Fill some, but not all sections with black lines or unfilled shapes. Each rectangle represents a garment. Turn your lines into pleats, seams, or surface stripes and your shapes into pockets, yokes, or appliqués. Add color using markers or colored pencils. Which is the best solution? Why?

REFERENCES

Beker, J. (2006, December 18). Jeanne talks Yohji Yamamoto. *Fashion Television.* Retrieved July 20, 2009, from http://www.fashiontelevision.com/images/Askjeanne/img_aj_Yohji_Yamamoto_Getty.jpg.

Brainard, S. (1998). *A design manual* (2nd ed.). Upper Saddle River, NJ: Prentice Hall.

Cox, C. (2009). Yohji Yamamoto. Answers.com. Retrieved July 20, 2009, from http://www.answers.com/topic/yohji-yamamoto.

Cunningham, R. (1994). *The magic garment: Principles of costume design.* Long Grove, IL: Waveland Press.

Dantzic, C. M. (1990). *Design dimensions: An introduction to the visual surface.* Englewood Cliffs, NJ: Prentice Hall.

Davis, M. L. (1996). *Visual design in dress.* (3rd ed.) Upper Saddle River, NJ: Prentice Hall.

Martinez, B., & Block, J. (1995). *Visual forces: An introduction to design* \ ed.). Upper Saddle River, NJ: Prentice Hall.

Parmal, Pamela A., Grumbach, D., Ward, S., & Whitley, L. D. (2007). *Fashio. show, Paris style.* Boston: MFA Publications.

Ocvirk, O. G., Stinson, R. E., Wigg, P. R., Bone, R. O., & Cayton, D. L. (2002). *Art fundamentals: Theory and practice* (9th ed.). New York: McGraw-Hill.

Stewart, M. (2008). *Launching the imagination, A Comprehensive Guide to Basic Design,* (3rd ed.) New York: McGraw-Hill.

Stoops, J., & Samuelson, J. (1983). *Design dialogue.* Worcester, MA: Davis Publications.

| # UNITY

To define the principles of unity, variety, and harmony

To list and describe Gestalt Principles, which are the ways in which individuals visually organize elements into unified wholes

To apply unity to a single fashion or across a group of fashions

To understand the design approach of high-priced designers, of designers for mass fashion, and behind designer brands

THIS BOOK BEGAN with the observation that fashion designers experience a sensual feeling of excitement when they see a successful design. That is because the design has **unity**, the most important and the final principle of design.

Unity facilitates the feeling of completeness, wholeness, cohesion, and finish. It guides the viewer's eye and contributes to the reaction. It pulls the design together and ensures that all parts belong and work together. Unity integrates all aspects of the design but cannot be separated from them. It results in the selection of the appropriate devices peculiar to the medium and the principles of design that relate to them. Line, shape, space, value, color, texture, and pattern all join forces to unite as a team. It also means that while one element is emphasized, others become subordinate, and that any opposing forces create vitality rather than confusion.

This chapter defines the related principles of **variety** and **harmony** and discusses **Gestalt Principles**, which furnish several tools to ensure that visual information is understood in its totality. It applies unity to fashion, providing examples of unified designs. Finally, it relates unity to the development of a group of fashions, with consideration of societal **ideals of beauty**, sources of **inspiration**, and marketing for mass fashion and designer brands.

VARIETY AND HARMONY

"Variety is the spice of life." This old adage emphasizes the importance of variety in everyday lives. Variety also has a role in design. Central to its definition is the concept of "difference"—a reminder that if too many of the elements in a design are similar, the risk is boredom. There is a necessary balance between sameness and variety; too much variety brings confusion.

Changing the character of one element presents the possibility of contrast. Contrast creates interest, and interest accounts for the ability to arouse curiosity and hold the viewer's attention.

Harmony is a term most associated with music, where an instrument or a singing quartet use similar, but not the same, musical notes. The result is pleasing—a feeling of restful resolution and the opposite of dissonance.

Harmony means that all of the elements work in agreement, and hence, harmony is a factor in cohesion. Artists and designers work constantly to adjust their work between harmony and variety in the achievement of balance, proportion, emphasis, and rhythm. Inherent in this process is the necessity for **economy**. Economy does not allow for anything superfluous in the design. Harmony has an interesting relationship with unity. Unity without harmony is impossible, while it is possible to have harmony without unity.

GESTALT PRINCIPLES

In the 1920s and 1930s, concurrent with the evolution of the Bauhaus, German psychologists Max Wertheimer (1880–1943), Wolfgang Kohler (1887–1967), and Kurt Koffka (1886–1941) grappled with the question of how individuals perceive the complex scenes around them that consist of many groups of objects against a background. Gestalt is a German word meaning "shape" or "form." Their conclusions, which were publicly presented then and continue to be studied today, were that visual information is understood holistically before it is examined separately.

LAW OF SIMPLICITY

Gestalt is also known as the **Law of Simplicity**, which means that every stimulus is perceived in its most simple form. Their studies resulted in a list of approaches that people use to organize visual elements into unified wholes.

SIMILARITY

One approach is called **similarity** or **grouping**. Similarity occurs when objects look similar. Elements (e.g., line, shape, color) that share visual characteristics belong together in the viewer's mind. Grouping also implies that visual units are linked by location and orientation. American designer Pauline Trigère's (1908–2002) "Turtle" dress from 1965 is a wonderful example (FIGURE 12.1). The turtle was a favorite inspiration for Trigère, so she had a turtle dress in almost every collection. In this one, the geometric shape representing the pattern of the turtle's shell unifies the dress, even though it changes size. The smaller ones are located along the border and in the bodice.

CONTAINMENT

Containment states that the edge of a composition or a boundary within it is a unifying force. Boundaries can "contain" elements, such as motifs,

12.1 The geometric shapes, groped by location and orientation, are a critical part of the design in Pauline Trigere's "Turtle" dress from 1965.

PAULINE TRIGERE (AMERICAN, 1912–2002), DRESS, 1973, PRINTED SILK CHIFFON, PHOTO BY KEN HOWIE, COLLECTION OF PHOENIX ART MUSEUM, GIFT OF MRS. ADELE ASTAIRE DOUGLASS

textures, shapes, or spaces. This approach is appropriate for fashion, because of the structural need for seams. Dior's "La Cigale" dress from fall–winter 1952 has unity because of the arrangement of seams (FIGURE 12.2). One seam occurs vertically at the center front of the bodice, and three seams run from a common point at the center top of the skirt. In addition, they are placed front to back from the hipbone on each side. Agreement between the lines of the garment and the body cause harmony. Dior was such an expert on the figure that this dress actually caused a subtle change in fashionable posture. It forced the hip forward, the stomach in, the shoulders down, and the back long and rounded.

12.2 The seams are a unifying force in Christian Dior's "La Cigale" dress of 1952.
© THE METROPOLITAN MUSEUM OF ART/ART RESOURCE, NY

REPETITION

Repetition occurs when the same visual effect occurs over and over. A repeat of any element, such as line, shape, and color, has the potential for unity. Jeanne Lanvin used this technique in her 1927 "Robe de Style" of eggshell moiré (FIGURE 12.3). Art Deco shapes repeat along the neckline, at the waist, and down the center front of the skirt. Lanvin's designs occurred relatively early in the history of haute couture. Her talent for unified designs should not be minimized (BOX 12.1).

PROXIMITY

Proximity refers to the distance between visual elements. Closeness of proximity builds unity, as in *The Creation of Adam,* one of Michelangelo's frescoes on the ceiling of the Sistine Chapel (FIGURE 12.4, page 268). The placement of the hands, as they reach out to touch each other, creates a tension that ties the composition and the concept behind the work together.

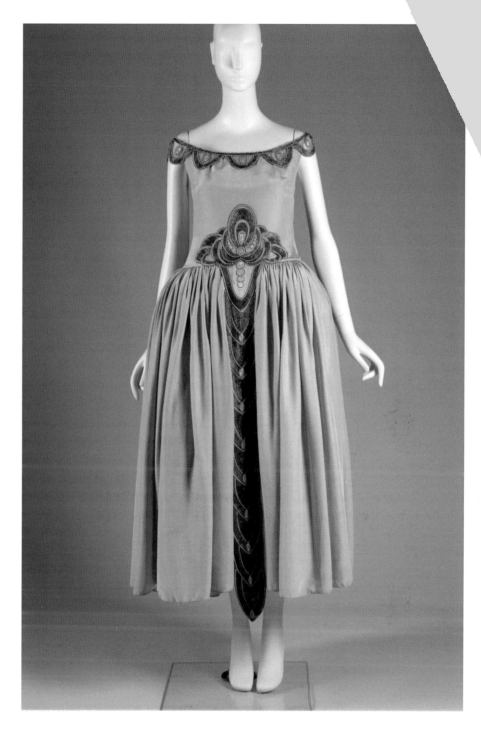

12.3 Repetition of shape provides unity in this 1927 "Robe de Style" designed by Jeanne Lanvin. DIA—1954.1, CHICAGO HISTORY MUSEUM

CONTINUITY

Another Gestalt Principle is called **continuity** or **good continuation**. It states that viewers tend to continue shapes beyond their ending points. Moving from one shape or object and continuing into another causes a fluid connection in the composition. Edgar Degas (1834–1917) used this dynamic in his 1886 pastel *The Tub* (FIGURE 12.5, page 268). The circular tub touches the bather's fingertips and hairline, as well as the shelf, from which the hairbrush overlaps.

(*Text continued on page 268.*)

JEANNE LANVIN WAS born in 1867 in Brittany, France, the eldest of 11 children. She was orphaned at a young age and had to take care of her younger siblings. In 1880, at the age of 13, she was apprenticed to the milliner Suzanne Talbot in Paris, and then by 1883, to the milliner Madame Félix. She was employed under contract in 1885 to Maria-Berta Valenti of Barcelona, a dressmaker who specialized in clothing for adults and children. It was Valenti who nurtured in her all of the skills necessary to create couture-quality garments. Lanvin returned to Paris, and by 1889, she set up her own millinery business.

She married and had a daughter named Marguerite. As a little girl, Marguerite was her inspiration, and she made beautiful dresses for her of pleating and English embroidery. When others saw them, they requested copies for their own daughters. Soon Lanvin was making dresses for their mothers as well from her Paris boutique. She made little distinction in the styling between the mothers and daughters. Both were considered fresh and young.

She joined the Syndicat de la Couture in 1909, and that marked her beginning as a couturière. The famous illustrator of the period, Paul Iribe, designed her famous logo, which was meant to capture the bond between a mother and a daughter. The logo became world famous, thanks to the later success of her fragrances, *My Sin* (1924) and *Arpege* (1927) (FIGURE BOX 12.1A).

In 1913, Lanvin designed dresses known as "robes de style," which were based on eighteenth-century designs (FIGURE BOX 12.1B). They had constructed waists with full skirts, and they remained popular for many years (FIGURE 12.3). Her designs had unity because the embellishments, crystal beads, pearls, metallic thread, and glass, were carefully placed and balanced by the soft drape of the fabrics.

RIGHT
FIGURE BOX 12.1A The logo for the House of Lanvin, originally designed by Paul Iribe and meant to capture the relationship between a mother and daughter.
© THE METROPOLITAN MUSEUM OF ART/ART RESOURCE, NY

OPPOSITE
FIGURE BOX 12.1B One of Jeanne Lanvin's "Robes de Style" from 1924, based on eighteenth-century designs.
© THE METROPOLITAN MUSEUM OF ART/ART RESOURCE, NY

Lanvin worked at the time of Paul Poiret, and like him, she was influenced by Orientalism. In the early 1920s, she made a simple chemise dress that became the imprint of the flapper style. She also opened a dye factory in Nanterre in order to cultivate exclusive colors, like rose polignac, Velasquez green, and Lanvin blue, a purplish blue thought to come from a Fra Angelico painting. Her color choices were also inspired by artists such as Edouard Vuillard (1868–1940), Odilon Redon (1840–1916), Jean-Honorè Fragonard (1732–1806), Pierre-Auguste Renoir (1814–1919), and Edgar Degas (1834–1917), whose works of art she collected (Merceron, 2007, 20). In the same decade she began a menswear division and was the first couturière to dress the entire family. Branches of the business opened in Nice, Cannes, and Biarritz. She dressed film stars Mary Pickford, Marlene Dietrich, and Yvonne Printemps, as well as the queens of Italy and Romania and English princesses.

Lanvin truly demonstrated her genius through her women's apparel. Her virtuoso embroideries, beadwork, and light, floral colors were her trademark. In 1921 she introduced Aztec embroidery. Her 1922 collection featured a Breton suit with a gathered skirt and short braided jacket featuring tiny buttons, a big white organdy collar, and a red satin bow. Her clients loved her penchant for femininity, which was expressed through fabrics like silk, taffeta, velvet, silk chiffon, organza, lace, tulle, and ornamentation such as free-flowing ribbons, ruffles, flowers, lace, mirrors, appliqué, couching, quilting, and parallel stitching.

ABOVE
FIGURE BOX 12.1C Jeanne
Lanvin's evening coat (1927) uses
both radiation and repetition of
radials to foster unity in the design.
© THE METROPOLITAN MUSEUM OF
ART/ART RESOURCE, NY

LEFT
FIGURE BOX 12.1D Featuring the
silhouette of the 1930s, this
Lanvin design draws the eye
to the shoulders.
© THE METROPOLITAN MUSEUM OF
ART/ART RESOURCE, NY

OPPOSITE LEFT
FIGURE BOX 12.1E The parallel
stitching in Lanvin's evening jacket
(1936–1937) provides unity
for the ensemble.
© THE METROPOLITAN MUSEUM OF
ART/ART RESOURCE, NY

OPPOSITE RIGHT
FIGURE BOX 12.1F Lanvin implemented unity in her "Cyclone"
gown using the repetition of
folds in the skirt tiers.
© THE METROPOLITAN MUSEUM OF
ART/ART RESOURCE, NY

She managed to grow with each period, as exemplified in her stunning spiral-designed evening coat of 1927 (FIGURE 12.1C). It is easy to spot the point of emphasis and follow the repetition of radials through the entire design. She slid easily into the feminine silhouette of the 1930s, as in her Oriental evening ensemble, which drew the eye to the shoulders (FIGURE 12.1D). That inspiration is also evident in her evening ensemble from 1936–1937, which featured contrast for emphasis and variety, as well as parallel stitching for repetition (FIGURE 12.1E). By 1939, her designs took a modern turn, where unity functioned in her "Cyclone" dress, due to the emphasis of the contrasting spangles, the repetition and rhythm of the skirt folds, and the proportion established by the skirt tiers (FIGURE 12.1F).

Lanvin managed to keep her business open through World War II, unlike many of her peers. She died in 1946 at the age of 79. Her daughter Marguerite continued the fashion house until her death in 1958.

(continued from page 263.)

12.4 The proximity of the hands in Michelangelo's *Creation of Adam* (circa 1511), from the ceiling of the Sistine Chapel, introduces tension and provides the image with unity.
ERICH LESSING/ART RESOURCE, NY

12.5 Edgar Degas uses continuity in the composition of *The Tub*, where the circular shape of the tub impinges on the model's fingertips and hairline, as well as the nearby shelf.
REUNION DES MUSEES NATIONAUX/ART RESOURCE, NY

FIGURE/GROUND

The next method is called **figure/ground**. This refers to the perceptual te dency to separate whole figures from their backgrounds, based on such ele ments as color, contrast, value. This phenomenon works like the relationship between positive and negative space, which was discussed in Chapter 3. In *Sky and Water I*, a woodcut from 1938 by M.C. Escher (1898–1972), the focus on the black areas easily changes to the white areas (FIGURE 12.6). That transition strengthens the feeling of unity in the piece.

The deliberate alteration of figure and ground so that the figure blends into the ground is **camouflage**. Also referred to as **ambiguity**, this unifying force hides lines and contours because it is visually disruptive. Fabric is often the source of camouflage in fashion. The typical camouflage pattern is shown in FIGURE 5.12.

12.6 Figure/ground is the phenomenon M.C. Ecsher explores in *Sky and Water I* from 1938.
COURTESY M.C. ESCHER GALLERY

When there are details missing from a familiar image or pattern, the brain tends to fill them in, and that tendency is called **closure**. From experience, the brain is encoded with the visual information, triggering a recognition response. It can complete a familiar shape, an anticipated line, or a common motif.

ORDER

Order is another contributor to unity. Sometimes there is an anticipated sense of order; at other times, it is up to the artist or designer to set the order. For instance, Gothic architecture results from a strict order or set of laws that govern the location of windows, doors, sculptures, and other decoration. Consider, for instance, the Cathedral of the Notre Dame in Paris (1163–1250) (FIGURE 12.7). Its façade is iconic. All of the visual elements are located, grouped, and assigned a size according to their relative importance to the whole of the design. So the architectural order is actually a hierarchy. Try to imagine how the cathedral would appear if window were moved to another location. What would that do to its appearance? The designer sets up a hierarchy unique to the design when developing emphasis, balance, and rhythm.

UNITY AND HARMONY IN FASHION

Unity, as the ultimate synthesizing principle, has a distinctive interpretation in fashion. It means that:

o The structural, functional, and decorative levels of the design work toward a unified result.

o There is unity in the selection and use of the materials.

o The back of the garment works with the front.

o The garments parts work with each other.

o The garment proportions agree in scale.

o The design avoids conflict and competition by organizing attention around a central theme.

o There is a sense of completion to the design.

Harmony operates within and among the elements of the design. The lines agree with each other in their type, placement, and relationship to the body.

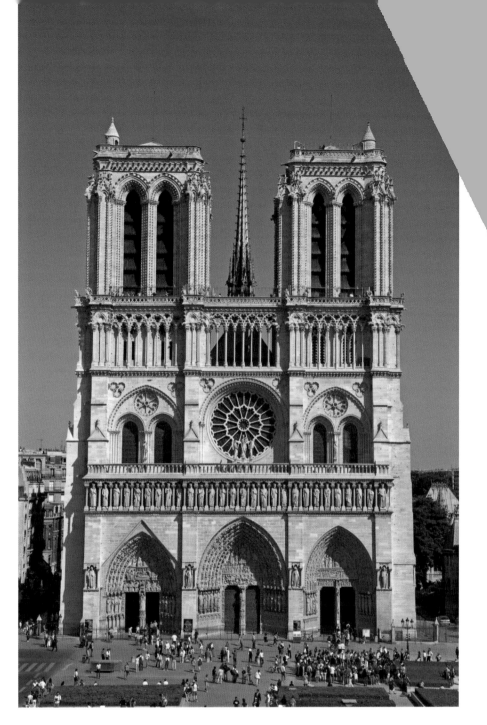

12.7 A strict order of laws governs the location of visual elements in Gothic architecture, which is evident in the stunning façade of the Cathedral of the Notre Dame in Paris.
© BRUNO MORANDI/GRAND TOUR/CORBIS

Shapes and spaces relate in proportion. Colors are harmonious. Values offer variety. Light reacts in a pleasing way to the surface of the fabrics. The pattern is appropriate in its arrangement and proportion.

Two examples of designs by Madame Grès exemplify both unity and harmony. In the first, shown in FIGURE 12.8, designed in 1950, it is easy to see the unity in the graceful transition from the front of the design to the back. The softness of the drape at the back of the neckline matches the quality of the gathers in the overskirt, which are influenced by the manner in which it is pulled under at the hem. The textures of the two fabrics are not the same, but their contrast is complementary rather than conflicting. The second design, shown in FIGURE 12.9, from 1954, is easily recognized for Grès' unique method of draping. Unity is the result of the repetition of the numerous folds. The softness of the silk jersey adds harmony. The balance is asymmetrical. Emphasis is employed by the use of the gold ribbon, while the lines of the folds furnish the rhythm to carry the eye throughout the rest of the design.

12.8 Madame Grès' gown from 1950 shows unity in design from front to back.
ILLUSTRATION BY
JANICE GREENBERG ELLINWOOD

12.9 Repetition of the lines of the numerous pleats unifies Madame Grès' asymmetrical gown from 1954.
© THE METROPOLITAN MUSEUM OF ART/ART RESOURCE, NY

There are more specific guidelines for arriving at a unified product for mass fashion. They are as follows:

○ All shapes employed in the garment reflect the same quality (if one has curved edges, the others should too).

○ The placement of style lines (darts and seams) should stay consistent (those above the waist should connect to those below the waist).

○ Hem lengths of garment parts should match unless a contrast is planned in the design (jacket sleeve-lengths should match jacket length, unless the sleeve is a short or three-quarter length).

○ Straight-grain stripes and plaids should match at seams and on sleeves that hang parallel to the bodice.

○ Style lines (darts and seams) should have compatible angles.

gners Noted for Particular Use of Design Elements & Principles

hion designers harness all of the elements of design and apply all of the principles in their work. he following tables note designers who exemplify particular aspects of design.

DESIGNERS NOTED FOR THEIR USE OF STRUCTURAL AND FUNCTIONAL DESIGN

Structural Design	Jeanne Lanvin, Madeleine Vionnet, Charles James, Yohji Yamamoto, Martin Margiela
Functional Design	Claire McCardell

DESIGNERS NOTED FOR THEIR USE OF AESTHETIC DESIGN

Line	John Galliano, Madame Grès, Yves Saint Laurent, Zac Posen, Coco Chanel, Karl Lagerfeld, Rudi Gernreich, Thierry Mugler, Christian Lacroix, Adrian
Form	Paul Poiret, Christian Dior, Madeleine Vionnet
Shape	Vivienne Westwood, Claire McCardell, Christian Lacroix, Christian Dior, Rei Kawakubo
Space	Rei Kawakubo, Issey Miyake, Claire McCardell, Pierre Cardin
Texture	Franco Moschino, Geoffrey Beene, Caroline Herrera, Cristóbal Balenciaga, Sonia Rykiel, Yves Saint Laurent, Norma Kamali, Paco Rabanne, Yohji Yamamoto, Isabel Toledo, Ralph Rucci
Light	Paco Rabanne, Emilio Pucci, Mariano Fortuny
Pattern	Gianni Versace, Bill Gibb, Oscar de la Renta, Christian Lacroix, Beer, Isaac Mizrahi, John Paul Gaultier, Giorgio Armani, Emilio Pucci, Laura Ashley, Lily Pulitzer
Color	Roberto Capucci, Sonia Delaunay, Coco Chanel, Valentino Garavani, Elsa Schiaparelli, Paul Poiret, Hubert de Givenchy, Madeleine Vionnet, Jean Paul Gaultier, Vivienne Westwood, John Galliano, Yohji Yamamoto
Balance	Halston, Madeleine Vionnet, Hubert de Givenchy, Karl Lagerfeld, André Courrèges, Hussein Chalayan, Stephen Burrows, Christian Dior, Madame Grès, Rei Kawakubo, John Galliano
Emphasis	Elsa Schiaparelli
Rhythm	Claire McCardell, Norman Norell, Madame Grès, Viktor & Rolf, Christian Dior, Madeleine Vionnet, Issey Miyake, Yves Saint Laurent, André Courrèges
Proportion	Yohji Yamamoto, Paul Poiret, Coco Chanel, Hubert de Givenchy, Bill Blass
Unity	Pauline Trigère, Christian Dior, Jeanne Lanvin, Madame Grès, Oscar de la Renta, Calvin Klein, Ralph Lauren, Donna Karan, Tommy Hilfiger, Michael Kors

FASHION INSPIRATION

History teaches that there is an ideal of beauty that prevails during [each] period. This ideal becomes a societal norm that has implications for b[ody] shape, so designers are necessarily influenced by it. James Jacques Josep[h] Tissot often painted the bustle-back ideal of the Victorian era (FIGURE 9.3). In the 1890s, the American ideal was the Gibson Girl, after the illustrations of Charles Dana Gibson (1867–1944) (FIGURE 12.10). Designer Paul Poiret originated the ideal of the early 1900s, showcasing his corset-freeing designs on his tall, slim wife (FIGURE 3.2). The flapper, the party girl with the cropped hair, was the ideal of the 1920s. Coco Chanel designed fashions for that look (FIGURE 11.8). The ideal became draped and feminine in the 1930s, helped along by designers such as Madeleine Vionnet and Elsa Schiaparelli. Actresses gained popularity in the 1930s and 1940s, the era of the "Sweater Girl." In the 1950s, Americans admired the iconic Marilyn Monroe (FIGURE 12.11). Celebrities, actresses, fashion models, and even royalty have defined the ideal of beauty in the decades since.

Designers are also inspired by whatever they find visually stimulating in the world around them. They look at the work of artists, historic costume and interiors, architecture, subcultures, and nature, as well as other areas. It is advisable to keep a journal of images. Survey the images before

12.10 The "Gibson Girl," from illustrations by Charles Dana Gibson, was the ideal of feminine beauty during the 1890s.
ART RESOURCE, NY

"BIG GAME"

"THE GIBSON GIRL"

In the early Nineties the famous "Gibson Girl" was the toast of the town. The gifted young artist, Charles Dana Gibson, was then at the beginning of his distinguished career. His brilliant cartoons, in *Life*, were the rivals of Du Maurier of *Punch* and each number of this popular periodical was eagerly awaited. Leading figures on the stage and in society aped the pose and the style of the "Gibson Girl" and every college had its devoted band of admirers. These two pictures give a slight idea of the beauty of these wonderful drawings, and of the styles of that day

..11 Actress Marilyn Monroe represented an ideal of beauty in the United States during the 1950s.
COURTESY OF EVERETT COLLECTION

designing, and group them into themes and subthemes. Examine them for shapes, lines, and colors, and adapt them into design ideas.

Designers also look at fabrics on a continual basis. Many are inspired by the color, pattern, or hand of fabric. They often keep a file of swatches or fabric lengths. In addition, they stay up-to-date on the research of fashion trends, like the research discussed in Chapter 7, "Color and Industry."

DESIGNING A GROUP OF FASHIONS

The fashion designer most often designs fashion as a group. The group designed by members of haute couture is called a **collection** (FIGURE 12.12). A collection may include a variety of styles for the same customer. Designers for mass fashion create a group referred to as a **line**. A line is typically designed with one **classification of apparel** in mind, such as evening wear, sportswear, or coats. Both types are broken into subgroups. Mass-produced dresses are designed in groups of three or six. A group of coordinated sportswear may consist of 6, 8, 12, or 16 pieces.

How is unity maintained across several garments? Designers start with a theme or story. That is reflected in the fabrics they choose for the group. Then they select a color story. As evident in FIGURE 12.12, when they identify the elements important to one design—such as lines, shapes, and

12.12 The models show a groups of fashions in the fall–winter 1950 collection designed by Christian Dior. The fashion show took place at the Alexander Palace in London.

TOPFOTO/THE IMAGE WORKS

construction details—they reorganize them differently for each of the other garments in the group. They remember not to design one so similar to the next that it steals that garment's visibility. Each garment has its own merit. Despite the repeated elements, they add variety to the group by varying the sleeves, necklines, and/or hem lengths, like these designs from the spring 2009 collection of Oscar de la Renta (FIGURES 12.13A–C). Of course, the designers are influenced by the preferences of the target market, the season, and the price category for which they design. Then they edit the line down to the best prospects.

DESIGN AS CORPORATE BRAND

Some American designers have successfully developed their collection and/or line of fashion into one corporate brand. That is the result of their keen sense of American markets, American lifestyles, and American ideals. They are able to associate their designs with a brand image and what is termed **lifestyle merchandising**. Lifestyle merchandising means the association of their names and their looks with a range of products—high-priced women's apparel, as well as men's sportswear and suits, children's apparel, accessories, casual sportswear, fragrances, and home products. Designers set up licensing agreements with other manufacturers of these products in order to produce them or develop the diversified lines in-house. They bring

the brand image, design elements, and logo throughout all the lines. A.
cans recognize the designer's name and associate it with prestige. T.
designers develop their brand internationally, so that customers of oth
countries become familiar with it.

Calvin Klein (1942–), Ralph Lauren (1939–), Tommy Hilfiger (1952–),
Donna Karan (1948–), and Michael Kors (1959–) are all designers who successfully established a corporate brand.

CALVIN KLEIN

Calvin Klein's designs were characterized by simple cut and plain colors,
which came to express a fresh, young spirit. The approach was called **minimalism**. Any detailing used by other designers—embroidery, prints,
shirring, obvious closures––were absent from Klein's apparel. Basic shapes
meant that the interest was confined to color and texture. A minimalistic
approach was applied to all the apparel bearing his name—swimwear,
dresses, jeans, and so on. The clean lines, spare shapes, and sexy cuts, combined with sexually provocative advertising campaigns, had great appeal to
customers who lived and worked in a complex, pressured culture.

RALPH LAUREN

Even before Calvin Klein, Ralph Lauren created a brand that appealed to an
American ideal. Ironically, the ideal reflected the lives lead historically by
British gentry. Lauren's designs largely portray the wealthy British at
leisure, alluding to the sports of yachting and polo. He married this ideal
image from the past with quality fabrics and details, all to convey the prom-
ise of good taste. A gold crest, a lace collar, or a wind tab on a lapel conveyed
a sense of wealth, so the consumer gained prestige with the purchase. In
addition, each season's product lines revolved around a single theme, also a
fantasy connected to an American ideal, such as Safari, Aviator, or Western
Frontier, among others. Fabric choice and details supported the theme,
such as suede fringe, cowboy boots, and cotton flannel for Western Frontier
and buttoned pockets with khaki fabric for Safari.

DONNA KARAN

Donna Karan had a different orientation to her market. She based her business on working women, not unlike herself. Her first line defined her philosophy of polished but understated clothing. Based on the universality of
black and the value of basic, functional, comfortable pieces that could be

mixed, she designed a black bodysuit, wrap skirt, trousers, jeans, and a suit. Her talent was in creating clothing that would complement a woman's figure, regardless of size. Working in front of a mirrored wall, sometimes working with her own body proportions, her designs would result from what her hands did with a fabric length, whether draping, tugging, twisting, or manipulating it. Her sense of fabric quality generated across all product lines, initiated with a quality line of hosiery.

TOMMY HILFIGER

Entering the fashion industry when these competitors were established, Tommy Hilfiger had to strive for a significantly different image. He did that by choosing the spirit of America's own dressing through which he emphasized many already classic and accepted fashions, but with a twist of color or a change of textile print repeat.

MICHAEL KORS

Michael Kors (1959–) is a designer who is working in the tradition of Calvin Klein, Ralph Lauren, Donna Karan, and Tommy Hilfiger. With fame buoyed by his participation as a judge on the television program *Project Runway,* Kors' clothes strike a delicate balance. They are luxurious yet sporty, embrace the past while looking contemporary, and look glamorous while being practical. He designs fashions that consistently combine the classic components of American sportswear with luxury, elegance, ease, and comfort. His spring 2010 designs reflect American sportswear sensibility with a futuristic quality, and they demonstrate unity via consistent design elements, while offering the customer variety in styling (FIGURE 12.14A–C).

Unity is the goal to which all design aspires, whether in relation to a single fashion or a group. With a sense of simplicity and logical organization, a command of the elements and principles of design, and knowledge of the structural, functional, and decorative parts of the garment, the fashion designer is assured of attaining it.

A

B

C

12.14A-C Michael Kors' designs for spring 2010 characterize his sportswear sensibility in looks geared to the future and in which design elements are repeated.
COURTESY OF WWD/ THOMAS IANNACCONE

KEY TERMS

ambiguity	Gestalt Principles	minimalism
camouflage	good continuation	order
classification of apparel	grouping	proximity
closure	harmony	repetition
collection	ideals of beauty	similarity
containment	inspiration	unity
continuity	Law of Simplicity	variety
economy	lifestyle merchandising	
figure/ground	line	

PROJECTS

1. In the sketchbook, develop a design with the ultimate goal of unity. Make a list of elements to use: a geometric shape, a type of line, two values of the same hue, a dull or shiny texture. Using markers and colored pencils, draw four different designs using your choice of these elements. Consider balance, emphasis, proportion, rhythm, and unity. Decide which of the four designs has the most unity. Which of the Gestalt Principles did you use? Which of the guidelines for obtaining unity in fashion did you use? Which is the most successful? Why?

2. Try again the problem described in Project 1. This time choose a compound geometric shape instead of a simple one and a monochromatic pattern with the same hue in place of the one with the darker value. For the pattern source, choose a scrapbook paper, a wrapping paper, or a length of fabric. Consider again which of the Gestalt Principles and/or guidelines for obtaining unity in fashion you used. Which is the most successful design? Why?

3. Research a designer brand for the present or upcoming season. Present to the class his or her apparel across all product categories. Show the advertising campaign(s). Describe the corporate image. Identify the design elements that are repeated. Explain how each line achieves variety. How did the designer attain unity? Note Gestalt Principles and/or guidelines for unity listed in this chapter.

4. Create a small group of fashions with the ultimate goal of unity—e.
   three dresses or six pieces of sportswear (separate tops and bottoms). W
   in your sketchbook first. Plan to execute your solution in a final presenta
   tion. Make the following choices:

   o A simple or compound geometric shape.

   o A type of line.

   o Two or three colors or one pattern and two colors.

   o One color in a darker value than the others.

   o A dull or shiny texture or both.

5. Create a minimum of three designs using your chosen elements for each of
   the fashions in the group. Build variety into the dress designs, varying the
   necklines, sleeves, and hem lengths. Vary the tops by including overtops,
   undertops, different sleeves, and lengths. Show both skirts and pants and
   vary the lengths. Locate one point of emphasis per dress and one point of
   emphasis per top with bottom. (Hint: Obtain appropriate fabric swatches
   for your designs. That will make the process of designing easier.) Which are
   the best designs of the group? Why? Does the group have unity and variety?
   Is there no duplication in the group?

   Once you settle on the best designs, render them at the same scale using
   markers on Bristol board. (A croquis figure used for flat, technical drawing
   is a useful guide for consistent scale.) Cut the shapes out with an X-ACTO
   knife. Mount the dresses in a row on black mat board. Mount the tops over
   the bottoms in two rows on the mat board. Use a glue stick or doublestick
   tape for the adhesive.

REFERENCES   Anthony-Dharan, S. (2008, January 5). Forgotten fashion heroes: Paul
                  Poiret and Jeanne Lanvin. *CultureKiosque*. Retrieved July 25, 2009,
                  from http://www.culturekiosque.com/nouveau/style/fashion_lanvin-
                  poiret114.html.
                  Bissonnette, A. (2009, February 26). Michael Kors designs from the Wendy
                  Zuckerwise Ritter collection. *Kentucky State University Museum*.

Retrieved September 25, 2009, from http://dept.kent.edu/museum/ exhibit/kors/main.htm.

Brainard, S. (1998). *A design manual* (2nd ed.). Upper Saddle River, NJ: Prentice Hall.

Chambers, B. G. (1951). *Color and design: Fashion in men's and women's clothing and home furnishings.* Englewood Cliffs, NJ: Prentice Hall.

Cunningham, R. (1994). *The magic garment: Principles of costume design.* Long Grove, IL: Waveland Press.

Dantzic, C. M. (1990). *Design dimensions: An introduction to the visual surface.* Englewood Cliffs, NJ: Prentice Hall.

Davis, M. L. (1996). *Visual design in dress.* (3rd ed.). Upper Saddle River, NJ: Prentice Hall.

Donovan, C. (1986, May 4). Designer Donna Karan: How a fashion star is born. *New York Times Magazine,* 26–33, 90–94.

Gestalt principles. (2009). Retrieved July 24, 2009, from http://facweb.cs .depaul.edu/sgrais/gestalt_principles.htm.

Hunter, V. (2007). *The ultimate fashion study guide: The design process.* Los Angeles: Hunter Publishing.

Jeanne Lanvin. (2009). The Internet Fashion Database. Retrieved July 25, 2009, from http://www.tifdb.com/people/jeanne_lanvin/74.

1867–1946 Jeanne Lanvin. (2009). *The Fashion Spot.* Retrieved July 25, 2009, from http://forums.thefashionspot.com/f116/1867-1946-Jeanne-lanvin-38391.html.

Martin, R., & Koda, H. (1996). *Christian Dior.* New York: The Metropolitan Museum of Art.

Martinez, B., & Block, J. (1995). *Visual forces: An Introduction to Design* (2nd ed.) Upper Saddle River, NJ: Prentice Hall.

Ocvirk, O. G., Stinson, R E., Wigg, P. R., Bone, R. O., & Cayton, D. L. (2002). *Art fundamentals: Theory and practice* (9th ed.). New York: McGraw-Hill.

Sanderson, L. (2009, April 6). Jeanne Lanvin: The oldest fashion house in Paris. *Suite101.com.* Retrieved July 25, 2009, from http://french-fashion-designers.suite101.com/article.cfm/jeanne_lanvin.

Spokane Falls Community College. (n.d.). The Gestalt principles. Retrieved July 24, 2009, from http://graphicdesign.spokanefalls.edu/ tutorials/process/gestaltprinciples/gestaltprinc.htm.

Steele, Valerie. (1985). *Fashion and eroticism: Ideals of feminine beauty j. the Victorian era to the Jazz Age.* New York: Oxford University Press.

Stewart, M. (2008). *Launching the imagination: A comprehensive guide to basic design* (3rd ed.). New York: McGraw-Hill.

Stoops, J., & Samuelson, J. (1983). *Design dialogue.* Worcester, MA: Davis Publications.

Tate, S. L. (1999). *Inside fashion design* (4th ed.) New York: Longmans & Green.

Todorovic, Dejan. (2008). Gestalt principles. *Scholarpedia.* Retrieved July 2, 2009, from http://www.scholarpedia.org/article/Gestalt_principles.

Trachtenberg, J. (1988). *Ralph Lauren: The man behind the mystique.* Boston: Little, Brown.

GLOSSARY

absorption 1. The taking up of moisture by a textile fiber, which adds comfort to the wearing of apparel. 2. The passing of light into a surface, as in the case of fabrics that are dark or dull.

abstract A motif where there is nothing representational or recognizable from the natural or man-made world.

abstract texture A simulated texture that is abstracted or simplified.

abstraction The removal of detail so that only the qualities and the properties of a thing remain.

acetate Generic fiber category established by the Federal Trade Commission (FTC) for manufactured fibers that are chemical variants of cellulose called cellulose acetate and that are manufactured from cellulose materials, such as wood chips.

achromatic Literally, without color; it describes a surface or object without a hue on the color wheel, such as white, gray, or black.

acrylic Generic fiber category established by the Federal Trade Commission (FTC) for a manufactured fiber primarily composed of a polymer material called acrylonitrile.

actual line A line where its evidence and placement are determined by intended design.

actual texture The form the surface takes that causes the sensation when it is touched.

additive color The dynamic of working with colored light rays; the more they are mixed with other colors, the lighter they become.

aesthetic design Of or in relation to the beauty of a design; evaluated by the elements and principles of design.

afterimage The idea that the cones in the eye can only register one color in a complementary pair at a time. When the cones fatigue, they revert to seeing that color's complement as an aftereffect of perception.

A-line The silhouette that takes the shape of the letter "A."

all-over layout A pattern that features motifs in a scattered or seemingly random arrangement where they are placed in all directions, also referred to as a *random* or *tossed layout*.

all-over pattern A pattern in which the viewer's eye moves from motif to motif; used as a vehicle to establish rhythm.

alpaca Fibers from a sheeplike animal of the camel family, related to the llama, native to the Andes in South America.

alternation A sequence of two units that change back and forth.

ambient light Light that encompasses an entire space.

ambiguity The deliberate alteration of figure and ground so that the figure blends into the ground.

analogous A color scheme made up of three to five adjacent hues on the color wheel.

angle of incidence The angle at which light hits an object.

angora Fibers or soft fuzzy yarn made from the underhair of the angora rabbit.

aniline dye Dyes made synthetically from a derivative of benzene.

anomaly A deviation from the norm.

appliqué Surface pattern made by cutting out fabric or lace designs and attaching them to another fabric by means of embroidery or stitching.

approximate symmetry The same distribution of elements on both sides of a design, but with a slight change.

architectural design The structural design of a garment that is conceived as an environment for the body and executed with an actual or visual rigidity of form that exists separately from the human body.

arrangement The organization of motifs into a layout.

Art Deco A pattern associated with the design influences during the 1920s and 1930s, the acceptance of industrialization, and the aesthetics of machines, which rejected the elaborate ornamentation of the preceding generations in favor of geometric shapes and simplicity of line.

art movement Support of an art style by a group of artists during a particular period.

Art Nouveau A pattern with organic elaboration, sinuous curved line, and asymmetrical arrangement of forms and patterns that descends specifically from the design period of the same name, 1890–1914, in Europe and North America.

Arts and Crafts movement A movement in response to the tastes of the Victorian era and the growth of the Industrial Age, and overlapped with and influenced the Art Nouveau period. Ornamentation was derived from Medieval Europe, Islamic influences, and Japanese ideas.

asymmetry The feeling of equally distributed weight due to decisions regarding the elements of design, but where the arrangement is different on either side of the median line.

back-fullness The silhouette that places fullness at the backside, or derriere.

balance The sense of evenly distributed weight, resulting in the overall feeling of stability.

balance of all-over pattern The existence of a regularly spaced pattern as an arrangement that leads the eye throughout the design.

batik A surface pattern that results from the dye process in which the fabric is covered in wax before it is immersed in dye. The dye penetrates cracks in the wax, yielding the effect that gives the pattern its character. The resist method originated in China or India but comes from Indonesia most commonly today.

bell-shaped The silhouette that takes the shape of a bell.

Bezold effect The idea that, by changing just one color in the color combination of a design, a completely different visual product is created.

bias When the lengthwise and crosswise yarns in a fabric structure are used on the diagonal.

bias cut When the fabric is cut off-grain, enabling it to drape over the contours of the body.

Black Tie Abbreviated term designating a man's semiformal evening attire.

bleaching The process of removing color from a substance.

border print A design that contrasts a border pattern with the one that covers the remainder of the fabric or the field.

botanical A pattern related to a floral, but the plants, flowers, and herbs are organized within blocks, reminiscent of the way they were pictured on pages of nineteenth-century books that enumerated plant species.

bouclé A novelty yarn with a loopy texture.

braid A narrow woven band with a structure of three interwoven strands for use as trimming, as binding, or for outlining lace and embroidery.

brightness The result of the amount of energy radiating from a light source.

brocade A heavy fabric with a complex, raised pattern that is woven on jacquard loom.

broken rhythm The term for what happens when a pattern is interrupted.

bustle A style that places exceptional fullness at the back of a skirt on a woman's dress.

calendaring Passing fabric between two heated rollers in order to produce a smooth, even appearance.

calico The name for patterns that have closely situated, tiny floral motifs in four-color combinations, usually with a dark or bright background.

camel's hair 1. Fibers from the crossbred Bactrian camel of Asia, which produces soft luxurious yarn. 2. Cloth made from these fibers.

camouflage 1. A pattern meant to present low visibility in the underbrush during a time of war. 2. The deliberate alteration of figure and ground so that the figure blends into the ground; also called ambiguity, it is a unifying visual force.

cashmere 1. Fibers from a fine, soft, downy wool undergrowth produced by the cashmere goat, which is raised in the Kashmir region of India and Pakistan and parts of northern India, Tibet, Mongolia, Turkmenistan, China, Iran, and Iraq. 2. Cloth woven from this fiber.

centricity A compositional center that, when emphasized, causes compressive compositional force, leading the eye further into the design.

challis Soft, plain-weave fabric made of wool, rayon staple, cotton, or manufactured fiber blends that is supple and lightweight, and often printed in small floral patterns.

checks A fabric design composed of alternate squares of colors in various sizes.

chiffon Thin transparent fabric made in a plain weave.

chintz A polished or glazed cotton that may feature a floral pattern with a realistic interpretation.

chiton Garment worn in ancient Greece that consisted of a rectangle of fabric wrapped around the body and fastened at the shoulders with one or more pins.

chroma A measure of a hue's purity or brilliance.

ciréing A finishing process in which wax or other compounds are applied to the surface of a fabric, after which a hot roller is passed over the surface to produce high polish.

classic Apparel that continues to be fashionable for a long period of time and that may return to high fashion at intervals.

classification of apparel A group of similar fashions, such as evening wear, sportswear. or coats.

closure 1. A device used to close or fasten a garment. 2. The tendency of the brain to fill in missing details from a familiar image or pattern (a Gestalt Principle).

collar Separate piece attached to an item of clothing at the neckline in order to finish the neckline edge.

collection 1. A group of fashions designed by members of the haute couture that may include a variety of styles

for the same customer. 2. A group of patterns that relate to each other by a common theme

color A specific hue that is determined by its wavelength.

color advisory association An organization of representatives of fiber companies, fashion services, retailers, and textile firms; it exists in a number of countries and meets in conferences twice per year in order to define and summarize their perception of color trends.

color constancy The phenomenon where people recognize color by past experience and do not make perceptual adjustments based on other variables, such as the changing light due to time of day.

color forecasting The analysis and interpretation of social and cultural events, the economy, and certain market sectors in order to make predictions about color based on insight, experience, and mathematics; forecasters identify what colors consumers are ready to consume.

color reporting service For-profit information services, available on a subscription basis, that research and report color trends across several classifications of apparel.

color spectrum 1. Colors organized in a particular order; the rainbow is one example. 2. A particular order in which color forecasters formulate their ideas to reflect the commonness of tones and intensities.

color temperature The warmth or coolness of colors based upon their associations with nature and their organization on the color wheel.

color trends Consumer preferences in color choice as revealed by research into their buying behavior; often paired with a prediction or forecast of future buying habits.

color wheel A system by which colors are organized.

colorfast The resistance of dye to migrate or fade from the fabric surface.

color-matching system A method of measuring colors according to hue, value, and chroma in order to determine the capacity for them to match with others.

lementary A color scheme that contains two opposite hues on the color wheel.

ompressibility How a fabric responds to squeezing.

concentricity The idea that a circular shape draws the eye to its center.

construction The act or process of constructing.

containment The edge of a composition or a boundary within which it acts as a unifying force.

continuity A Gestalt Principle which states that viewers tend to continue shapes beyond their ending points.

contour The outside line of a shape or the outside surface of a three-dimensional form.

contrast 1. When two forces operate in opposition, causing a significant difference. 2. The amount of difference between values.

conversational Patterns which tell a story or communicate a message.

cool Colors such as the blues and greens summoning thoughts of sky, grass, foliage, and water, and that occupy one side of the color wheel

coordinates 1. A group of garments designed to coordinate with one another, as in the case of sportswear. 2. A group of patterns designed to coordinate with one another.

corset A bodice stiffened with wood, bone, or metal, based on a historic garment from the eleventh century, but existent in some form through the early twentieth century.

cotton A soft white vegetable fiber that comes from the fluffy boll of the cotton plant.

Country French Patterns that originated in the Provence region of France in the eighteenth century and were the result of the artisan's process of printing with woodblocks.

coverage To what extent the arrangement of a pattern is highly concentrated or not.

crepe 1. A general classification of fabrics made from almost any fiber and characterized by a broad range of crinkled or grained surface effects. 2. A crepe yarn that is given a high twist during spinning.

crochet Fabric made from a continuous series of loops of yarn made with a single hooked needle

croquis The artwork that features the textile designer's communication of an original design, complete with main motif(s) and colors.

culture Characteristics such as ideas, customs, skills, and arts of a people or group in a particular period.

curved line A line having no straight part; bend having no angular part.

curvilinear line A line that has a repetitive organic quality, as in a series of curves.

cut of the fabric Whether the fabric is cut with its yarns on-grain or on the bias.

damask A fabric or scroll patterned fabric that is produced by a weaving process.

dart A method of stitching out a fold of fabric to remove excess in length or width that enables the fabric to fit a body curve.

deconstruction A concept whereby in the search for hidden or alternative meanings, new and diverse forms express new meanings, which are offered as alternatives to what was previously accepted. In fashion, clothing appears inside out, unfinished, or deteriorated.

density The weight per volume of the texture of a fabric.

design Both product and process; as a product, a tangible visual solution that integrates materials and function; the result of the organization and arrangement of parts into a final form.

design process The result of many stages of thought, including research and analysis.

details Garments parts, such as necklines, sleeves, waistlines, pockets, trims, and surface embellishments, such as embroidery, fringes, buttons, appliqués, and bows. Also refers to fashion accessories.

diagonal line A line that moves or extend obliquely, especially at a 45-degree angle.

diffused light Rays that scatter in different directions.

direct printing A process that imparts motifs to the fabric via engraved rollers, wooden blocks, or a photo process.

directed light   Localized light that is focused like a spotlight.

discharge printing   A process in which dark dyes are removed from dark backgrounds, causing light-colored motifs to occur.

dobby   Weave forming small repeated geometric patterns.

documentary designs   Patterns that originate in historic periods, other countries, and cultures, and international or ethnic styles.

dot   A tiny spot or point; the smallest entity in design.

double complementary   A color scheme that consists of two colors on either side of a hue and the two on either side of its complement.

double knit   Knits produced on rib machines that have two sets of needles set at angles to each other.

double split complement   A color scheme that uses four colors that are equidistant on the color wheel; also called a *tetrad*.

drape   The way in which a fabric falls.

draped design   The structure of the garment design when the fabric is bias cut.

dye   The natural or synthetic coloring agent used for the coloring of fibers, yarns, fabrics, furs, and leather.

eccentricity   The effect if emphasis is located close to the outside edge(s) of the composition, causing expansive compositional force.

economy   Management of a design using careful planning and restrained or efficient use of the elements and details.

electromagnetic waves   Waves propagated through space or matter by oscillating electric and magnetic fields.

elements of construction   Techniques used to enable fabric to take the shape of the body.

elements of design   The ingredients of a design.

embroidery   Fancy needlework or trimming using colored yarn, embroidery floss, soft cotton, silk, or metallic thread.

emphasis   The location where the eye first settles on the garment.

empire   Refers to the fashion prevalent during the Empire period in the beginning of the nineteenth century during which Napoleon was in power. The dress tubular silhouette with the waistline placed just be the bust.

engineered design   A design created for a particular area or shape, signifying an important relationship between the pattern and the garment.

epaulettes   Ornamental shoulder trims originally used on military uniforms.

extensibility   The extent of stretch in a fabric.

eyelet   A fabric in which holes are punched as decoration and are embroidered around the edges to keep them from fraying.

fabric   The medium in which a fashion designer works.

fabric trends   Predictions about the consumer acceptance of fabrics based on research of previous consumption.

fagoting   Stitch used to join two edges of fabric together in decorative openwork effect.

faille   Fabric with a flat-ribbed effect running crosswise that is flatter and less pronounced than grosgrain.

fashion reporting service   For-profit informational service, based on purchase by subscription, that reports predictions about the consumption of fashion based on research.

felt   A fabric constructed by fibers adhering to one another without first being spun.

fiber   The chemical substance from which fabrics are made.

fiber dyeing   Coloring that occurs during the production of the fiber.

Fiberglas   Fine-spun filaments of glass made into yarn that is woven into textiles.

field   In textile design, the wide space of the fabric that contrasts with the border. Also referred to as the background on the design of a flag.

figure and ground   The relationship of shape to space in which there is a visual cue that the shape is advancing closer to the viewer and the space is receding.

figure/ground   The perceptual tendency to separate whole figures from their backgrounds, based on such elements as color, contrast, and value.

ent A long fiber, like those in silk and synthetic fibers.

sh A chemical or mechanical treatment that applies heat, pressure, and/or chemicals to affect the fabric surface and penetrate its fibers.

fit To take the size and shape that is appropriate for the end use of a garment, which includes consideration of the comfort of the wearer.

flannel Fine soft fabric made in tightly woven twill or plain weave and finished with a light napping.

flat pattern A system of adjusting the basic pattern shapes.

flax Fiber from the stem of the flax plant.

fleece A fabric with a thick, heavy, fleece-like surface; it may be a pile fabric or simply one with nap, and may be woven or knitted.

flexibility The term used to express the suppleness or rigidity of a fabric.

floral A pattern in which flowers constitute the motifs.

focal point What the designer wants the viewer to see, the center of attraction or the area of greatest visual importance; also called the point of emphasis.

folk Patterns that originate in specific regions or countries.

form A three-dimensional area enclosed by a surface.

formal balance When each element on one side of the design has a counterpart on the other.

foulard Patterns with tiny geometric motifs that repeat in a set layout, often used in neckties.

four way A layout in which motifs are placed up and down as well as left and right in the same design.

fraction A mathematical expression of a ratio .

frequency The speed of wave vibrations.

functional design Refers to the way in which a design works or performs physically.

gabardine Durable, closely woven fabric with diagonal ridges created by a warp-faced twill weave and made from wool, rayon, or other fibers or blends.

gathering A seam where the stitches are larger and looser so the fabric gathers into puffs of fabric.

Gazar A heavily sized woven silk originated by designer Cristóbal Balenciaga along with the textile designer Gustav Zumsteg and the Swiss textile manufacturer Abraham.

geometric Patterns with motifs that are characterized by geometric shapes, but that also occur in woven structures defined by lines, such as stripes, plaids, and checks.

Gestalt principles The ways in which visual information are understood holistically before it is examined separately; also called the *Law of Simplicity*; they explain different approaches for the creation of unity.

gingham A yarn-dyed checked fabric made of cotton or of cotton blended with polyester.

glazing Process of pressing fabric with heated rollers to give it a high gloss.

golden mean The concept attributed to the Greek mathematician Euclid that a small part relates to a larger part as the larger part relates to the whole. It suggests "the moderation in all things" or a place between two extremes.

golden section Another name for the golden mean.

good continuation Another term for "continuity," meaning that viewers tend to continue shapes beyond their ending points.

gradation A sequence of adjacent units that change in steps from one to the next; also called progression.

grain Yarns run lengthwise, parallel to the fabric selvage, and crosswise in the fabric structure.

gravity As a result of the force that draws things to the earth or ground, the idea that elements provoking greater visual weight appear most appropriate in the bottom area of a design.

grid A structure where vertical and horizontal lines create a tension that suggests stillness and formality and is a framework for repetition.

grosgrain Fabric with a large rib that is made by grouping several crosswise yarns together. Used for ribbons, sashes, trim, bows, neckwear, and millinery.

grouping Also called "similarity"; elements that share similar characteristics are grouped together in the viewer's mind.

hand The way in which fabric feels to the skin.

harmony All of the design elements work in agreement.

haute couture The term means "high sewing" in its literal translation but refers to the level of the industry in which clothing is made of the best quality at the highest prices on a custom-order basis.

hem The lower edge of an item of clothing, such as a skirt or blouse, or of sleeves.

hemp A coarse, strong, lustrous fiber from the stem of the hemp plant.

herringbone A pattern made of short, slanting parallel lines adjacent to other rows slanting in reverse direction, creating a continuous V-shaped design like the bones of a fish.

Hierarchical Principle Authored by costume curator James Laver, the idea that people dress to indicate position in society.

high contrast Related to the value scale, the concept that a vast difference in contrast draws attention and provides clarity.

high-key values The range of values between white and middle gray.

historic period A particular period of years in history characterized by common cultural forces.

holographic materials Of or having the quality of holography, which is a method of making three-dimensional photographs without a camera, but by the use of splitting a laser beam.

horizontal balance An approach commonly utilized to determine weight distribution in which an imaginary vertical line is drawn down the center of a fashion and each side examined for distribution.

horizontal line A line that runs parallel to the horizon.

houndstooth Irregular colored checks like squares with two points at the corners. The checks alternate with white, produced by a yarn-dyed twill weave.

hourglass The silhouette that takes the shape of an hourglass, with some fullness at the bust and hip and fit at the waist.

hue The general term for or the family name of a color, which is determined by its wavelength on the light spectrum.

ideals of beauty An ideal during a certain period which becomes a societal norm and that has implications for body shape, and therefore necessarily influences designers.

ikat A pattern that results from a yarn-dying method where yarns are individually tied and then dyed along different lengths.

image A decision which rests primarily on the opinions of others.

imagination The act or power of forming mental images of what is not actually present.

implied line A series of shapes or dots placed in a linear arrangement suggests a line.

indigo 1. Dark blue. 2. The dye used originally for jeans. 3. The only shade of a particular hue on the color wheel that performs generally like a neutral.

informal balance When the elements on either side of the imaginary vertical line achieve equality in weight but with variety in line, shape, value, texture, or color.

inspiration Any stimulus to creative thought or action.

intensity The range of brightness to dullness of a hue, also referred to as saturation.

interlining A layer used between the fabric and lining for the purpose of adding shape to a garment without rigidity.

interpretation The expression of a person's conception of a work of art, subject, and so forth.

invented texture The pure invention of texture by the artist or designer through the use of media.

inverted pyramid The reversed form of a structure that has a square base and four triangular sides. In fashion, it is another term for a wedge silhouette.

isolation A shape that stands by itself.

jacquard A woven structure that has designs of considerable size in a pattern, due to the use of punched cards or an electronic device added to a loom; examples of a jacquard fabric include brocade, damask, and tapestry.

Laver The late curator of the Victoria and Albert Museum who developed the three theories about fashion from a desire to date images accurately through the clothing depicted in them—the Utility Principle, the Hierarchical Principle, and the Seduction Principle

jersey Classification of knitted fabrics that are made in a plain stitch without a distinct rib.

kimono A traditional costume of Japan that is a loose, straight-cut cotton or silk robe made in various lengths and sashed at the waist; loose straight sleeves are cut on at right angles.

kinetic line A line from which one perceives movement.

knit A fabric structure in which needles are used to form a series of interconnecting loops from one or more yarns or a set of yarns.

lace Decorative openwork fabric made by hand or machine, often with a repeated motif.

Law of Simplicity Every stimulus is perceived in its most simple form (Gestalt Principle).

layout Refers to the placement of one motif relative to another.

level of illumination The result of the amount of energy radiating from a light source; brightness.

Liberty The term for prints that are named for the British department store called Liberty of London. They have small floral motifs, fruits, and birds of small and medium scale, and they are used in women's and children's apparel.

lifestyle merchandising The association of designer names and their looks with a range of products, including but not limited to high-priced women's apparel, as well as men's sportswear and suits, children's apparel, accessories, casual sportswear, fragrances, and home products.

light The electromagnetic energy making things visible or radiant energy resulting from the vibration of electrons.

line 1. A moving point or dot; a connection between two points. 2. A group of fashions created by designers for mass fashion, typically designed with one classification of apparel in mind.

line direction The point toward which a line travels.

line network Vertical and horizontal lines used in combination and with repetition.

linen 1. Fibers of the flax plant that are used to make linen yarn. 2. Fabrics made of linen yarns.

looks Particular styles.

low contrast A description of subtle difference.

low-key values The range of values between middle gray and black.

Lurex Trademark for a decorative metallic fiber and yarn made of aluminum-coated plastic to prevent tarnishing.

luster The way light is reflected from the fabric surface.

macramé A fabric structure in which two, three, four, or more strands of cord, string, or yarn are knotted in groups to form patterns.

man-made fibers Manufactured or synthetic fibers.

man-made objects Those objects that are familiar as a result of experience, such as teapots, beach balls, golf clubs, and birdhouses.

mass-produced brand A manufacturer or distributor-assigned name, mark, or label assigned to product aimed at the mass market in order to encourage recognition of the product.

men's shirting Fabric that is traditionally used for men's shirts; a light cotton or cotton blend with stripes or other appropriate patterns.

metallic fibers Fibers made from metals.

microfiber An extremely fine polyester filament.

minimalism An approach characterized by simple cut and plain colors.

modacrylic Generic category of manufactured fiber made from acrylic resins.

moderate price point The middle price ranges for fashion apparel, as opposed to the budget- or popular-, better-, or designer-price range.

mohair Fiber obtained from the hair of the angora goat or fabric made from that hair.

moiréing The implementation of a water pattern on fabric by applying heated rollers that flatten some of the heavy crosswise yarns, thus changing the light reflection.

monochromatic A color scheme where a garment design rests on one hue.

motif The building blocks of a pattern, making it recognizable by their repetition and arrangement.

movement Another term for rhythm.

muse An individual who especially inspires a fashion designer to design.

napping Creating a fuzzy appearance on the surface of fabric by brushing it with loosely twisted yarn.

natural fibers Fibers that come from animal or plant sources.

natural objects Objects that originate in nature, like flowers, leaves, waves, snowflakes, and seashells.

negative space The dark or secondary space that may interact with another space, perceived as a light or positive space.

netting A fabric often made with hexagonal meshes.

neutral Colors that are achromatic or without a hue thought to harmonize with all hues and with each other, and not found on the color wheel.

New Look of 1947 The style of Christian Dior's initial collection in 1947, also called the *Corolle* line. It was characterized by a sweeping skirt, close-fitted bodice, nipped-in waist, rounded breasts, padded hips, and de-emphasized shoulders.

nonobjective Art that does not have representational forms or recognizable forms from the world around us.

notan The Japanese principle that is the interaction between positive (light) and negative (dark) space. The two parts together make a whole created through opposites that have equal and inseparable value, contributing to a new unity.

nylon Generic fiber category established by the FTC for a manufactured fiber composed of a long chain of chemicals called polyamides.

occult balance Also called *asymmetrical balance*, it refers to designs that are different on either side of the median,

but still convey the feeling of equally distributed due to the decisions regarding shape, line, color, value, pattern, size, arrangement, or construction.

ombre From the darkest value of a hue to its tint to white.

one way A layout where one or more motifs are placed "right-side-up."

on-grain When the warp yarns (which run lengthwise in a woven fabric) and the weft yarns (which run crosswise) are at right angles.

open A layout where there is a lot of distance between motifs, also called spaced.

opponent theory The term for the fact that cones can only register one color in a complementary pair at a time.

optical center A bit higher than the actual center.

order All of the visual elements are located, grouped, and assigned a size according to their relative importance to the whole of the design; a contributor to unity.

organdy Light sheer cotton fabric with a permanently crisp feel.

organic line A line that has the properties of life forms, such as curves like the body.

Orphism The idea that movement, light, and rhythm are more important than the presentation of an object; also called *simultaneity*.

out of proportion Not consistent with the proportion of the human figure.

packed A layout where motifs are highly concentrated, with little space between them; also called a "tight" layout.

paillettes Spangles made of metal or plastic, usually a round disk larger than a sequin.

paisley A design inherited from the cashmere shawls of India that were woven in Paisley, Scotland, defined by the palm shape and repeated at either a very large or small scale.

pannier A historic undergarment with the framework of a basket meant to support skirts into the space outside of the hips.

parallelism An element which utilizes equidistant units on the same plane.

An amount that is less than the whole that can be separated from the whole either physically or in the imagination.

patchwork A method of sewing small pieces of various colors and patterns together to form a fabric or a quilt.

pattern The result when any visual element is repeated over an extended area.

pattern drafting The system by which pattern shapes are developed from a combination of measurements.

pattern piece One of the set of forms to the shape of which material is cut for assembly into a finished garment.

percale Plain-weave lightweight fabric made originally in cotton, but in a blend of polyester and cotton in recent years.

personal coloring The composite of skin, hair, and eye colors of a consumer.

personal space The space immediately surrounding a person.

physical texture Another term for "actual texture," which is the form the surface takes that causes the sensation when it is touched.

piece dyeing Adding the dye to the garment at the fabric stage.

pigment Coloring matter, usually in the form of an insoluble powder, mixed with liquids such as oil or water to make paints.

pile Cut yarns in a woven structure that cause a plush surface.

pile knit A type of weft knit in which deep-pile fabrics or simulated fur pile fabrics are made on a jersey knit machine by the addition of a special attachment.

piping A folded piece of bias binding used for trimming.

piqué A group of durable fabrics characterized by corded effects either lengthwise or crosswise.

placement In relation to emphasis, the phenomenon of a designer distinguishing a part of the design by visual selection.

plaid Common term for pattern woven of various colored yarns in stripes of different widths running at right angles to form blocks.

plaid layout A design offering intersecting lines or bands of color.

plain weave The simplest woven structure, in which the warp and weft yarns intersect singly with one another.

pleats Folds of fabric usually pressed flat but sometimes left unpressed.

ply The strands in a yarn.

pocket A piece of fabric shaped to fit either on the outside or inside of clothing used for decorative purposes or to carry small articles.

point of emphasis What the designer wants the viewer to see, the center of attraction or the area of greatest visual importance; also called the *focal point*.

polyester Generic fiber name for manufactured fibers made from acids and alcohols derived from petroleum.

Pop Art movement An art movement that began in the 1950s in the United Kingdom and the United States, which drew its techniques and themes from popular mass culture, such as television, movies, advertising, and comic books.

portion One of a number of equal parts into which the whole is divided.

positive space The light or primary space that may interact with another space, perceived as dark or negative space.

pouf A wide, puffy skirt with a light, airy appearance, made in both short and long styles, and often constructed by gathering the bottom, turning it up, and stitching it to a lining.

primary colors Those that cannot be mixed by combining any other colors, identified as red, green, and blue.

principles of design The methods by which the elements combine in a design.

product dyeing Adding dye once the garment is formed.

progression A sequence of adjacent units that change in steps from one to the next; also called *gradation*.

proportion The result of the comparative relationships of distances, sizes, amounts, degrees or parts to the whole.

proximity The distance between visual elements.

quilting The technique of joining together layers of fabrics using hand or machine stitching, sometimes with batting or other filling in between.

radial balance A system of arrangement that occurs around a central point.

radiation A wheel-shaped form where emphasis begins at the center and the eye moves outward, along the radials, from the center.

ramie Strong, soft, lustrous fiber, somewhat similar to linen, from the inner bark of the ramie plant.

random layout A pattern that features motifs in a scattered or seemingly random arrangement where they are placed in all directions, also referred to as an all-over layout.

ratio A comparison of two quantities.

rayon Generic fiber name for manufactured cellulosic fibers regenerated from short cotton fibers or wood chips.

realistic The condition where motifs have their true colors, highlights, and shadows, and where the overlapping of them provides depth and perspective.

reflective The quality of bouncing light back into space after it hits a surface.

refracted light When light is bent, as in the case of hitting a transparent surface.

repeat The adaptation of the design to the industry printing process.

repetition The repeating of a design element when the same visual effect occurs over and over.

resilience The ability of the fabric to spring back from squeezing or twisting.

resist Methods that indicate a medium is applied to the fabric surface to prevent dye from reaching it.

rhythm The movement of the eye from the point of contact throughout the rest of the design or a recurrence of movement.

ribbed knit A knitted fabric structure where the stitches are drawn to both sides of the fabric and that is characterized by distinct lengthwise rib effects on both sides of the fabric.

ribbon A long, narrow strip of silk, cotton, or rayon woven with selvages on both sides used mainly for trimming.

rotary screen printing A process in which dye is moved through a finely perforated drum.

ruching A trimming using the pleating a strip of material such as lace, ribbon, or silk so that it ruffles on both sides; made by stitching through the center of the pleating. Contemporary usage also applies the term to clothing with large rippled areas formed by gathers.

ruffle A strip of cloth, lace, or ribbon gathered along one edge or cut in a curve to produce a ripple.

satin A smooth lustrous fabric woven with floating yarns in the warp.

saturation The range of brightness to dullness of a hue; also referred to as *intensity*.

scale Used to describe size proportions in comparison with human size.

schreinering The etching of hundreds of fine lines on a fabric's surface to add a subtle luster.

screen printing A process in which dye meets the fabric through a cutout adhered to a fine fabric screen.

seam A line of stitching that attaches two pieces of fabric.

season Any of the divisions of the year characterized by differences in temperature, rainfall, light, and plant growth. The fashion industry gears the creation of garment lines or collections to a particular time of year, such as fall, holiday, winter (sometimes marketed in terms of vacations in warm climates and therefore called "resort"), and spring.

secondary colors When colors of light overlap in varying amounts forming other interesting colors

Seduction Principle Authored by costume curator James Laver, the idea that people dress to attract others.

seersucker A medium-weight fabric made with lengthwise crinkled stripes alternating with plain woven stripes and puckering, achieved by releasing the tension at intervals on the lengthwise yarns.

self-expression A decision that is made primarily on aesthetics and may involve experimentation.

ge The edge of a pattern or border.

uencing An arrangement where one unit follows another in a particular order.

sequins Small shiny iridescent disks of metal or plastic pierced in the center and sewn on garments in a decorative design or in rows to cover a portion or the entire surface,

set layout A pattern that is based upon an invisible grid where the motifs are arranged in the squares.

sett The sequence in which bands of different colors and varying widths repeat in a plaid.

"sex appeal" theory The Seduction Principle, authored by costume curator James Laver, which states that people dress to attract others.

shade The addition of black to a hue.

shape A two-dimensional area enclosed by a line.

shearing The process of clipping nap of fabric to its desired length.

shirring Three or more rows of gathers made by small running stitches in parallel lines.

signature color A color which defines the house's image and the continuing collections.

silhouette The outer contour or shape of a fashion.

silk A fiber obtained from the cocoon of the silkworm.

similarity Elements that share visual characteristics belong together in the viewer's mind; also called *grouping*.

simulated texture The faithful rendering of a real texture.

simultaneity The idea that movement, light, and rhythm are more important than the presentation of an object; also called *Orphism*.

simultaneous contrast The idea that a color looks different when placed in proximity to another color.

single knit A knitted fabric structure created by a single set of needles.

size 1. The magnitude or quantitative degree in relation to a particular standard of measurement. 2. A scale of numbers or letters that correspond to garment measurements in order to fit a variety of body types.

sleeve The part of an item of clothing that covers the arm.

source The origin from which a motif's design emerges; origins include natural objects, man-made objects, imagination, and symbolism.

space An empty area or extent; a two-dimensional emptiness or three-dimensional void.

spaced A layout where there is a lot of distance between motifs; also called *open*.

spandex Generic fiber term for manufactured fibers, composed largely of segmented polyurethane, which are stretchable and lightweight.

spectrum A particular order of colors.

Standard Color Wheel The system of color that is the most relevant for fashion design; an organizational chart of color sensations that offers a guide for discovering the color combinations, schemes, or relationships that should have the greatest visual impact.

staple 1. Short fibers that are dull, rough, and fuzzy, like those characteristic of cotton and wool. 2. A fashion that does not change and remains a basic in the wardrobe.

stencil An instrument that allows dye to be poured through its holes but not through the plate itself

stomacher In women's dress, a heavily embroidered or jeweled V-shaped panel over the chest and extending down to a point over the stomach.

straight line A line that has the same direction throughout its length.

stripe The most common repetition of the line in pattern.

stripe layout A pattern organized in colored bands, sometimes alternating with rows of motifs, a typical arrangement for documentary designs.

structural design That which determines the form of the design.

structural texture The result of the elements of a substance or material and the method of its construction.

stylize The condition where a motif is simplified, flattened, distorted, changed in color, or edged in line.

subculture A group (within a society) of persons of the same age, social or economic status, or ethnic background, and having its own characteristics such as interests and goals.

subtractive color The process of experiencing sensations when wavelengths are absorbed and few are reflected.

successive contrast The idea that if one stares at a color for a long time and looks away, the complementary color appears in an afterglow.

surface contour Divergence from a flat plane on the fabric surface.

surface friction How the fabric slides over itself.

symbolism Motifs that represent a non-concrete idea, like a political movement, religion, or organization, such as logos or flags.

Symbolism movement A late-nineteenth-century movement that espoused the evocation of feelings and ideas rather than representational nature and objects.

symmetry A strict adherence to the balance of elements on either side of the median line.

synthetic fiber Textile fiber that is not found in nature but is produced by various chemical processes.

tactile texture The actual feel of the surface texture.

taffeta Crisp fabric with a fine, smooth surface made in a plain weave with a small crosswise rib.

target market Also referred to as *target customer*; the particular customer range envisioned by a fashion company and defined by gender, age range, geographic location, and lifestyle.

tartan Name for the kinds of plaid that come from Scotland and represent a different family clan; they are distinctive because the bands of colors and various widths repeat in a sequence that is the same crosswise and lengthwise.

tattersall Plaid consisting of narrow lines in two alternating colors, crossed to form a checked design on a plain light-colored ground; named for Richard Tattersall, British founder of Tattersall's London Horse Auction Mart.

terry cloth Fabric made in the pile weave with uncut loops and a background weave of plain or twill.

tertiary colors The colors that result when secondary colors combine.

tetrad A color scheme that uses four colors that are equidistant on the color wheel; also called a *double-split complement*.

texture The visible and tangible structure of a surface.

Theory of the Shifting Erogenous Zone The idea that the human body can be so desirable that one cannot take it all in at once but must concentrate on one part at a time, including the erotic zones or sexually secondary characteristics, such as the breasts, hips, derriere, or even the legs, feet, back, shoulders, or waist.

thermal character The apparent fabric temperature by comparison to skin temperature.

tie-dyeing A process in which fabric is tied into gathers, pleats, tucks, or puckers and then is released after being submerged into dye.

tight A layout where motifs are highly concentrated, with little space between them, also called *packed*.

tint The addition of white to a hue.

Toile de Jouy A pattern that features romanticized landscapes and figures, referring to a French town known for the print works that were founded in 1760.

tone on tone A color scheme that involves two hues that lie next to each other on the color wheel.

topstitching Stitching visible from the outer or "top" side of a garment that consists of one or more rows of machine stitching made through all layers of fabric.

tossed A layout in which motifs occur in all directions.

traditional Designs which have been treated the same way over many years.

transition When an element's change is so subtle that it is difficult to notice but nevertheless keeps the eye moving along the design.

translucent When some light can pass through a surface, because the surface is neither fully transparent or fully opaque.

transmission The passing of light through a surface.

transparent Characterized by the ability to see through a substance.

nto Type of quilting in which design is outlined and then stuffed from the back of the fabric to achieve a raised or embossed effect.

trends Direction in which styles, colors, fabrics, and designs are tending to change.

triad A color scheme featuring three hues equidistant on the color wheel.

triangle A geometric figure having three angles and three sides; a garment may take on the shape of a triangle.

trim A material used specifically to decorate or embellish a garment.

trompe l'oeil French term meaning "to fool the eye," a technique used in painting and in fashion where the viewer expects the authentic feel of the object depicted.

tubular The fashion silhouette that takes the shape of an oblong rectangle.

tuck A means of controlling fullness in a garment in which part of the garment piece is made smaller by folding the fabric and stitching line parallel to the fold.

tulle Fine, sheer net fabric made of silk, nylon, or rayon with hexagonal holes.

twill Basic weave characterized by diagonal wales, as in denim jean fabric.

two way A layout that has motifs placed both up and down in a design.

unity Integrates all aspects of the design.

Utility Principle Authored by costume curator James Laver, the idea that people dress for concerns such as warmth and comfort.

value The degree of a color's lightness or darkness.

value scale The sequence of values from white to black.

variety Difference in the elements of a design and in the comparison of one design to the next.

velvet A fabric with short, closely woven pile created from extra lengthwise yarns that is known for its soft, rich texture.

vertical balance An approach commonly utilized to determine weight distribution in which an imaginary horizontal line is drawn down the center of a fashion and each side examined for distribution.

vertical line A line that runs from the top to the bottom of a design.

visible spectrum Each of the colors thought to distinguish itself to the human eye due to different ranges of wavelengths of radiant energy.

visual texture The structure of the surface based on perception.

visual weight An element that denotes the relative importance of an element in the design.

waistband A band of fabric, usually faced and interfaced, seamed to the waistline of skirt or pants and fastened to hold garment firmly around the waist.

wardrobe consultant A professional who is compensated for advising the consumer on the selection of personal clothing.

warm Colors that are yellow-based, oranges and reds to violets, occupy half of the color wheel, and convey associations with the sun or fire.

warp The yarns that run from back to front on a loom.

warp knit A knitted fabric structure in which the yarns run the length of the fabric, vertical loops form in the crosswise direction, and then more diagonally in the subsequent course, making the yarns zigzag along the length of the fabric

warp printing A process in which warp yarns alone are first printed and then woven with a single-colored weft.

wavelength The distance between the crests in a wave of energy.

weave A fabric structure in which yarns are woven together.

wedge The silhouette that takes the shape of a wedge, with the greater width at the shoulders tapering to narrowness at the hem.

weft The yarns that run crosswise on a loom.

weft knit Also called a *filling knit*, a knitted structure that is formed by a single yarn fed into a number of needles in the horizontal direction, building loops on top of each other. Weft knits are made on circular or flat knitting machines and include plain knits, purl knits, and rib knits.

wool Animal fiber from fleece of sheep or lambs.

workmanship Excellence in the construction techniques used in fashion design.

worsted wool Wools made from combed and carded fibers.

yarn The result of fibers spun together.

yarn dyeing Adding dye at the yarn stage of the garment.

yoke The portion of a garment that provides fit across the shoulders in front or back or fit at the top of a skirt to which the lower part of the skirt is attached by means of clothing construction techniques such as shirring, gores, or pleats.

INDEX

Page numbers in italics refer to images.